FINAL DRAFT 3

Series Editor: **Jeanne Lambert**
The New School

Andrew Aquino-Cutcher
Harold Washington College at the City Colleges of Chicago
Wendy Asplin
University of Washington
David Bohlke
Jeanne Lambert
The New School

with
Monica F. Jacobe, The College of New Jersey
Alan S. Kennedy, Columbia University
Emily Ann Mathis, University of Oregon
Sara Stapleton, North Seattle College
Linda Van Doren, Emily Griffith Technical College

CAMBRIDGE
UNIVERSITY PRESS

Shaftesbury Road, Cambridge CB2 8EA, United Kingdom

One Liberty Plaza, 20th Floor, New York, NY 10006, USA

477 Williamstown Road, Port Melbourne, VIC 3207, Australia

314–321, 3rd Floor, Plot 3, Splendor Forum, Jasola District Centre, New Delhi – 110025, India

103 Penang Road, #05-06/07, Visioncrest Commercial, Singapore 238467

Cambridge University Press & Assessment is part of the University of Cambridge.

It furthers the University's mission by disseminating knowledge in the pursuit of education, learning and research at the highest international levels of excellence.

www.cambridge.org
Information on this title: www.cambridge.org/9781009345460

First published 2016
Update published 2022

20 19 18 17 16 15 14 13 12 11 10 9 8 7 6 5 4 3 2 1

Printed in Mexico by Litográfica Ingramex, S.A. de C.V.

A catalog record for this publication is available from the British Library.

Cataloging in Publication data is available at the Library of Congress.

ISBN 978-1-009-34546-0 Student's Book with Digital Pack Level 3
ISBN 978-1-107-49554-8 Teacher's Manual Level 3

Additional resources for this publication at www.cambridge.org/finaldraft

Cambridge University Press & Assessment has no responsibility for the persistence or accuracy of URLs for external or third-party Internet Web sites referred to in this publication and does not guarantee that any content on such Web sites is, or will remain, accurate or appropriate. Information regarding prices, travel timetables, and other factual information given in this work is correct at the time of first printing but Cambridge University Press & Assessment does not guarantee the accuracy of such information thereafter.

Art direction, book design, and photo research: emc design limited
Layout services: emc design limited

CONTENTS

SCOPE AND SEQUENCE

All academic vocabulary words appear on the Academic Word List (AWL) or the General Service List (GSL). 👁 All academic collocations, academic phrases, and common grammar mistakes are based on the Cambridge Academic Corpus.

WRITING SKILLS	GRAMMAR FOR WRITING 👁	AVOIDING PLAGIARISM
Thesis statements and writing prompts	Infinitives	Recognizing plagiarism
Words and phrases that show differences	*That* clauses	Strategies for paraphrasing
Words and phrases that show comparison Avoiding sentence fragments	Identifying relative clauses	What is common knowledge?
Phrases that show cause and effect Parallel structure Paragraph unity	Real conditionals	Citing sources
Purpose, audience, and tone	Reporting verbs	Evaluating Internet sources
Coherence 1: Transition words and phrases Coherence 2: Ways to connect ideas across sentences	Passive voice	Taking effective notes
Avoiding run-ons and comma splices	Reduced relative clauses	Strategies for managing your time
Avoiding faulty logic Sentence variety	Modals for hedging	Synthesizing information

TOUR OF A UNIT

ACADEMIC WRITING AND VOCABULARY

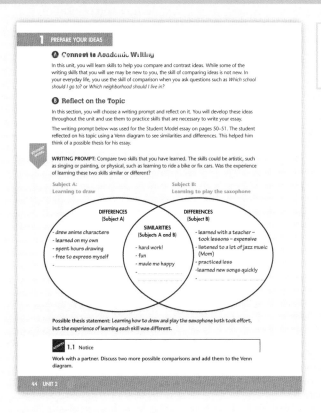

Students begin to explore a rhetorical mode and connect it to their everyday lives.

Next, students prepare for their writing by learning corpus-informed academic vocabulary, collocations, and phrases.

The first model shows students how the rhetorical mode is applied in a real-world setting, helping them recognize that academic writing is all around them.

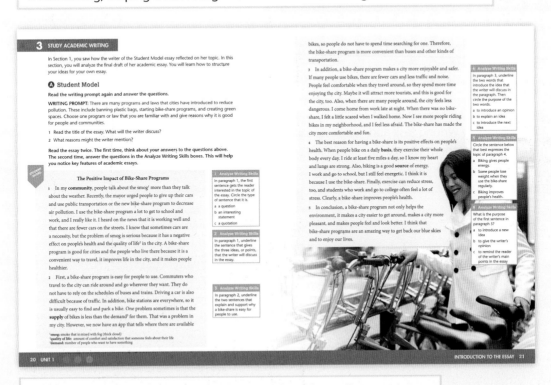

The second model shows a typical assignment from a college writing course. Students analyze this in detail, preparing for their own writing.

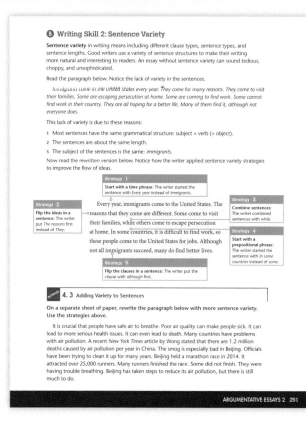

❺ Writing Skill 2: Sentence Variety

Sentence variety in writing means including different clause types, sentence types, and sentence lengths. Good writers use a variety of sentence structures to make their writing more natural and interesting to readers. An essay without sentence variety can sound tedious, choppy, and unsophisticated.

Read the paragraph below. Notice the lack of variety in the sentences.

Immigrants come to the United States every year. They come for many reasons. They come to visit their families. Some are escaping persecution at home. Some are coming to find work. Some cannot find work in their country. They are all hoping for a better life. Many of them find it, although not everyone does.

This lack of variety is due to these reasons:

1 Most sentences have the same grammatical structure: subject + verb (+ object).
2 The sentences are about the same length.
3 The subject of the sentences is the same: *immigrants.*

Now read the rewritten version below. Notice how the writer applied sentence variety strategies to improve the flow of ideas.

Strategy 1
Start with a time phrase: The writer started the sentence with *Every year* instead of *Immigrants.*

Strategy 2
Flip the ideas in a sentence: The writer put *The reasons* first instead of *They.*

Strategy 3
Combine sentences: The writer combined sentences with *while.*

Strategy 4
Start with a prepositional phrase: The writer started the sentence with *In some countries* instead of *some.*

Strategy 5
Flip the clauses in a sentence: The writer put the clause with *although* first.

Every year, immigrants come to the United States. The reasons that they come are different. Some come to visit their families, while others come to escape persecution at home. In some countries, it is difficult to find work, so these people come to the United States for jobs. Although not all immigrants succeed, many do find better lives.

4. 3 Adding Variety to Sentences

On a separate sheet of paper, rewrite the paragraph below with more sentence variety. Use the strategies above.

It is crucial that people have safe air to breathe. Poor air quality can make people sick. It can lead to more serious health issues. It can even lead to death. Many countries have problems with air pollution. A recent *New York Times* article by Wong stated that there are 1.2 million deaths caused by air pollution per year in China. The smog is especially bad in Beijing. Officials have been trying to clean it up for many years. Beijing held a marathon race in 2014. It attracted over 25,000 runners. Many runners finished the race. Some did not finish. They were having trouble breathing. Beijing has taken steps to reduce its air pollution, but there is still much to do.

ARGUMENTATIVE ESSAYS 2 251

Students develop an extensive skill set, preparing them for every aspect of academic writing.

Students study specific applications of grammar for the writing task and learn to avoid common mistakes (informed by the Cambridge Learner Corpus).

Avoiding Common Mistakes 👁

Research tells us that these are the most common mistakes that students make in academic writing when reducing relative clauses.

1 Use the correct form of the verb in the reduced clause.
    studying
    Researchers ~~studied~~ the effects of diversity on the economy do not always agree.

2 Put the verb after the noun – not before the noun.
    provided
    The ~~provided~~ facts by the researchers support her argument.

3 Omit the verb *be* before the noun when you omit the relative pronoun.
    The author, ~~is~~ an economist, has written many books on the subject of diversity.

4 For reduced clauses with single adjectives, put the adjective before the noun.
    multicultural
    The city ~~multicultural~~ has residents from over 100 countries.

4.3 Editing Task

Find and correct six more mistakes in the paragraph below.
                    competing
    For many companies ~~competed~~ in today's global market, a diverse workforce is one strategy to increase success, but there are challenges. Some businesses recruited people from different backgrounds believe that it increases creativity, but it can increase conflict, too. While employees with diverse backgrounds offer perspectives unique on problems, they may also be unable to see each other's points of view. Ted Park, is a management consultant, says that employees must be trained to work together. Some employees upset can cause additional problems and conflicts. Training on cultural diversity giving regularly is more effective than training that is given once. Companies thought about diversifying their workforce should prepare carefully for it.

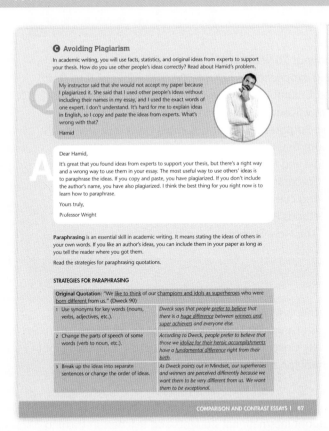

Students learn to acknowledge others' work and ideas and appropriately incorporate them into their writing.

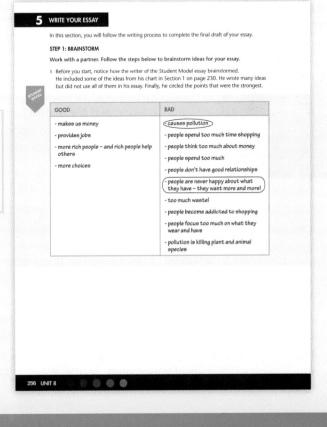

Equipped with the skills and language they have developed throughout the unit, students pull their ideas into the writing process to produce a final draft.

THE TEAM BEHIND *FINAL DRAFT*

SERIES EDITOR

Jeanne Lambert brings 20 years of ESL classroom, teacher training, and materials writing experience to her role as series editor of *Final Draft*. Jeanne has taught at Columbia University, City University of New York (CUNY), and The New School, specializing in academic writing and English for Academic Purposes. While at Columbia University, she taught writing courses in both the American Language Program and for the School of International and Public Affairs. At CUNY, she co-designed a faculty development program to help high school teachers align their ESL reading and writing curriculum with college standards. She has worked as an ESL Methods Practicum instructor and currently teaches academic writing at The New School.

AUTHORS

Andrew Aquino-Cutcher is a Language Coordinator and Assistant Professor in the English Language Learning and World Languages Department at the City Colleges of Chicago. Prior to this, Andrew taught ESL in France and Brazil for 20 years.

Wendy Asplin has taught international students and teachers-in-training in Turkey and the United States. For the past 20 years, she has been a lecturer at the University of Washington in Seattle and is an author of the Cambridge academic reading series *Read This!*

David Bohlke has been actively involved in ELT since 1987. He has taught in Asia, Africa, and the Middle East and frequently conducts teacher-training sessions around the world. He has served as a writer and series editor of numerous ESL publications.

ACADEMIC WRITING ADVISORY PANEL

The Advisory Panel is comprised of experienced writing instructors who have helped guide the development of this series and have provided invaluable information about the needs of ESL student writers.

Laszlo Arvai, Borough of Manhattan Community College, New York, NY
Leo Kazan, Passaic County Community College, Paterson, NJ
Amy Nunamaker, San Diego State College, San Diego, CA
Amy Renehan, University of Washington, Seattle, WA
Adrianne Thompson, Miami Dade College, Miami, FL

Final Draft was influenced by the opinions and insights of classroom teachers from the following institutions:

UNITED STATES **Alabama**: Cleburne County High School, Gadsden State Community College, University of Alabama; **Arizona:** Arizona State University, Northern Arizona University, Pima Community College; **Arkansas**: Arkansas State University, University of Arkansas, University of Central Arkansas; **California:** Allan Hancock College, Berkeley High School, California State Polytechnic University, California State University East Bay, California State University Fullerton, California State University Long Beach, California State University Los Angeles, City College of San Francisco, College of San Mateo, De Anza College, Diablo Valley College, East Los Angeles College, El Camino College, The English Center, Evergreen Valley College, Foothill College, Fullerton College, Gavilan College, Glendale Community College, Hollywood High School, Imperial Valley College, Las Positas College, Los Angeles City College, Los Angeles Southwest College, Mendocino College, Mills College, Mission College, Modesto Junior College, Monterey Peninsula College, Palomar College, Pasadena City College, Placer High School, Roybal Learning Center, Sacramento City College, Sacramento State, San Diego Community College District, San Francisco State University, San Jose City College, Santa Ana College, Santa Barbara City College, Santa Monica College, Santa Rosa Junior College, Skyline College, Stanford University, Taft College, University of California Berkeley, University of California Davis, University of California Irvine, University of San Diego, University of San Francisco, University of Southern California, West Valley Community College; **Colorado:** Community College of Aurora, Front Range Community College, Red Rocks Community College, University of Colorado; **Connecticut:** Central Connecticut State University, Enfield High School, Naugatuck Valley Community College, Norwalk Community College, Post University, University of Bridgeport, University of Hartford; **Florida:** Barry University, Florida SouthWestern State College, Florida State University, Hillsborough Community College, Indian River State College, Miami Dade College, Robinson High School, St. Petersburg College, University of Central Florida, University of Florida, University of Miami, University of South Florida; **Georgia:** Augusta State University, Emory University, Georgia Institute of Technology, Georgia Perimeter College, Georgia State University, Interactive College of Technology, Pebblebrook High School, Savannah College of Art and Design, West Hall High School; **Hawaii:** Hawaii Community College, Hawaii Tokai International College, Kapiolani Community College, Mid-Pacific Institute, University of Hawaii; **Idaho:** College of Western Idaho, Northwest Nazarene University; **Illinois:** College of DuPage, College of Lake County, Elgin Community College, English Center USA, Harold Washington College, Harper College, Illinois Institute of Technology, Lake Forest Academy, Moraine Valley Community College, Oakton Community College, Roosevelt University, South Suburban College, Southern Illinois University, Triton College, Truman College, University of Illinois, Waubonsee Community College; **Indiana:** Earlham College, Indiana University, Purdue University; **Iowa:** Divine Word College, Iowa State University, Kirkwood Community College, Mercy College of Health Sciences, University of Northern Iowa; **Kansas:** Donnelly College, Johnson County Community College, Kansas State University, Washburn University; **Kentucky:** Bluegrass Community & Technical College, Georgetown College, Northern Kentucky University, University of Kentucky; **Maryland:** Anne Arundel Community College, Howard Community College, Montgomery College, Johns Hopkins University; **Massachusetts:** Boston University, Mount Ida College, New England Conservatory of Music, North Shore Community College, Phillips Academy, Roxbury Community College, The Winchendon School, Worcester State University; **Michigan:** Central Michigan University, Eastern Michigan University, Grand Rapids Community College, Lansing Community College, Macomb Community College, Michigan State University, Saginaw Valley State University, University of Detroit Mercy, University of Michigan, Wayne

State University, Western Michigan University; **Minnesota:** Century College, Saint Paul College, University of Minnesota, University of St. Thomas; **Mississippi:** Mississippi College, Mississippi State University; **Missouri:** Missouri State University, St. Louis Community College, Saint Louis University, University of Missouri, Webster University; **Nebraska:** Union College, University of Nebraska; **Nevada:** Truckee Meadows Community College, University of Nevada; **New Jersey:** Bergen Community College, The College of New Jersey, Hudson County Community College, Kean University, Linden High School, Mercer County Community College, Passaic County Community College, Rutgers University, Stockton University, Union County College; **New Mexico:** University of New Mexico; **New York:** Alfred State College, Baruch College, Borough of Manhattan Community College, City University of New York, Columbia University, Fashion Institute of Technology, Hofstra University, Hostos Community College, Hunter College, John Jay College of Criminal Justice, Kingsborough Community College, The Knox School, LaGuardia Community College, LIC/LISMA Language Center, Medgar Evers College, New York University, Queens College, Queensborough Community College, Suffolk Community College, Syracuse University, Zoni Language Centers; **North Carolina:** Central Carolina Community College, Central Piedmont Community College, Duke University, Durham Technical Community College, South Piedmont Community College, University of North Carolina, Wake Technical Community College; **North Dakota:** Woodrow Wilson High School; **Ohio:** Columbus State Community College, Cuyahoga Community College, Kent State University, Miami University Middletown, Ohio Northern University, Ohio State University, Sinclair Community College, University of Cincinnati, University of Dayton, Wright State University, Xavier University; **Oklahoma:** University of Oklahoma; **Oregon:** Chemeketa Community College, Clackamas Community College, Lewis & Clark College, Portland Community College, Portland State University, Westview High School; **Pennsylvania:** Pennsylvania State University, University of Pennsylvania, University of Pittsburgh; **Puerto Rico:** Carlos Albizu University, InterAmerican University of Puerto Rico; **Rhode Island:** Johnson & Wales University, Salve Regina University; **South Carolina:** University of South Carolina; **South Dakota:** Black Hills State University; **Tennessee:** Southern Adventist University, University of Tennessee, Vanderbilt University, Williamson Christian College; **Texas:** Austin Community College, Colleyville Heritage High School, Collin College, Dallas Baptist University, El Paso Community College, Houston Community College, Lone Star College, Northwest Vista College, Richland College, San Jacinto College, Stephen F. Austin State University, Tarrant County College, Texas A&M University, University of Houston, University of North Texas, University of Texas, Victoria College, West Brook High School; **Utah:** Brigham Young University, Davis Applied Technology College, Weber State University; **Vermont:** Green Mountain College; **Virginia:** College of William & Mary, Liberty University, Northern Virginia Community College, Tidewater Community College; **Washington:** Bellevue College, EF International Language Centers, Gonzaga University, The IDEAL School, Mount Rainier High School, North Seattle College, Peninsula College, Seattle Central College, Seattle University, Shoreline Community College, South Puget Sound Community College, Tacoma Community College, University of Washington, Whatcom Community College, Wilson High School; **Washington, DC:** George Washington University, Georgetown University; **West Virginia:** West Virginia University; **Wisconsin:** Beloit College, Edgewood College, Gateway Technical College, Kenosha eSchool, Lawrence University, Marquette University, St. Norbert College, University of Wisconsin, Waukesha County Technical College

CANADA British Columbia: Vancouver Island University, VanWest College; **Nova Scotia**: Acadia University; **Ontario**: Centennial College, University of Guelph, York University; **Québec**: Université du Québec

MEXICO Baja California: Universidad de Tijuana

TURKEY Istanbul: Bilgi University, Özyeğin University

INTRODUCTION TO THE ESSAY

ENVIRONMENTAL STUDIES: GREEN LIVING

"I feel more confident than ever that the power to save the planet rests with the individual consumer."

Denis Hayes (1944–)

About the Author:

Denis Hayes is an environmental activist. He was the main organizer of the first Earth Day in 1970.

Work with a partner. Read the quotation about protecting the environment. Then answer the questions.

1 What does Hayes mean when he says that the individual consumer can save the planet?

2 What are some things that people do every day that are harmful to the environment?

3 What is something that you could do to help the environment?

Ⓐ Connect to Academic Writing

In this unit, you will learn skills for writing clear, well-organized academic essays. While some of the skills you will use may be new, others are not. Writing essays requires you to explain and organize your ideas in a clear and logical way. You do this in everyday life, too. For example, you use similar skills to consider the advantages and disadvantages of two different careers or to describe an experience you have had in your life.

Ⓑ Reflect on the Topic

In this section, you will choose a writing prompt and reflect on it. You will develop these ideas throughout the unit and use them to practice skills that are necessary to write your essay.

The writing prompt below was used for the Student Model essay on pages 20–21. After reflecting on her topic, the student decided to make a list to generate ideas. This helped her think of a possible thesis statement.

WRITING PROMPT: There are many programs and laws that cities have introduced to reduce pollution. These include banning plastic bags, starting bike-share programs, and creating green spaces. Choose one program or law that you are familiar with and give reasons why it is good for people and communities.

Reasons for a Bike-Share Program
more freedom
no looking for parking!
never get stuck in traffic
save money
convenient to travel around city
feel safer because more people everywhere
fun – I go more places

Possible thesis statement: A bike-share program is good for a city and people because it saves money and the city is safer and more fun.

 1.1 Notice

Work with a partner. Discuss how someone's life would change if he or she rode a bike rather than drove a car.

1.2 **Apply It to Your Writing**

Follow the directions to reflect on your topic.

A Choose a prompt:

- Choose a product that is not good for the environment, such as plastic bags or paper towels. Write three reasons why people should stop using them.
- Describe a green place, such as a park, where you live. Describe how people use the space.
- Imagine that your town or city wants to start a program to improve the city, such as a bike-sharing program, a car-sharing program, or a program to create more green spaces. Choose one and tell how it would affect the quality of life.
- A topic approved by your instructor

B Complete the following tasks:

1 Reflect on the topic and make a list.

2 Write a possible thesis statement.

3 Compare lists and possible thesis statements with a partner.

Possible thesis statement: ....

In this section, you will learn academic language that you can use in your academic essay. You will also notice how a professional writer uses this language.

Academic Vocabulary

The words below appear throughout the unit. Many are from the Academic Word List. Using these words in your writing will make your ideas clearer and your writing more academic.

basis (n)	cooperation (n)	source (n)	supply (n)
community (n)	scope (n)	sufficient (adj)	transition (n)

ACTIVITY **2.1** Focus on Meaning

Match the words in bold with their definitions. Write the letters.

A

.... 1 The **scope** of a problem such as pollution is large. It involves many complex social, economic, and scientific issues.

   a the people in a particular area or who share interests or background

.... 2 We want the recycling program to succeed, so the entire **community** must participate.

   b enough

.... 3 The government and the citizens are working on ways to solve the problem of air pollution. This **cooperation** is necessary.

   c the range or area of something

.... 4 There is **sufficient** research that recycling is effective. It is has been shown to reduce negative effects on the environment.

   d the process of people working together

B

.... 1 Making the **transition** from oil to solar energy is expensive because people have to buy equipment.

a origin

.... 2 Solar energy is a good **source** of power because it comes from the sun.

b the process of change

.... 3 The **supply** of oil in the world is limited, and we will run out of it one day.

c the facts or beliefs that support a claim or idea

.... 4 The **basis** for the argument is that recycling reduces land pollution.

d the amount of something that is available for use

B Academic Collocations

Collocations are words that are frequently used together. Research tells us that the academic vocabulary in Part A is commonly used in the collocations in bold below.

ACTIVITY **2.2** Focus on Meaning

Work with a partner. Circle the correct meanings.

1 "Simple living" includes a **wide scope** of actions. These actions range from recycling to growing your own food. **Wide scope** means

   a a small range.

   b a large range.

2 Car sharing helps people in a community get to know each other better, and it gives them a **sense of community**. A **sense of community** is

   a the feeling of being connected to others.

   b the feeling of pride.

3 The **water supply** in the community has improved in recent years. However, many people still do not have enough clean, safe water. The **water supply** is

   a the water available to a community.

   b the water that is sold in stores.

4 There is a **limited supply** of oil in the world. However, there is plenty of solar energy because it comes from the sun. A **limited supply** is

   a poor quality of something.

   b an amount of something that is not large.

5 We can improve the environment every day. For example, we can save energy **on a daily basis** if we unplug appliances and turn off lights when we leave the house each day. **On a daily basis** means

   a occasionally.

   b every day.

C Writing in the Real World

The author of "Going Off the Grid: Why People Are Choosing to Live Life Unplugged" uses features of academic essays to present his ideas in an organized way that is convincing and interesting.

Before you read, answer these questions: Look at the title. What do you think it means to "live life unplugged"? Why do you think some people want to live very simply?

Now read the article. Think about your answers to the questions above as you read.

GOING OFF THE GRID:
Why More People Are Choosing to Live Life Unplugged (adapted)

by John Platt

1   Imagine living off the land. See yourself growing your own food, producing your own energy, and getting away from the consumption economy[1] that influences so many of our decisions. For more and more people, this simple lifestyle, called off-grid living, has become a real option. Although statistics on Americans who choose off-grid living are unavailable, trends suggest that the number is increasing. Some people do it to be self-reliant[2] or more in touch with nature. Others do it on the **basis** that there is a limited **supply** of traditional energy, such as oil. Still others do it because it is the best financial option available to them. For people who want to get away from today's consumerist society or help protect the environment, living off-grid can be an attractive option.

2   Although a desire to go green isn't always the top reason for people going off-grid, the lifestyle has many environmental benefits. For one thing, most off-grid homes or communities are in places where nature plays an important part of their everyday lives. Many people in these communities want to make sure they treat their environment with respect. And they want the choices that they make on a daily basis to help the environment rather than hurt it. In these communities, people often convert from oil to solar power for regular home heating or bike rather than drive to reduce the use of gasoline. Making the **transition** from traditional energy to a renewable **source** may take getting used to at first, but many in off-grid communities are willing to sacrifice for the chance to make a positive impact on the environment.

[1]**consumption economy:** economy that relies on consumer spending
[2]**self-reliant:** capable of relying on oneself rather than others

3 For others, living off-grid is a rejection of consumerism.[3] "Going off the grid is not a game," says Nick Rosen, founder of the Off-Grid website. "It is real life and a real choice for real people." And many of these people are starting to ask themselves, "How much do we really need?" They reject overly large homes in favor of small homes based on the idea that we are less happy when we have a lot more than we need. They feel overconsumption leads to being less grateful for what we do have. And doing something like buying a smaller home also fits into the environmentally friendly lifestyle because smaller homes require less energy for heating and cooling.

4 For others, going off-grid is an economic necessity because they have faced economic hardships,[4] and many have lost their own homes. They end up living a more eco-friendly[5] lifestyle because they need to reduce electric bills or grow their own food to survive. Rosen reports, "A lot of the people I met when I was traveling around the States writing my book were people who had to hand back the keys to their properties and find a new lifestyle. In one case they bought some land on eBay and moved themselves into a trailer. And they find themselves living a more ecological lifestyle just by the fact that they're generating their own electricity and growing their own food, but they were motivated by financial matters rather than by a more pure desire to tread more lightly[6] on the planet." So, financial concerns also play a role in many people's decision to live off the grid.

5 The **scope** of the off-grid movement is not fully known. However, we do know what motivates many off-grid **community** members – the desire to protect the environment, to be self-reliant, to embrace simple living, and sometimes to live more economically. For many of these members, the benefits outweigh the inconveniences of giving up some of the features of a modern life – using as much oil and electricity as you want or buying prepackaged food. Living off the grid might not be for everyone, but the lifestyle of people who do so certainly gives us all something to consider.

[3]**consumerism:** culture where people focus a lot on buying things
[4]**economic hardships:** economic suffering
[5]**eco-friendly:** good for the environment

[6]**tread more lightly:** speak or behave carefully to avoid upsetting anyone or causing harm

 2.3 Check Your Understanding

Answer the questions.

1 What are the main reasons people want to live in off-grid communities?

2 How would you explain the benefits of off-grid living to someone who has never heard of it before?

3 How would you feel about living in an off-grid community?

 2.4 Notice the Features of Essay Writing

Answer the questions.

1 Look at the first two sentences in the introductory paragraph. How does the author get the reader's attention?

2 In which sentence in the introductory paragraph does the writer tell us what he will discuss in the rest of the essay?

3 Look at paragraphs 2, 3, and 4. What is their purpose?

In Section 1, you saw how the writer of the Student Model essay reflected on her topic. In this section, you will analyze the final draft of her academic essay. You will learn how to structure your ideas for your own essay.

(A) Student Model

Read the writing prompt again and answer the questions.

WRITING PROMPT: There are many programs and laws that cities have introduced to reduce pollution. These include banning plastic bags, starting bike-share programs, and creating green spaces. Choose one program or law that you are familiar with and give reasons why it is good for people and communities.

1 Read the title of the essay. What will the writer discuss?

2 What reasons might the writer mention?

Read the essay twice. The first time, think about your answers to the questions above. The second time, answer the questions in the Analyze Writing Skills boxes. This will help you notice key features of academic essays.

The Positive Impact of Bike-Share Programs

1 In my **community**, people talk about the smog[1] more than they talk about the weather. Recently, the mayor urged people to give up their cars and use public transportation or the new bike-share program to decrease air pollution. I use the bike-share program a lot to get to school and work, and I really like it. I heard on the news that it is working well and that there are fewer cars on the streets. I know that sometimes cars are a necessity, but the problem of smog is serious because it has a negative effect on people's health and the quality of life[2] in the city. A bike-share program is good for cities and the people who live there because it is a convenient way to travel, it improves life in the city, and it makes people healthier.

2 First, a bike-share program is easy for people to use. Commuters who travel to the city can ride around and go wherever they want. They do not have to rely on the schedules of buses and trains. Driving a car is also difficult because of traffic. In addition, bike stations are everywhere, so it is usually easy to find and park a bike. One problem sometimes is that the **supply** of bikes is less than the demand[3] for them. That was a problem in my city. However, we now have an app that tells where there are available

[1]**smog:** smoke that is mixed with fog (thick cloud)
[2]**quality of life:** amount of comfort and satisfaction that someone feels about their life
[3]**demand:** number of people who want to have something

1 Analyze Writing Skills

In paragraph 1, the first sentence gets the reader interested in the topic of the essay. Circle the type of sentence that it is.

a a question

b an interesting statement

c a quotation

2 Analyze Writing Skills

In paragraph 1, underline the sentence that gives the three ideas, or points, that the writer will discuss in the essay.

3 Analyze Writing Skills

In paragraph 2, underline the two sentences that explain and support why a bike-share is easy for people to use.

bikes, so people do not have to spend time searching for one. Therefore, the bike-share program is more convenient than buses and other kinds of transportation.

3   In addition, a bike-share program makes a city more enjoyable and safer. If many people use bikes, there are fewer cars and less traffic and noise. People feel comfortable when they travel around, so they spend more time enjoying the city. Maybe it will attract more tourists, and this is good for the city, too. Also, when there are many people around, the city feels less dangerous. I come home from work late at night. When there was no bike-share, I felt a little scared when I walked home. Now I see more people riding bikes in my neighborhood, and I feel less afraid. The bike-share has made the city more comfortable and fun.

4   The best reason for having a bike-share is its positive effects on people's health. When people bike on a daily **basis**, they exercise their whole body every day. I ride at least five miles a day, so I know my heart and lungs are strong. Also, biking is a good **source** of energy. I work and go to school, but I still feel energetic. I think it is because I use the bike-share. Finally, exercise can reduce stress, too, and students who work and go to college often feel a lot of stress. Clearly, a bike-share improves people's health.

5   In conclusion, a bike-share program not only helps the environment, it makes a city easier to get around, makes a city more pleasant, and makes people feel and look better. I think that bike-share programs are an amazing way to get back our blue skies and to enjoy our lives.

4   Analyze Writing Skills

In paragraph 3, underline the two words that introduce the idea that the writer will discuss in the paragraph. Then circle the purpose of the two words.

a   to introduce an opinion

b   to explain an idea

c   to introduce the next idea

5   Analyze Writing Skills

Circle the sentence below that best expresses the topic of paragraph 4.

a   Biking gives people energy.

b   Some people lose weight when they use the bike-share regularly.

c   Biking improves people's health.

6   Analyze Writing Skills

What is the purpose of the first sentence in paragraph 5?

a   to introduce a new idea

b   to give the writer's opinion

c   to remind the reader of the writer's main points in the essay

3.1 Check Your Understanding

Answer the questions.

1 What is the essay about?

2 Which reason is the most convincing or important in your opinion? Explain.

3 How do you feel about bike-share programs?

 3.2 Outline the Writer's Ideas

Complete the outline for "The Positive Impact of Bike-Share Programs." Write the thesis statement. Then use the phrases in the box.

coming home from work – feel safer	exercises whole body
easy to find and park a bike	fewer cars, less traffic and noise
easy to use	reduces stress

ESSAY OUTLINE

I. Introductory paragraph

Thesis Statement
....
....
....

Body Paragraph 1
II. ....

Supporting Idea 1
    A. Commuters – can ride and go everywhere

Detail
      1. Do not have to rely on bus/train schedules

Detail
      2. Car – too much traffic

Supporting Idea 2
    B. Bike stations are everywhere

Detail
      1. ....

Detail
      2. One problem – supply

Detail
      3. App – to find bikes

Body Paragraph 2	III. City more enjoyable and safer
Supporting Idea 1	A.
Detail	1. Feel comfortable traveling
Detail	2. Spend more time enjoying city
Detail	3. Attract tourists
Supporting Idea 2	B. City feels less dangerous
Detail	1.
Body Paragraph 3	IV. Positive effects on health
Supporting Idea 1	A.
Detail	1. I ride 5 miles a day
Supporting Idea 2	B. Good source of energy
Detail	1. My experience – feel energetic
Supporting Idea 3	C.
	V. Concluding paragraph

B The Essay in Academic Writing

Writers use the essay structure to communicate their ideas clearly and convincingly. There are several types of essays that you will review in this book, including comparison and contrast, cause-effect, and argumentative. Academic essays typically have the following structure:

1 An **introductory paragraph** that explains the topic and the writer's purpose in writing. It includes:
   - a hook *zayenca*
   - background information
   - a thesis statement

2 **Body paragraphs** (usually 2–4 paragraphs) that develop the writer's main points. Each body paragraph includes:
   - a topic sentence
   - supporting sentences and details
   - a concluding sentence

3 A **concluding paragraph** that restates the thesis statement and provides a final comment. It includes:
   - a restatement of the thesis
   - an insight, an opinion, a recommendation, a prediction, or a call to action

 3.3 Notice

Circle the answers.

1 Which of the following does an introductory paragraph include?
   a   a topic sentence   b   a prediction   c   a thesis statement

2 In which paragraph(s) does the writer explain the main points of the essay?
   a   introductory paragraph   b   body paragraphs   c   concluding paragraph

3 In which paragraph(s) does the writer say something he or she has learned or wants the reader to do?
   a   introductory paragraph   b   body paragraphs   c   concluding paragraph

THE INTRODUCTORY PARAGRAPH

The **hook** is usually the first one or two sentences in an introductory paragraph. It makes the reader interested in reading the essay. Writers use different types of **hooks**.

Hooks can be:

- **A thought-provoking question**

   What's more important, having the convenience of plastic water bottles or having a healthy, clean environment?

- **A request to reflect on or visualize a situation to help the reader make a personal connection to the issue**

   Think about how much paper and plastic you throw away in one day. Multiply that amount by 365 days in the year. Think about how many rooms it all would fill.

- **A relevant or memorable quotation**

  Former U.S. President Franklin D. Roosevelt once said, "A nation that destroys its soils destroys itself. Forests are the lungs of our land, purifying the air and giving fresh strength to our people."

- **A surprising statistic**

  According to the Environmental Protection Agency, Americans throw away roughly 32 million tons of plastic each year.

- **An interesting and relevant observation**

  On every college campus, you see many students walking around with plastic water bottles.

 3.4 Notice

Work with a partner. Discuss these questions.

1. Look at the professional author's essay on pages 18–19. What kind of hook did the author use? Do you think it was effective? Why or why not?

2. Look at the Student Model essay on pages 20–21. What kind of hook did the writer use? Do you think it was effective? Why or why not?

BACKGROUND INFORMATION

In an introductory paragraph, **background information** is information on the topic that sets up the reader for the thesis statement. It explains the topic in a way that makes the thesis statement seem logical. For example, if a writer's thesis is "A bike-share program is good for cities and the people who live there because it is a convenient way to travel, it improves life in the city, and it makes people healthier," then the background information should introduce bike-share programs in a way that shows that bike-share programs have advantages.

Some types of background information are:

- a general explanation of the topic
- historical information on the topic
- a personal story that relates to the topic
- relevant data and statistics

Read the following student paragraphs. Notice the type of background information each one contains.

Student Paragraph 1

What's more important, having the convenience of plastic water bottles or having a healthy, clean environment? According to the Environmental Protection Agency, Americans threw away roughly 32 million tons of plastic in 2012. This has a large impact on the environment. It takes more than 17 million barrels of oil to produce the energy to make and deliver these bottles. Furthermore, burning oil and other fossil fuels is a main cause of pollution.

Relevant data and statistics

Student Paragraph 2

Did you know that shipping an apple 3,000 miles from California to New York hurts the environment? Most of the produce we buy in grocery stores is not grown locally. Instead, it is produced in one area and then shipped hundreds and often thousands of miles to another area. The trucks that carry the produce use a lot of oil for fuel. This oil causes carbon emissions that pollute our air. Buying produce that comes from local farmers is an effective way to use less oil and create less pollution.

General explanation of the topic

 3.5 Notice

Work with a partner. Discuss these questions.

1 Look at the introductory paragraph of the professional author's essay on pages 18–19. What kind of background information did the author use? Do you think it was effective? Why or why not?

2 Look at the introductory paragraph of the Student Model essay on pages 20–21. What kind of background information did the writer use? Do you think it was effective? Why or why not?

3.6 Apply It to Your Writing

Look at the list that you created in Section 1 on page 15. Use your brainstorm ideas to write some background information for your topic.

....

....

....

THE THESIS STATEMENT

The **thesis statement** in an essay:

- is usually the last sentence in the introductory paragraph
- tells the reader what ideas will be developed in the body of the essay

The thesis statement has two parts: a topic and a point of view. The point of view often states the individual ideas or points that the writer will develop in the essay. Below is an example of a thesis statement that states the points. The points are numbered.

POINT OF VIEW

TOPIC   1   2   3

<u>Bringing your own bag to the store</u> saves trees, reduces waste, and saves money.

Sometimes the thesis statement is more general. This means that the writer does not actually state the individual points. However, it is still clear what he or she will write about. The thesis statement below is an example of this. We know the writer will discuss benefits related to the environment and to riders, but we do not know the exact benefits.

TOPIC   POINT OF VIEW

<u>Taking public transportation</u> benefits both the environment and riders.

 3.7 Notice

Look at the professional author's essay on pages 18–19 and the Student Model essay on pages 20–21. Find the thesis statement for each one. Do the thesis statements state the points that will be developed?

FACTS VS. POINTS OF VIEW

It is important to remember that a thesis is not a statement of fact that everyone agrees on. A point of view is debatable. People may not agree with the specific ideas. They may have a different point of view. Compare the two thesis statements for the following prompt:

WRITING PROMPT: What are the benefits of using solar power?

Thesis Statement 1: Solar power saves money, is a renewable source of energy, and reduces global warming.

Thesis Statement 2: Solar power is an important part of photosynthesis and the water cycle process.

Note that Thesis Statement 1 is debatable. The writer must support the point of view with explanation, facts, and examples. Thesis Statement 2 is a fact. It is not debatable, so it cannot be developed further like a point of view can. As a result, it is not a good thesis statement.

3.8 Evaluate Thesis Statements

Work with a partner. Read the topics. Circle the thesis statements that include a debatable point of view.

1 **Topic:** Prefabricated homes

    a Prefabricated homes are built in one location and then moved to another location.

    (b) Prefabricated homes benefit the environment and the people who live in them.

2 **Topic:** Solar power

    (a) Solar power can reduce our use of dangerous sources of power, such as nuclear energy.

    b The supply of power from the sun is unlimited.

3 **Topic:** Community gardens in city neighborhoods

    (a) Community gardens benefit the environment and help build a sense of community.

    b Many cities have community gardens.

4 **Topic:** Car sharing

    (a) Car sharing should be mandatory in cities in order to reduce air pollution.

    b Car sharing is one way to share the cost of gasoline.

 3.9 Apply It to Your Writing

Think about what you have learned. Revise the possible thesis statement that you wrote on page 15. Then share it with a partner.

....

....

....

....

BODY PARAGRAPHS

Body paragraphs present the main points of an essay. Each body paragraph logically and thoroughly explains, describes, or argues one aspect of the thesis statement.

A body paragraph includes:

- **a topic sentence** that states one aspect of the thesis. A good topic sentence clearly connects to the thesis by reusing or paraphrasing key words. The underlined words below connect to the words "makes people healthier" in the thesis statement of the Student Model essay.

    The best reason for having a bike-share is its underline{positive effects on people's health}.

- **supporting sentences** that give specific information about the main idea. Writers also include sentences that offer **details**, or more information about the ideas in the supporting sentences. The information that writers give in their supporting sentences and details includes explanations, examples, and facts.

    When people bike on a daily basis, they exercise their whole body every day. I ride at least 5 miles a day, so I know my heart and lungs are strong. Also, biking is a good source of energy.

- **a concluding sentence** that ties all the ideas in the paragraph together. Writers signal the conclusion by starting this sentence with a word or phrase such as *clearly*, *for these reasons*, *therefore*, or *in brief*.

     Clearly, a bike-share program improves people's health.

 3.10 Notice

Read the body paragraph from the Student Model essay on pages 20–21. Double underline the topic sentence. Underline the supporting sentences. Circle the concluding sentence.

First, a bike-share program is easy for people to use. Commuters who travel to the city can ride around and go wherever they want. They do not have to rely on the schedules of buses and trains. Driving a car is also difficult because of traffic. In addition, bike stations are everywhere, so it is usually easy to find and park a bike. One problem sometimes is that the supply of bikes is less than the demand for them. That was a problem in my city. However, we now have an app that tells where there are available bikes, so people do not have to spend time searching for one. Therefore, the bike-share program is more convenient than buses and other kinds of transportation.

 3.11 Practice Writing Topic Sentences

Read the thesis statements. Write topic sentences for the body paragraphs.

1 **Thesis statement:** Community gardens benefit cities by improving air quality, providing healthy food, and teaching children valuable skills.

   ....
   .... Many urban areas have pollution because of the carbon emissions from cars. This pollution can cause asthma and other breathing problems. The green plants in gardens make oxygen. This oxygen makes it easier for everyone to breathe. Clearly, cleaner air is one benefit of community gardens.

2 **Thesis statement:** Biking to work instead of driving reduces air pollution, saves money, and makes people healthier.

   ....
   .... Cars are very expensive to maintain, while bikes are easy to maintain. For example, if a car engine breaks, it can cost hundreds of dollars to repair. On the other hand, if the chain on a bike breaks, it costs a lot less to fix. Gas and insurance for cars are expensive, too, but bikes do not need them. Bikers often have to register their bikes, but this does not usually cost very much. There is no doubt that biking to work costs less.

3.12 Apply It to Your Writing

Look at the thesis statement that you revised in Activity 3.9 on page 28. Write a topic sentence for one of the body paragraphs. Then share it with a partner.

 3.13 Practice Writing Supporting Sentences

Work with a partner. Read the essay prompt. Write three drawbacks of bike-share programs.

WRITING PROMPT: Many communities in the United States have started bike-share programs. People use the bikes to get around and return them to bike lots that are located in convenient places around town. What are the possible drawbacks of using a bike from a bike share program?

Advantage 1: ....

Advantage 2: ....

Advantage 3: ....

3.14 Practice Writing a Thesis Statement

Write a thesis statement based on your ideas from Activity 3.13.

Thesis statement: ....

3.15 Practice Writing Topic Sentences

Write topic sentences for three body paragraphs based on your thesis statement in Activity 3.14 and your ideas from Activity 3.13. Use the expressions in the box.

another drawback is	first,	finally,

Body Paragraph 1 Topic Sentence: ....
....

Body Paragraph 2 Topic Sentence: ....
....

Body Paragraph 3 Topic Sentence: ....
....

3.16 Write Supporting Sentences

Work with a partner. Choose one of your topic sentences from Activity 3.14. Think of supporting sentences and details for it and write a paragraph.

....

....

....

....

CONCLUDING PARAGRAPH

The concluding paragraph reminds the reader of your thesis by restating it and then ends with an interesting comment, recommendation, or prediction. A conclusion never adds new information or ideas to your essay.

The first sentence in the concluding paragraph usually begins with a transition phrase such as the following: *in conclusion, in short, in sum,* and *to conclude.*

> **In conclusion,** *biking instead of driving has many benefits.*

The final **comment** is often:

- **an insight or opinion:** *I have more respect for people who choose off-grid living because they are committed to it even though it is difficult and inconvenient sometimes.*
- **a prediction:** *These changes require cooperation, but if everyone biked or took public transportation just three days a week, most communities would be cleaner and healthier places to live.*
- **a recommendation:** *Instead of spending money on new roads and buildings, communities should create more parks and green spaces.*
- **a call to action:** *Consumers must demand that their city officials pass laws banning plastic bags.*

3.17 Notice

Read the concluding paragraph of the Student Model essay on pages 20–21. What kind of comment is it? ....

HOW TO RESTATE THE THESIS STATEMENT

Good writers paraphrase their thesis statement in the conclusion instead of repeating it word for word. Notice how the writer of the Student Model essay used synonyms for "convenient," "improves life," and "makes people healthier" in restating the thesis statement:

Thesis statement: *A bike-share program is good for cities and the people who live there because it is a <u>convenient</u> way to travel, it <u>improves life</u> in the city, and it <u>makes people healthier</u>.*

Concluding sentence: *In conclusion, a bike-share program not only helps the environment, it <u>makes a city easier to get around</u>, <u>makes</u> a city <u>more pleasant</u>, and <u>makes people feel and look better</u>.*

Remember to restate the points in the same order as they appeared in the thesis statement.

3.18 Practice Choosing Restatements of the Thesis Statement

Work with a partner. Choose the best restatement for each thesis statement.

1 **Thesis statement:** Consumers can reduce their use of energy on a daily basis by unplugging appliances, turning off lights when not in a room, and washing clothes with warm water.

   a In short, unplugging appliances, turning off lights when not in a room, and washing clothes in warm water are three ways that consumers can reduce their use of energy on a daily basis.

   b In conclusion, shutting off lights when no one is there, unplugging appliances when you're not using them, and using warm water to wash clothes are ways we can all help to cut down on energy use.

   c To conclude, disconnecting appliances, shutting off lights in rooms when no one is there, and using warm water to wash clothes are ways that everyone can reduce energy consumption.

2 **Thesis statement:** Eliminating plastic bags reduces water pollution, produces less garbage, and saves communities money.

   a In short, if there were no plastic bags, there would be less water pollution, less litter, and more money for communities.

   b In conclusion, if plastic bags are eliminated, it would save communities money, reduce litter, and decrease water pollution.

   c To conclude, eliminating plastic bags reduces water pollution, produces less garbage, and saves communities money.

 3.19 Practice Restating a Thesis Statement

Restate the thesis statement below. Keep the original meaning, but use different words.

Thesis statement: Biking rather than driving to work helps people to get in shape, save money, and reduce stress.

Restatement: ....

....

In this section, you will learn the writing and grammar skills that will help make your writing more sophisticated and accurate.

Ⓐ Writing Skill: Thesis Statements and Writing Prompts

A good thesis statement answers the writing prompt. That may seem obvious, but sometimes writers can become confused if they do not fully understand the prompt. As a result, their thesis statements do not match the writing prompt.

One way to make sure that your thesis statement answers the writing prompt is to repeat key words from the prompt in your thesis statement. Read the examples below. Notice how Thesis Statement 2 repeats key words, making it a better thesis statement.

WRITING PROMPT: Consumers spend thousands of dollars each year on **bottled water** even though they know plastic is **damaging the environment**. What are some ways to **persuade** the **public** to use **fewer plastic products**?

Thesis Statement 1: People could use **fewer plastic products** if the government taxed plastic and talked to people about the negative effects of it.

Thesis Statement 2: Taxing **plastic bottles**, explaining how **plastic damages** the **environment**, and offering **consumers** alternatives to **plastic products** will **persuade the public to use** fewer of them.

 4.1 Choose Thesis Statements

Work with a partner. Choose the best thesis statements. Discuss the reasons for your choices.

1 **WRITING PROMPT:** Green spaces, such as parks and community gardens, are considered good for cities for many reasons. How do they improve the lives of residents in a city?

   a Green spaces are nice for cities because people can enjoy nature, they can relax and play games, and they can hear concerts and go to other events.

   b Green spaces improve the lives of residents in a city because these spaces help people enjoy nature, they reduce air pollution, and they build a sense of community among people.

   c Green spaces are good for people because these places are relaxing and beautiful, they are fun to go with friends and family, and they reduce air pollution in the city.

2 **WRITING PROMPT:** Many people have habits that are bad for the environment. For example, they drive everywhere, they keep the lights on even when they leave a room, they keep the TV on even when they are not watching it, or they use paper towels or sponges instead of reusable cloth towels for cleaning. Choose a habit that you have that you know is not very good for the environment and give three reasons why it would be difficult to give it up.

a I use a lot of electricity every day because I often keep the TV on, I usually keep electric appliances plugged in all the time, and I usually keep lights on in rooms when I am not in them.

b I know driving everywhere is bad for the environment but it would be difficult for me to give it up because I hate to walk, I love driving, and I hate taking public transportation.

c Buying bottled water is bad, but I cannot stop it because I do not like carrying bottles around, I like fresh water, and I recycle the bottles so it is not damaging the environment.

B Grammar for Writing: Infinitives

An infinitive is *to* + the base form of a verb. It can follow verbs, nouns, or adjectives.

Below are some common structures with infinitives.

COMMON STRUCTURES WITH INFINITIVES	
1 An infinitive follows verbs such as the following: *attempt, decide, need, plan, want*	VERB + INFINITIVE *They **want to protect** the environment.*
2 To make an infinitive negative, put *not* before it.	*The city is asking the public **not to use** plastic bags for groceries.*
3 An infinitive can also follow certain nouns such as the following: *ability, chance, energy, opportunity, time, way*	NOUN + INFINITIVE *Off-grid living is a good **way to live** simply.*
4 An infinitive of purpose answers the question *why*.	*Some people go off the grid **to save** money.* (Why do some people go off the grid? To save money.) *Some people go off the grid **to help** the environment.* (Why do some people go off the grid? To help the environment.)

ACTIVITY 4.2 Practice Infinitive Forms

Work with a partner. Complete the sentences with the infinitive forms of the verbs in the box.

be	create	heat
cost	enjoy	protect

1 Many people use green cleaning products .... their health.
2 Community gardens help .... a sense of belonging.
3 Solar power uses the sun .... homes.
4 Organic fruits and vegetables tend .... more than regular produce.
5 Parks in cities give residents the chance .... the beauty of nature.
6 Off-grid living gives people a way .... more connected to nature.

Avoiding Common Mistakes

Research tells us that these are the most common mistakes that students make when using infinitives in academic writing. Avoid these mistakes when you write your essay in Section 5.

1 **Use correct word order with the negative form of an infinitive.**

               not to

The city decided ~~to not~~ switch to a renewable energy source.

2 **Remember that some verbs – for example,** *avoid, require, finish, keep, discuss,* **and** *consider* **– require a gerund.**

                  exploring

Many governments avoid ~~to explore~~ new energy sources because of financial concerns.

3 **Do not confuse the preposition** *for* **with the infinitive** *to* **when the meaning is "in order to."**

                to

Cooperation is necessary ~~for~~ ensure the success of zero-waste programs.

 4.3 Editing Task

Find and correct five more mistakes in the paragraph below.

               to live

Some people want ~~living~~ in very small houses because these homes use fewer natural resources. Because they are small, it costs less for heat these homes. Also, they use less electricity than large houses because it costs much less per month for supply electricity to a small house than to a large house. This is because small houses have fewer rooms, fewer electrical outlets, and less need for light fixtures than larger houses. Small houses use less water, too. Finally, they tend to not be on large lots. Therefore, they do not have large gardens that require to water. The decision to not have a lot of space means that owners of small homes not only reduce energy consumption, but save valuable resources and money as well.

C Avoiding Plagiarism

Academic writing has special challenges. One of the challenges for writers is recognizing and avoiding plagiarism.

I got my first essay back from my instructor. I worked really hard on it, so I thought I'd get a good grade. I was so surprised when I saw a big, red X at the top of the paper! When I asked my instructor about it, she said I had plagiarized it. I don't understand what I did wrong! Help! What is plagiarism?

Gitta

Dear Gitta,

Plagiarism is using someone else's exact words or ideas in your writing, and not naming the original writer or book, magazine, video, podcast, or website where you found them. Maybe you copied the exact words or images from some of these places and didn't include the source references.

Most schools in North America have an academic integrity policy. This policy is an agreement that members of an academic community sign. When you sign this agreement, you promise to be honest in how you present your ideas. That means you promise that you won't plagiarize another person's work.

Yours truly,

Professor Wright

RECOGNIZING PLAGIARISM

In order to avoid plagiarizing, you must first recognize it. Read the original text from author Emily Sohn's article "Revving Up Green Machines."

ORIGINAL TEXT: "In the United States alone, 17 million new cars hit the road in 2004. But the freedom to travel anywhere, anytime in a car or truck comes at a price. It's not just the cost of gasoline, insurance, and repairs. Automobiles are a major source of pollution. Most cars burn gasoline, which releases carbon dioxide gas into the air, along with other particles and pollutants."

Now read the paragraphs by students who used the information in the original text. Student A plagiarized it, and Student B did not.

Student A (plagiarized text)	Student B (did not plagiarize text)
I believe that we need to reduce the number of cars. <u>In the United States alone, 17 million new cars hit the road in 2004. Automobiles are a major source of pollution. Most cars burn gasoline, and it releases carbon dioxide into the air.</u>	Use of gasoline-powered cars is a problem in the world. According to Emily Sohn, there were 17 million new cars in America. She says there is a price to traveling freely in cars. She states, "It's not just the cost of gasoline, insurance, and repairs." Pollution is also a cost.
This student: • copied and pasted the underlined sentences from the original source. • did not cite, in other words, give the author's name or title and page number (if there is one) of the article from which the information came.	This student: • wrote the ideas in her own words. • cited her source, in other words, gave the name of the author of the article in which she found the information. • used quotation marks when she used the author's *exact words*.

 4.4 Practice

Read the original text. Then read the paragraphs by Student A and Student B. Check (✓) the student who plagiarized. Discuss your reasons with a partner.

ORIGINAL TEXT: "Landfills and garbage dumps are full of plastic. But scientists are working on a new generation of plastics that are better for the environment. Some are made from natural materials, like parts of corn or sugar plants. These are called bioplastics. Already, Earth-friendlier plastics are being used to make water bottles, gift cards, forks, and more." (Adapted from the article "Planting Seeds for Better Plastic," by Emily Sohn)

☐ **Student A:** According to Sohn, scientists can use plants to make special new plastics. That means they are natural, so they are not so bad for the environment. Now, many common products are being made from these new plastics.

☐ **Student B:** There is a lot of plastic in garbage dumps. Scientists are working on a new generation of plastics that are better for the environment. Some are made from natural materials. These are called bioplastics. They are being used to make many new products.

 4.5 Practice

Rewrite one of the plagiarized sentences from Activity 4.4 in your own words.

....

....

5 WRITE YOUR ESSAY

In this section, you will follow the writing process to complete the final draft of your essay.

STEP 1: BRAINSTORM

Work with a partner. Follow the steps below to brainstorm ideas for your essay.

1 Before you start, notice how the writer of the Student Model essay brainstormed. She wrote a lot of ideas. She included some of the ideas from the list that she made in Section 1 on page 14. Then she circled the three points that she thought were the strongest.

Reasons for a Bike-Share Program
more freedom
no looking for parking
never get stuck in traffic
save money
⟨convenient to travel around city⟩
get more exercise
⟨feel safer because more people everywhere⟩
⟨city – more fun⟩
no worry about bus schedules
BUT supply can be a problem – app!
can go anywhere
fun – I go more places
reduce stress
better health

2 Write the ideas that you wrote in Section 1 on page 15 in the space below. Include ideas from the Your Turns throughout the unit. Brainstorm more ideas.

3 Circle the three strongest points in support of your thesis and write them below.

1 ....

2 ....

3 ....

STEP 2: DO RESEARCH

If your topic requires research, see page 261 for advice on how to find information.

STEP 3: MAKE AN OUTLINE

Making an outline helps you organize your ideas. Complete the outline below with your ideas from the previous steps.

ESSAY OUTLINE

I. Introductory paragraph

Thesis Statement

Body Paragraph 1 II.

Supporting Idea 1 A.

Detail 1.

Supporting Idea 2 B.

Detail 1.

Body Paragraph 2 III.

Supporting Idea 1 A.

Detail 1.

Supporting Idea 2 B.

Detail 1.

Body Paragraph 3 IV.

Supporting Idea 1 A.

Detail 1.

Supporting Idea 2 B.

Detail 1.

V. Concluding paragraph

STEP 4: WRITE YOUR FIRST DRAFT

Now it is time to write your first draft. Here are some suggestions on how to get started:

1 Use your outline, notes, and the sentences you wrote in the Your Turns and in Step 3 on page 41.

2 Focus on making your ideas as clear as possible.

3 Remember to add a title.

After you finish, read your essay and check for basic errors:

1 Check that all sentences have subjects and verbs.

2 Go through and look at every comma. Is it correct? Should it be a period?

3 Check that you have used a comma after dependent clauses with *Although/While/Because*, etc., when they start a sentence.

4 Make sure your thesis statement and topic sentences are clear.

STEP 5: WRITE YOUR FINAL DRAFT

Before you write your final draft, do the following:

1 After you receive feedback on your first draft, review it carefully. Fix any errors.

2 Make a note of errors that were most frequent (wrong verb tense, using commas instead of periods, etc.). Try to avoid them as you write.

3 Review the Academic Vocabulary and Collocations from this unit. Are there any that you can add to your essay?

4 Turn to page 262 and use the Self-Editing Review to check your work one more time.

5 Write your final draft and hand it in.

② COMPARISON AND CONTRAST ESSAYS 1
EDUCATION: APPROACHES TO LEARNING

"One of the reasons people stop learning is that they become less and less willing to risk failure."

John W. Gardner
(1912–2002)

About the Author:

John W. Gardner was an educator and a philanthropist. He devoted his life to civil rights and education.

Work with a partner. Read the quotation about learning. Then answer the questions.

1 What does Gardner mean when he says that a person becomes "less and less willing to risk failure"?

2 What are some other reasons that people stop learning?

3 In your opinion, what is the most important reason that people stop learning? Why is it more significant than the other reasons you have discussed?

Ⓐ Connect to Academic Writing

In this unit, you will learn skills to help you compare and contrast ideas. While some of the writing skills that you will use may be new to you, the skill of comparing ideas is not new. In your everyday life, you use the skill of comparison when you ask questions such as *Which school should I go to?* or *Which neighborhood should I live in?*

Ⓑ Reflect on the Topic

In this section, you will choose a writing prompt and reflect on it. You will develop these ideas throughout the unit and use them to practice skills that are necessary to write your essay.

The writing prompt below was used for the Student Model essay on pages 50–51. The student reflected on his topic using a Venn diagram to see similarities and differences. This helped him think of a possible thesis for his essay.

WRITING PROMPT: Compare two skills that you have learned. The skills could be artistic, such as singing or painting, or physical, such as learning to ride a bike or fix cars. Was the experience of learning these two skills similar or different?

Subject A:
Learning to draw

Subject B:
Learning to play the saxophone

DIFFERENCES
(Subject A)

- drew anime characters
- learned on my own
- spent hours drawing
- free to express myself
- ....

SIMILARITIES
(Subjects A and B)

- hard work!
- fun
- made me happy
- ....
....

DIFFERENCES
(Subject B)

- learned with a teacher – took lessons – expensive
- listened to a lot of jazz music (Mom)
- practiced less
- learned new songs quickly
- ....

Possible thesis statement: Learning how to draw and play the saxophone both took effort, but the experience of learning each skill was different.

 1.1 Notice

Work with a partner. Discuss two more possible comparisons and add them to the Venn diagram.

Follow the directions to reflect on your topic.

A Choose a prompt:

- Compare the life of a college student in two countries – for example, the life of a college student in the United States with the life of a college student in Turkey.

- Some people learn a language mostly by taking classes and studying the grammar. Other people learn a language by interacting with people in that culture. Compare the two ways of learning. How are these two ways similar or different?

- Compare two people's attitudes toward school and learning. Some ideas: think about how they feel about studying, how motivated they are, and how they behave in class.

- A topic approved by your instructor

B Complete the following tasks:

1 Complete the Venn diagram below. Think of everything you know about both subjects.

2 Write a possible thesis statement.

3 Compare Venn diagrams and possible thesis statements with a partner.

Subject A:
....

Subject B:
....

DIFFERENCES
(Subject A)

SIMILARITIES
(Subjects A and B)

DIFFERENCES
(Subject B)

Possible thesis statement: ....

2 EXPAND YOUR KNOWLEDGE

In this section, you will learn academic language that you can use in your comparison and contrast essay. You will also notice how a professional writer uses the language and features of academic essays.

Academic Vocabulary

The words below appear throughout the unit. Many are from the Academic Word List. Using these words in your writing will make your ideas clearer and your writing more academic.

assume (v)	factor (n)	gap (n)	rely on (v)
expectation (n)	fundamental (adj)	persistence (n)	task (n)

ACTIVITY 2.1 Focus on Meaning

Work with a partner. Match the words in bold with their definitions. Write the letters.

A

.... 1 Some students are not confident about their ability to learn. Before they take a test, they **assume** that they will fail.

.... 2 Parents usually have high **expectations** of their children. They think that their children can achieve anything.

.... 3 Researchers have studied students who do well in school. One key **factor** for their success was the support that they got from their family.

.... 4 Students who do well have a confident attitude, while students who do poorly are much less confident. Confidence is a **fundamental** difference.

a a fact or situation that has an influence

b very important or essential

c to feel that something is true or will happen without proof

d a strong hope or belief that something will happen

B

.... 1 Students in the United States score lower in math compared to students in many other countries. Some say this **gap** exists because schools in the United States do not emphasize math enough.

.... 2 Some students believe that they will succeed if they work hard enough. They have **persistence**.

.... 3 Students need to **rely on** someone to help them when they feel stressed or have challenges.

.... 4 When classroom **tasks** are difficult, some students give up and do not finish them.

a the act of continuing to try to do something although it is difficult

b an activity or a chore

c to depend on someone or something for help or information

d the difference or space between two things; a missing part

B Academic Phrases

Research tells us that the phrases in bold below are commonly used in academic writing.

ACTIVITY **2.2** Focus on Purpose

Read the paragraph. Then match the phrases in bold to the reasons that the writer used them.

    While some people **argue that** it is easier for children to learn another language, adult learners have some clear advantages. Adult learners benefit from a teacher's motivation, but they are also self-motivated. Adult learners have specific goals, such as getting a degree, so they rely less on others to motivate them. Also, adult learners are able to pay attention in class for longer periods of time. More importantly, adults can learn more quickly because they can find patterns of language and ideas. **As** Sara Ferman and Avi Karni **point out in** their article "No Childhood Advantage in the Acquisition Skill in Using an Artificial Language Rule," adults can figure out rules, such as grammar rules, and use them in new situations. **According to** Ferman and Karni, children have not learned this skill (7). These advantages are encouraging to all adult learners.

PHRASE	PURPOSE
.... 1 **While** some people **argue that** …	a to introduce the authors and article
.... 2 **As** Ferman and Karni **point out in** their article …	b to introduce an opposing idea
.... 3 **According to** Ferman and Karni, …	c to introduce the authors' ideas

C Writing in the Real World

The author of "The Trouble with Talent" uses comparison and contrast to strengthen her argument.

Before you read, answer these questions: What does it mean to be "smart"? Can people get smart or are they born smart?

Now read the article. Think about your answers to the questions above as you read.

THE TROUBLE WITH TALENT: ARE WE BORN SMART OR DO WE GET SMART? (adapted)

BY KATHY SEAL

1   Jim Stigler was in an awkward position.[1] He was fascinated to see that Asian students usually do better than American students at elementary math. The psychologist suspected that **persistence** might be the key **factor**. So he did an experiment in which he gave the same insolvable math problem to separate groups of Japanese and American children.

2   As expected, most American students started the problem, struggled briefly, and then gave up. The Japanese students, however, worked on and on. Finally, Stigler stopped the experiment. If the Japanese students were uninterrupted, they seemed willing to continue indefinitely.[2]

3   "The Japanese kids **assumed** that if they kept working, they'd eventually get it," Stigler recalls. "The Americans thought 'either you get it or you don't.'"

4   Stigler's work, detailed in his book *The Learning Gap,* shatters the assumption that Asian education **relies on** rote and drill.[3] In fact, Japanese and Chinese teachers believe that their chief **task** is to stimulate thinking. In addition, they tell their students that anyone who thinks long enough about a problem can move toward its solution.

5   Stigler concludes that the belief in hard work is one reason why Asians outperform us academically. Americans believe that success in school requires inborn talent. "If you believe that achievement is mostly caused by ability," Stigler says, "at some **fundamental** level you don't believe in education. You

believe in sorting kids, and that kids in some categories can't learn. The Japanese believe everybody can master the curriculum if you give them the time."

6   Stigler and his co-author, Harold W. Stevenson, are among a group of psychologists who argue that the American fixation[4] on talent causes us to waste many children's potential. He feels that this focus on talent is producing kids who give up easily.

7   Respect for hard work is present throughout Asian culture. Many folk tales demonstrate the idea that if you work hard, you can achieve any goal. For example, the poet Li Po tells about a woman who grinds a piece of iron into a needle. The accent on effort in Asian countries demonstrates how **expectations** for children are both higher and more democratic there than in America. "If learning is gradual and proceeds step by step," says Stigler, "anyone can gain knowledge."

8   Americans, on the other hand, group children by ability. So students know who the teacher thinks is "very smart, sorta smart, and kinda dumb," says Jeff Howard of the Efficacy Institute, a firm that specializes in education issues. "The idea of genetic intellectual inferiority is widespread in [American society]."

9   A consequence is that many students face lower expectations. "A student who is bright is expected to just 'get it,'" Stigler says. "Duller kids are **assumed** to lack the necessary ability for ever learning certain material."

[1]**awkward position:** difficult situation
[2]**indefinitely:** without a clear end
[3]**rote and drill:** learning by memorizing and repeating over and over

[4]**fixation:** unnaturally strong interest

10   Psychologist Carol Dweck has conducted a series of studies showing the dangers of believing that geniuses are born rather than made. In one study, Dweck and researcher Valanne Henderson asked 229 seventh graders whether people are "born smart" or "get smart" by working hard. Then they compared the students' sixth and seventh grade achievement scores. The scores of students with the get-smart beliefs stayed high or improved. In contrast, the scores of students who believed in the born-smart assumption stayed low or declined. Surprisingly, even students who believed in working hard but who had low confidence did very well. And the students whose scores dropped the most were the born-smart believers with high confidence.

11   Although getting Americans to give up their worship of ability and replace it with a belief in effort seems like a huge task, Dweck believes that it is possible to train students to believe in hard work. According to Dweck, the key is for the adults close to them to believe that effort is what counts.

12   The Efficacy Institute is working on exactly that. The Institute conducts a seminar for teachers which helps them reject the born-smart belief system. They use the slogan "Think you can; work hard; get smart."

13   "We tell teachers to talk to kids with the presumption[5] that they can all get As in their tests," explains specialist Kim Taylor. Most kids respond immediately, Howard says. As proof, he cites test scores of 137 third grade students from six Detroit public schools who were enrolled in the program in 1989 and 1990. The students' scores rose 2.4 grade levels in one year. That was compared with a control group[6] whose scores went up by less than half of one grade level.

14   Although efforts for change are modest, even the U.S. government is weaving this new thinking into its education agenda. During a talk to the California Teachers Association, the U.S. Secretary of Education pledged to work on setting national standards in education. "These standards," he says, "must be for all of our young people, regardless of their economic background. We must convince people that children aren't born smart. They get smart."

[5]**presumption:** a belief that something is true without any proof that it is true
[6]**control group:** a group of people in an experiment that does not receive any treatment

 2.3 Check Your Understanding

Answer the questions.

1   What two groups of subjects did Stigler compare in his experiment?

2   What are the differences in attitude between the two groups of subjects?

3   Which attitude is more similar to your attitude about learning: the Asian students' or the American students'? Explain.

 2.4 Notice the Features of Comparison and Contrast Writing

Answer the questions.

1   Look at paragraph 2. Which word does the author use to make a difference between the two subjects clear?

2   Look at paragraphs 7 and 8. What is the author comparing? What phrase does the writer use in paragraph 8 to introduce how Americans are different?

3   Look at paragraph 10. What does the comparison help the writer prove?

In Section 1, you saw how the writer of the Student Model essay reflected on his topic. In this section, you will analyze the final draft of his comparison and contrast essay. You will learn how to structure your ideas for your own essay.

Ⓐ Student Model

Read the writing prompt again and answer the questions.

WRITING PROMPT: Compare two skills that you have learned. The skills could be artistic, such as singing or painting, or physical, such as learning to ride a bike or fix cars. Was the experience of learning these two skills similar or different?

1   What is the essay prompt asking the writer to compare? Circle the words in the prompt that you expect the writer to use in his or her thesis statement.

2   What are some similarities or differences that you think the writer might mention?

Read the essay twice. The first time, think about your answers to the questions above. The second time, answer the questions in the Analyze Writing Skills boxes. This will help you notice key features of comparison and contrast essays.

STUDENT MODEL

Learning Two Skills

1   Thanks to my parents, I have always had a passion for the arts. When I was young, my father bought me manga, which are Japanese comic books. All my friends loved to read manga, but I was fascinated by the drawings. Then I became obsessed with anime and began drawing the characters. I have an interest in music, too, because my mother always played jazz at home. Hearing great musicians like Astrud Gilberto and Miles Davis every evening inspired me to take saxophone lessons at school. I enjoyed learning to draw and play the saxophone, but they were very different experiences in terms of how I learned, how much I practiced, and how they made me feel.

2   I learned to draw on my own because there were no art schools near our house. I started by tracing my favorite anime characters. Later, I was able to draw them on paper without looking. After several years, I could draw images from my imagination. I improved because I practiced whenever I could. I had **persistence** and spent many hours each day perfecting my drawings. When I was drawing, I felt a real sense of freedom because I experimented with new ideas and techniques. I was free to express myself, because there was no right or wrong way to do things.

1 Analyze Writing Skills

In paragraph 1, circle the two subjects that the writer is comparing.

2 Analyze Writing Skills

Underline the writer's thesis statement in paragraph 1. What will the writer focus on in his essay?

a   similarities

b   differences

c   both similarities and differences

3 Analyze Writing Skills

In paragraph 2, the writer talks about the three points below. Number them in the order that he talks about them.

a   how he felt when drawing

b   how he learned to draw

c   how often he practiced

3   In contrast, my experience learning to play the saxophone was different. I took lessons at my school in Brazil. I had class once a week. I **relied on** a teacher to help me learn how to read music, use the instrument, and play rhythms. Although I practiced less than drawing, I improved faster. I only practiced on Saturdays for an hour, but I learned new songs quickly because I was good at memorizing notes and rhythms. Unlike drawing, playing the saxophone felt less free because I played songs that my teacher chose. Also, I had to play them the way my teacher wanted me to. **According to** her, there was a right way to play each song. Her **expectation** was that I should sound like everyone else. This was not an easy **task**.

4   In conclusion, learning to draw felt different from learning to play the saxophone in important ways. Even though learning the saxophone produced quicker results, I enjoyed the time and freedom I had when I was teaching myself how to draw. Today I still listen to jazz music, but I do not play. I have realized that drawing comes more naturally to me and gives me greater satisfaction. Playing the saxophone taught me the importance of teamwork, but drawing is my true passion because it has allowed me to express myself.

4 Analyze Writing Skills

In paragraph 3, underline the first sentence. What is the function of this sentence?

a   to show contrast

b   to introduce the second subject

c   both a and b

5 Analyze Writing Skills

Which statement is true about the ideas in paragraph 3?

a   The writer focuses only on playing the saxophone.

b   The writer contrasts learning to play the saxophone with learning to draw.

6 Analyze Writing Skills

In paragraph 4, underline the two sentences that restate the author's thesis.

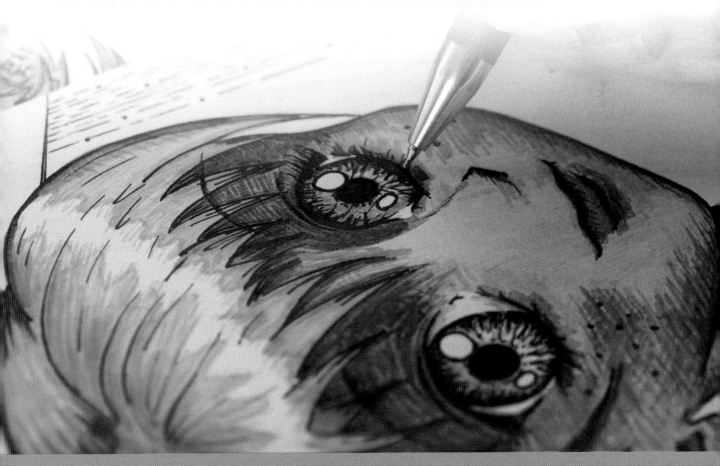

3.1 Check Your Understanding

Answer the questions.

1 The writer compared his experiences learning to draw and play the saxophone in three ways. What are they?

2 How much freedom did the writer feel when drawing and playing the saxophone? How did these feelings affect his experiences?

3 What are the benefits of having a teacher to help you learn something new?

 3.2 Outline the Writer's Ideas

Complete the outline for "Learning Two Skills." Write the thesis statement. Then use the phrases in the box.

could draw from my imagination	felt less free
expectation – sound like everyone else	practiced one hour on Saturdays
felt a sense of freedom	relied on my teacher to learn

ESSAY OUTLINE

I. Introductory paragraph ....

Thesis Statement ....

....

....

Body Paragraph 1 II. Learning to draw ....

Point 1   A. Learned on my own ....

Detail   1. Started by tracing anime characters ....

Detail   2. Able to draw them without looking ....

Detail   3. ....

Point 2   B. Practiced whenever I could ....

Detail   1. Spent hours perfecting drawings ....

Point 3	C. ....
Detail	1. Experimented with new ideas and techniques ....
Detail	2. Free to express myself ....
Body Paragraph 2	III. Learning to play the saxophone ....
Point 1	A. Took lessons at school ....
Detail	1. Had class once a week ....
Detail	2. ....
Point 2	B. Practiced less, but improved faster ....
Detail	1. ....
Detail	2. Learned new songs quickly ....
Point 3	C. ....
Detail	1. Played songs teacher chose ....
Detail	2. A right way to play each song ....
Detail	3. ....
	IV. Concluding paragraph ....

Ⓑ Comparison and Contrast Essays: Block Organization

Writers compare subjects to help reveal important differences and/or similarities between them.

There are two basic ways to organize ideas in comparison and contrast essays: block organization and point-by-point. In this unit, you will learn **block organization**. In Unit 3, you will learn **point-by-point organization**.

In block organization, writers compare their subjects in two body paragraphs, or two "blocks" of text. Each paragraph has a different purpose:

- The first body paragraph describes Subject A using specific points of comparison.
- The second body paragraph describes Subject B using the same points of comparison to show how the two subjects are similar or different.

The Student Model essay is an example of block organization. Below is the organization of his ideas and three points of comparison.

LEARNING TWO SKILLS

Introduction

Body Paragraph 1: Subject A: learning to draw

    Point 1: How I learned – by myself

    Point 2: How much I practiced – every day

    Point 3: How I felt – free to express myself

Body Paragraph 2: Subject B: learning to play the saxophone *compared to* learning to draw

    Point 1: How I learned – in a class

    Point 2: How much I practiced – on Saturdays

    Point 3: How I felt – less free

Conclusion

 3.3 Notice

Look at the Student Model essay outline above. Circle the answers.

1 The writer describes each point of comparison in

  a body paragraph 1.   b body paragraph 2.   c both body paragraphs.

2 The writer focuses only on learning to draw in

  a body paragraph 1.   b body paragraph 2.   c both body paragraphs.

3 The writer discusses how he felt about learning in

  a body paragraph 1.   b body paragraph 2.   c both body paragraphs.

4 The writer explains how learning to play the saxophone was different from learning to draw in

  a body paragraph 1.   b body paragraph 2.   c both body paragraphs.

POINTS OF COMPARISON

Writers use the same **points of comparison** for their subjects. **Points of comparison** are the ways the writer will compare the two subjects. For example, the writer of the Student Model essay used *how he learned, how much time he practiced*, and *how he felt* as his three points of comparison. Reflecting on these points of comparison revealed important differences.

Below is an example of how to organize ideas using block organization. The writer compares young learners and adult learners. This helps her think about possible similarities and differences, which helped her decide whether to focus only on similarities, only on differences, or on both similarities and differences. Look at how she organized her ideas. What do you think she focused on?

WRITING PROMPT: Compare young language learners and adult language learners. What are some important similarities or differences between them?

Points of Comparison	Young Learners	Adult Learners
1 motivation	teacher motivates	teacher motivates and self-motivated
2 ability to pay attention	shorter attention spans	longer attention spans
3 how they learn	playing, socializing	socializing, alone

 3.4 Apply It to Your Writing

Look at your Venn diagram on page 45. Use the ideas to complete the chart below.

Points of Comparison	Subject A	Subject B

INTRODUCTORY PARAGRAPH

In a comparison essay, the introductory paragraph gives readers background information about the two subjects that the writer will compare. As you learned in Unit 1, the introduction also includes the writer's thesis statement. In a comparison essay, the thesis statement shows readers whether the essay will focus on similarities, on differences, or on both.

A good thesis statement:

- includes the two subjects the writer is comparing
- uses parallel structure to list the points of comparison
- uses language that shows if the writer will focus on similarities, on differences, or on both

Parallel structure means that each point is listed using the same part of speech. Read the examples below to see how to make the points parallel.

Learning to sing and learning to read were different in how I learned, ~~*I learned from different people,*~~ who taught me *and why I learned.*

Online and traditional classes **are similar because** *they both require students to participate, take exams, and* ~~*they have to work in groups*~~ work in groups.

3.5 Practice Noticing Parallel Structure

Complete the thesis statements with the correct point of comparison.

1 Higher education today is very different from higher education 20 years ago, especially in the technology in the classroom, the subjects that you can major in, and ....
....

    a there are more students in a class

    b how many students are in a class

    c the number of students in a class

2 Good teachers are like good parents because they care about you, they listen when you are troubled, and ....

    a helpful when you need it

    b they offer help when you need it

    c are helpful when you need advice

3 Successful students are different from unsuccessful students in how much time they study, how they deal with stress, and ....

    a they deal with failure

    b ways to deal with failure

    c how they deal with failure

3.6 Practice Writing Parallel Structure

Work with a partner. Complete the thesis statements with your own ideas. Use parallel structure.

1 Learning another language is like learning a musical instrument because they both require time, ..., and ....

2 Young learners and adult learners differ in how they study, ..., and ....

3 Learning to read is like learning to drive a car because for both you must have patience, you ...., and you ....

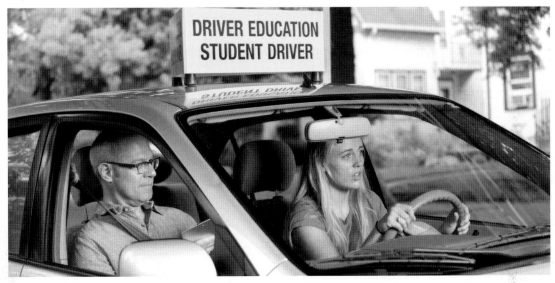

THESIS STATEMENTS THAT FOCUS ON SIMILARITIES AND DIFFERENCES

Below are examples of thesis statements. The words and phrases in bold focus on differences, on similarities, or on both. You can use these words and phrases to create your thesis statement. Notice the parallel structure of the points of comparison.

Thesis statements that focus on differences:

*I enjoyed learning to draw and play the saxophone, **but** they **were different in** <u>how I learned</u>, <u>how much I practiced</u>, and <u>how each one made me feel</u>.*

*It is clear that young learners and adult learners **have different** needs that affect how they learn.*

Thesis statements that focus on similarities:

***Both** teachers and students are motivated when classroom tasks are <u>relevant</u>, <u>fun</u>, and <u>creative</u>.*

*Online and traditional classes **are similar because** they both require <u>studying</u>, <u>working in groups</u>, and <u>taking exams</u>.*

Thesis statement that focuses on both similarities and differences:

***Although** young learners and adult learners **are different because** of their motivation and ability to pay attention, they **both** learn from playing games.*

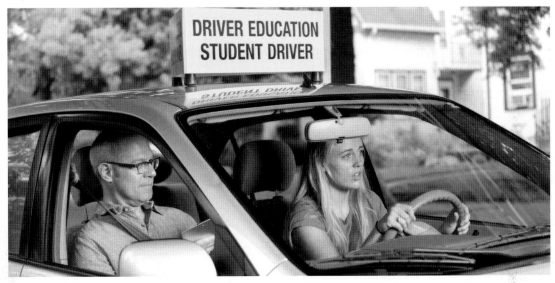

ACTIVITY 3.7 Analyze Thesis Statements

Write S if the statement focuses on similarities, D if the statement focuses on differences, or B if the statement focuses on both. Underline the words that helped you decide.

D   1   Although many private language schools and community colleges offer ESL programs, they <u>are different in</u> their costs, class sizes, and facilities.

       2   When I compare how I learned to fix cars and how to repair computers, I realize that my experiences were similar in many ways.

       3   Online learning and traditional learning have some fundamental differences that students should consider in their decision-making process.

       4   Japanese and American college students have some similarities; however, they differ in one important way.

       5   It is clear that learning how to play baseball and learning how to play soccer are similar because they both require practicing a lot, being a team player, and obeying rules.

ACTIVITY 3.8 Apply It to Your Writing

Think about the writing prompt and the ideas in your Venn diagram in Section 1 on page 45. Write a possible thesis statement based on what you have learned. Then share your thesis statement with a partner. Does the statement make it clear whether the essay will focus on similarities and/or differences?

....

....

....

BODY PARAGRAPHS IN BLOCK COMPARISON AND CONTRAST ESSAYS

As you learned earlier, the body paragraphs of a block comparison and contrast essay describe the two subjects in separate paragraphs. The first paragraph introduces Subject A and describes each point of comparison with specific details, such as explanations and examples.

Notice how the writer of the Student Model essay organizes his points for Subject A and discusses each one by giving specific details.

Body Paragraph 1: Subject A

How I learned	I learned to draw on my own because there were no art schools near our house. I started by tracing my favorite anime characters. Later, I was able to …		
	How much I practiced	I improved because I practiced whenever I could. I had persistence and spent many hours each day perfecting my drawings.	
		How I felt	When I was drawing, I felt a real sense of freedom because I experimented with new ideas and techniques. I was free to express myself …

Now notice below how the writer introduces Subject B and compares it to Subject A using the same points in the same order as in body paragraph 1. In order to make these comparisons clear for the reader, the writer uses words and phrases such as *in contrast*, *but*, *unlike*, and *although*.

Body Paragraph 2: Subject B Compared to Subject A

How I learned	*In contrast*, my experience learning to play the saxophone was different. I took lessons at my school in Brazil. I had class once a week. I relied on my teacher …		
	How much I practiced	*Although* I practiced less than drawing, I improved faster. I only practiced on Saturdays for an hour, but I learned new songs quickly because …	
		How I felt	*Unlike* drawing, playing the saxophone felt less free because I was playing songs that my teacher chose. Also, I had to …

 3.9 Notice

Read the thesis statement and first body paragraph below. Then read the sentences from the second body paragraph at the top of page 62. Number them in order from 1 to 3.

Thesis statement: Although students in Morocco and the United States begin college about the same time, there are some fundamental differences between them, including who supports them, where they live, and what course options they have.

Body paragraph 1:

Moroccan students have a lot of family support because many live with their families while they study. Their families want them to do well, and students try hard because they want to please their families. Also, most Moroccan students do not work and study at the same time. People there think that children should focus on studying and not on a job. Because Moroccan students focus solely on their education, they can be more successful. Finally, in Morocco, students do not have choices about classes when they start college. Everyone takes the same classes and follows the same schedule. Their classes are in both French and Arabic since both of these languages are widely used in society.

Body paragraph 2:

.... a Furthermore, American students have more course options than Moroccans do. Although there are several classes all students must take, most colleges offer many different schedules to fit students' needs, and students can try classes in various subjects.

.... b In contrast, many American students live away from home. They prefer to live in dormitories on campus, which means they do not have the same kind of family support that Moroccan students do.

.... c Unlike Moroccan students, many students in the United States also have a part-time job so that they can pay for their classes and living expenses. Some work all day and then take classes at night, so they are busier and struggle to complete all their schoolwork.

 3.10 Write Ideas

Work with a partner. Read the writing prompt and the first part of the essay. Then complete the second body paragraph at the top of page 61 using the same points of comparison.

WRITING PROMPT: Sometimes high school students are not prepared for the transition to college. Compare high school classes and college classes. What are their differences? Why do students need to understand these differences?

From High School to College: A Giant Leap

Transitioning from high school to college can be challenging. When students go to college, the environment is very different. In college, students are treated like adults, and they have more responsibilities. It is important for students to understand these differences so that they are better prepared and therefore more successful. They need to understand that high school and college classes have significant differences in terms of class schedules, amount of homework, and types of instruction.

High school classes usually last all year. Students study the same subjects, such as science and mathematics, for the whole school year. They use the same books and have the same teachers. They are in school from early morning to late afternoon every day. Students also have homework for each class every night and projects; however, if a student is well organized, he or she can usually complete all the assignments in a few hours. High school teachers help their students stay organized. They remind them about important assignments and deadlines often, and they talk to students about missing homework.

In contrast, the schedule for college classes is different ....

....

.... Unlike homework for high school, homework for college

....

....

Finally, compared to high school teachers, college professors ....

....

CONCLUDING PARAGRAPH

The **concluding paragraph** in a comparison and contrast essay can restate the thesis in two sentences. The first sentence includes the two subjects and restates whether the focus was on similarities, on differences, or on both. The second sentence then restates the points of comparison. Finally, the writer ends with a comment, such as an opinion or a realization.

Read the two example concluding paragraphs below.

In sum, learning how to fix cars and learning how to repair computers were actually quite similar experiences. They both required attention to detail, patience, and trial and error. <u>I believe that these skills will become more similar in the future because of technological advances.</u> (opinion)

In conclusion, there are several key differences between high school and college classes. In college, students must get used to different schedules, more homework, and higher expectations from professors. I realize now why my parents wanted me to go to a good high school. When I started college, I was already used to a lot of homework and to higher expectations from teachers, and that has helped me succeed. (realization)

 3.11 Notice

Look at the concluding paragraph in the Student Model essay on pages 50–51. Discuss the questions with a partner.

1 Does the writer restate the thesis statement in one or two sentences?
2 What is his final comment about learning to draw and to play the saxophone? Restate it in your own words.

In this section, you will learn writing and grammar skills that will help make your writing more sophisticated and accurate.

Ⓐ Writing Skill: Words and Phrases That Show Differences

Writers connect and compare ideas that show contrast, or differences between two subjects, using specific words and phrases.

Below are common words and phrases that show difference and how to use them in sentences.

WORDS AND PHRASES THAT SHOW DIFFERENCES	
However,	Online learning is convenient for busy students. **However,** students have to be self-motivated or they may not succeed.
On the other hand,	Students who are bright often learn quickly. **On the other hand,** they sometimes become easily frustrated and stop learning if they can't understand an idea right away.
In contrast,	Students who believe that they are smart expect that they will learn. **In contrast**, students who believe that they are not smart are not confident that they can learn.
Although / Even though	**Although / Even though** most of the interaction in online education is through the Internet, students say that they form strong relationships with other students through online discussions.
While	**While** there have been huge changes in education since 1960, a skilled teacher is still important for students to be successful.
	Women in the 1960s were expected to be housewives, **while** women today are much more likely to have careers.
Unlike	**Unlike** the college population in the 1960s, female students make up almost 50 percent of today's student body.

Notice the differences in meaning of the words and phrases.

1 In sentences with *although / even though*, the idea in the main clause is surprising. Sentences with *while* show only a contrast of ideas.

   Although / Even though *most of the interaction in online education is through the Internet,* <u>*students say that they form strong relationships with other students through online discussions*</u>. (It is surprising that students can form strong relationships with people they have never met face-to-face.)

2 *On the other hand* and *In contrast* show two contrasting meanings that seem to contradict each other.

   Students who are bright often learn quickly. **On the other hand,** *they sometimes become easily frustrated and stop learning if they can't understand an idea right away.* (It seems contradictory that these bright students stop learning because of frustration.)

4.1 Combine Sentences

Read the first sentence. Check (✓) the sentence that shows a contrast of ideas. Connect the two sentences using the word or phrase in parentheses. You may need to change or delete words.

1 Print textbooks are heavy and hard to carry.

☐ Electronic textbooks are environmentally friendly.

☑ Electronic textbooks fit on a lightweight electronic reader.

(unlike) *Unlike print textbooks, electronic textbooks fit on a lightweight electronic reader. OR Unlike electronic textbooks, print textbooks are heavy and hard to carry.*

2 Electronic textbooks are quick and easy to purchase and download.

☐ Print textbooks take more time to buy.

☐ Print textbooks can last many years.

(unlike) ....

....

3 Electronic textbooks are convenient.

☐ They can be out of stock.

☐ You have to have an electronic reader to use them.

(on the other hand) ....

....

4 The number of students buying electronic textbooks is rising.

☐ Some students say that they would rather read a print textbook.

☐ Print textbooks are less popular.

(while) ....

....

5 Young learners and adult learners have striking differences.

☐ Activities for young learners must be shorter because of their short attention spans.

☐ They both enjoy and learn from tasks that are interesting to them.

(even though) ....

....

6 A good teacher is an important motivator for both young learners and adult learners.

☐ Young learners rely on the help of a teacher much more.

☐ Young learners play games more.

(though) ....

....

7 Both young learners and adult learners learn through socializing and games.

☐ Young learners like to have fun.

☐ Adult learners can also learn by themselves.

(however) ....

....

8 Young learners generally accept the information that the teacher gives them.

☐ Adult learners ask questions and may disagree with the teacher.

☐ Adult learners are motivated learners.

(in contrast) ....

....

B Grammar for Writing: *That* Clauses

Writers use certain verbs and nouns to describe the thoughts, feelings, and attitudes of others. These verbs and nouns are followed by *that* clauses. Below are some examples.

VERBS AND NOUNS + *THAT* CLAUSES TO DESCRIBE THOUGHTS, FEELINGS, AND ATTITUDES	
1 Some common verbs that writers use to describe ways of thinking are: *argue, assume, believe, conclude, feel, see, show, think*	Stigler **argues that** the born-smart mentality hurts children. Japanese teachers **believe that** their chief task is to stimulate thinking. Stigler **concludes that** the belief in hard work is one reason that Asians outperform Americans academically.
2 Some common nouns that writers use to describe ways of thinking are: *assumption, belief, claim, conclusion, fact, idea*	Asians hold the **belief that** everyone can learn through effort. The **claim that** Asian education relies on rote and drill is inaccurate. Some students have trouble believing in the **idea that** they can get As if they work hard enough.
3 In academic writing, writers include *that*. In less formal writing, *that* is often omitted.	ACADEMIC WRITING: *Studies show that teachers' expectations influence children's achievement.* LESS FORMAL WRITING: *Studies show teachers' expectations influence children's achievement.*

4.2 Combine Ideas

Combine each pair of ideas into one sentence with the word or phrase in parentheses and a *that* clause. Use the correct form of the verb or noun in parentheses to introduce the *that* clause.

1 Successful students are more likely to use study strategies. There is research on this.

(show) Research shows that successful students are more likely to use study strategies.

2 Adults are more challenging to teach than children. This is what the author claims.

(make the claim)

3 The born-smart mindset hurts students. The author makes the argument for this.

(argue)

4 Online classes are not as difficult as traditional classes. Some students say this.

(feel)

5 Online learning is as effective as traditional learning. Researchers cannot say this.

(draw the conclusion)

Avoiding Common Mistakes

Research tells us that these are the most common mistakes that students make when using *that* clauses in academic writing.

> 1. **Remember to use a complete verb in a *that* clause.**
>
>   He says that this focus on talent _{is} producing kids who give up easily.
>
> 2. **Do not omit the word *that* in a *that* clause in academic writing.**
>
>   Some teachers believe _{that} some students cannot learn.
>
> 3. **Remember to use a subject in a *that* clause.**
>
>   Children must be convinced that _{they} can achieve if they work hard.

 4.3 Editing Task

Find and correct six more mistakes in the paragraph below.

Most people assume _{that} success in life for many means getting a college education. In fact, many high school students spend their last few years assuming that will go to college and prepare for it. Once in college, however, their optimistic belief they can achieve their goal weakens. College is hard. Current research shows students who are successful have different mindsets from other less successful students. Low-performing students may have the impression that they failing because they are not smart enough. Researchers have found that is often not true. They claim intelligence has less to do with success than people think. Successful students are different from other less successful students in their persistence and ability to deal with failure. They simply have the belief that can succeed through hard work.

C Avoiding Plagiarism

In academic writing, you will use facts, statistics, and original ideas from experts to support your thesis. How do you use other people's ideas correctly? Read about Hamid's problem.

My instructor said that she would not accept my paper because I plagiarized it. She said that I used other people's ideas without including their names in my essay, and I used the exact words of one expert. I don't understand. It's hard for me to explain ideas in English, so I copy and paste the ideas from experts. What's wrong with that?

Hamid

Dear Hamid,

It's great that you found ideas from experts to support your thesis, but there's a right way and a wrong way to use them in your essay. The most useful way to use others' ideas is to paraphrase the ideas. If you copy and paste, you have plagiarized. If you don't include the author's name, you have also plagiarized. I think the best thing for you right now is to learn how to paraphrase.

Yours truly,

Professor Wright

Paraphrasing is an essential skill in academic writing. It means stating the ideas of others in your own words. If you like an author's ideas, you can include them in your paper as long as you tell the reader where you got them.

Read the strategies for paraphrasing quotations.

STRATEGIES FOR PARAPHRASING

Original Quotation: "We like to think of our champions and idols as superheroes who were born different from us." (Dweck 90)

1	Use synonyms for key words (nouns, verbs, adjectives, etc.).	*Dweck says that people prefer to believe that there is a huge difference between winners and super achievers and everyone else.*
2	Change the parts of speech of some words (verb to noun, etc.).	*According to Dweck, people prefer to believe that those we idolize for their heroic accomplishments have a fundamental difference right from their birth.*
3	Break up the ideas into separate sentences or change the order of ideas.	*As Dweck points out in Mindset, our superheroes and winners are perceived differently because we want them to be very different from us. We want them to be exceptional.*

To successfully paraphrase text, you must:

1 Use at least two of the strategies on page 67 to change the text so that it looks like your writing – but make sure you do *not* change the ideas.

2 Include the name of the source. In other words, give credit to the source in one of the following ways:

[Author] reports/states/says/claims that …

According to [Author], …

As [Author] points out in [title of article/book], …

 4.4 Practice the Strategies

Read the original text and the two paraphrases below. Check (✓) the strategies that the writer used for each paraphrase. Then answer the questions below.

Original Text: *"If you believe that achievement is mostly caused by ability," Stigler says, "at some fundamental level you don't believe in education."*

Paraphrase 1: According to Stigler, people who think that inborn talent is essential for success probably do not think fundamentally that education matters much.

Paraphrase 2: You fundamentally do not believe in education if you believe that achievement is mostly the result of ability.

	Use synonyms.	Change parts of speech.	Break up or change the order of ideas.	Introduce ideas with: *X reports/ states/believes that …* *According to X, …*
Paraphrase 1	✓			
Paraphrase 2				

1 Which paraphrased version does not plagiarize the original text? Why?

2 Rewrite the version that plagiarizes the original text so that it is a better paraphrase.

....

....

....

....

5 WRITE YOUR ESSAY

In this section, you will follow the writing process to complete the final draft of your essay.

STEP 1: BRAINSTORM

Work with a partner. Follow the steps below to brainstorm ideas for your essay.

1 Before you start, notice how the writer of the Student Model essay brainstormed. He wrote many ideas. Then he chose three points of comparison that he thought were the strongest.

STUDENT MODEL

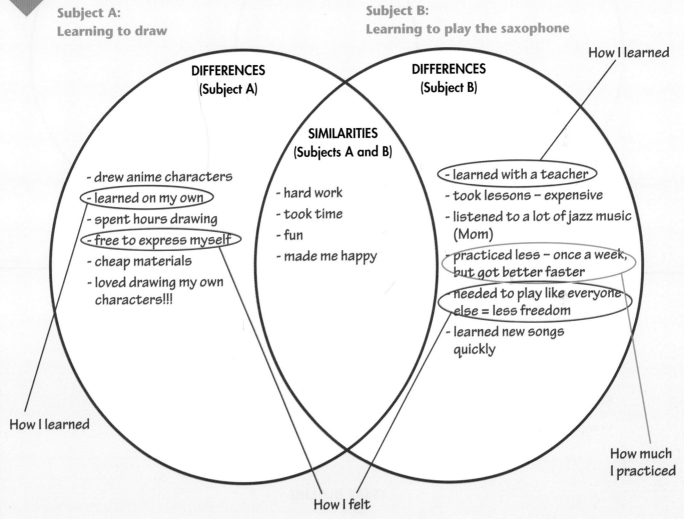

Subject A:
Learning to draw

Subject B:
Learning to play the saxophone

How I learned

DIFFERENCES
(Subject A)

DIFFERENCES
(Subject B)

SIMILARITIES
(Subjects A and B)

- drew anime characters
- learned on my own
- spent hours drawing
- free to express myself
- cheap materials
- loved drawing my own
  characters!!!

- hard work
- took time
- fun
- made me happy

- learned with a teacher
- took lessons – expensive
- listened to a lot of jazz music
  (Mom)
- practiced less – once a week,
  but got better faster
- needed to play like everyone
  else = less freedom
- learned new songs
  quickly

How I learned

How much
I practiced

How I felt

2 Write the ideas that you wrote in Section 1 on page 45 in the Venn diagram below. Include ideas from the Your Turns throughout the unit. Brainstorm more ideas.

Subject A: ....   Subject B: ....

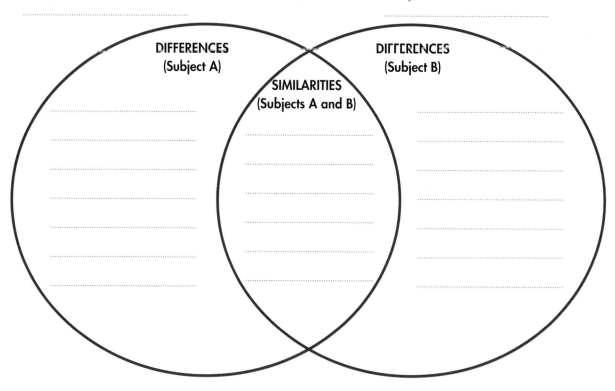

When you are finished, circle the three strongest points of comparison and write them here.

1 ....   2 ....   3 ....

STEP 2: DO RESEARCH

If your topic requires research, see page 261 for advice on how to find information.

STEP 3: MAKE AN OUTLINE

Complete the outline below with your ideas from the previous steps.

ESSAY OUTLINE

I. Introductory paragraph ....

Thesis Statement ....

....

Body Paragraph 1	II. ....
Supporting Idea 1	A. ....
Detail	1. ....
Detail	2. ....
Supporting Idea 2	B. ....
Detail	1. ....
Detail	2. ....
Supporting Idea 3	C. ....
Detail	1. ....
Detail	2. ....
Body Paragraph 2	III. ....
Supporting Idea 1	A. ....
Detail	1. ....
Detail	2. ....
Supporting Idea 2	B. ....
Detail	1. ....
Detail	2. ....
Supporting Idea 3	C. ....
Detail	1. ....
Detail	2. ....
	IV. Concluding paragraph ....

STEP 4: WRITE YOUR FIRST DRAFT

Now it is time to write your first draft. Here are some suggestions on how to get started:

1 Use your outline, notes, and the sentences you wrote in the Your Turns and in Step 3 on pages 70–71.

2 Focus on making your ideas as clear as possible.

3 Remember to add a title.

After you finish, read your essay and check for basic errors:

1 Check that all sentences have subjects and verbs.

2 Look at every comma. Is it correct? Should it be a period?

3 Check that you have used a comma after dependent clauses with *Although/While/Because*, etc., when they start a sentence.

4 Make sure your thesis statement is clear.

STEP 5: WRITE YOUR FINAL DRAFT

1 After you receive feedback on your first draft, review it carefully. Fix any errors.

2 Make a note of errors that were most frequent. Try to avoid them as you write.

3 Review the Academic Vocabulary and Phrases from this unit. Are there any that you can add to your essay?

4 Turn to page 263 and use the Self-Editing Review to check your work one more time.

5 Write your final draft and hand it in.

3 COMPARISON AND CONTRAST ESSAYS 2
SOCIOLOGY: COMMUNITIES AND RELATIONSHIPS

"Life is a constant struggle between being an individual and being a member of the community."

Sherman Alexie (1966–)

About the Author:

Sherman Alexie is a poet, novelist, and filmmaker. He grew up on the Spokane Indian Reservation and now lives in Seattle, Washington.

Work with a partner. Read the quotation about communities. Then answer the questions.

1 What kind of struggles do you think Alexie is referring to?

2 What does it mean to be a member of a community? What responsibilities do people have as part of a community?

3 Which is more important to you: being able to do what you want or being part of a community of people?

Ⓐ Connect to Academic Writing

In this unit, you will learn to write a comparison and contrast essay using point-by-point organization. While some of the skills may be new to you, others are not. In your daily life, you already use many of the skills – for example, when you compare careers or when you compare neighborhoods.

Ⓑ Reflect on the Topic

In this section, you will choose a writing prompt and reflect on it. You will develop these ideas throughout the unit and use them to practice skills that are necessary to write your essay.

The writing prompt below was used for the Student Model essay on pages 80–81. After reflecting on the topic, the student decided to use a Venn diagram to reveal the changes in her community. This helped her think of a possible thesis statement.

WRITING PROMPT: Describe how your community has changed in recent years. How have the changes had an impact on the community? Explain why.

Subject A:
My Neighborhood Before the Light Rail

Subject B:
My Neighborhood Now

DIFFERENCES (Subject A)

- cheap housing
- hard to find a job
- only buses – hard to get around
- ugly streets
- mostly poor people
- some music clubs

SIMILARITIES (Subjects A and B)

- lots of different cultures – Vietnamese, Filipinos, Somalis, East Africans
- friendly people
- ethnic restaurants

DIFFERENCES (Subject B)

- better housing, but more expensive
- a lot more businesses – more interesting
- easier to get a job
- much easier to get around
- prettier streets
- more music clubs and bands

Possible thesis statement: *Compared to a decade ago, Royalville today is more expensive and more attractive, but there are still a lot of different cultures.*

 1.1 Notice

Think about a town or city. Compare what it was like in the past and what it's like now. Share ideas with a partner.

1.2 Apply It to Your Writing

Follow the directions to reflect on your topic.

A Choose a prompt:

- Compare two groups of people that you know in your school – for example, two different extracurricular clubs. Some ways that you might compare them are by their purpose, the kinds of interaction among the club members, and the traits that they all share.

- Discuss the lifestyles and relationships of two families that you know – for example, the relationship between parents, the amount or kinds of interaction between parents and children, and the amount or kinds of interaction between siblings.

- A topic approved by your instructor

B Complete the following tasks:

1 Complete the Venn diagram below. Think of everything you know about both subjects.

2 Write a possible thesis statement.

3 Compare Venn diagrams and possible thesis statements with a partner.

Subject A: ....   Subject B: ....

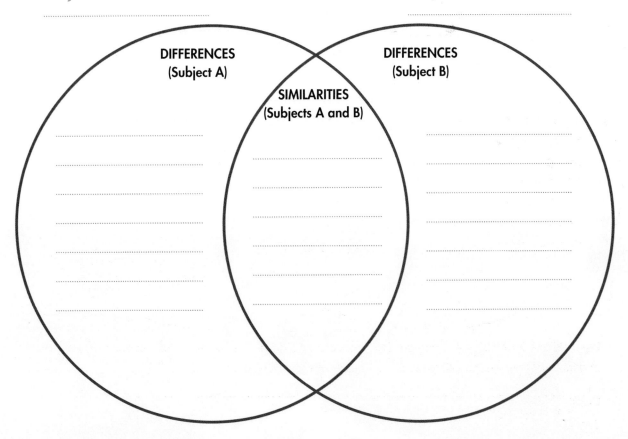

Possible thesis statement: ....

In this section, you will learn academic language that you can use in your comparison and contrast essay. You will also notice how a professional writer uses the language and features of academic essays.

Ⓐ Academic Vocabulary

The words below appear throughout the unit. All are from the Academic Word List. Using these words in your writing will make your ideas clearer and your writing more academic.

adapt (v)	identical (adj)	infrastructure (n)	participate (v)
framework (n)	impact (n)	network (n)	survive (v)

 2.1 Focus on Meaning

Work with a partner. Match the words in bold with their definitions. Write the letters.

A

.... 1 Some places have special community centers that help new immigrants **adapt** to their new home. It takes time to get used to a new place.

a the basic systems of a community, like transportation, energy, and communication

.... 2 Humans can **survive** for three weeks without food, but they will die after only three days without water.

b to be involved in an activity with other people

.... 3 During winter storms, a part of the **infrastructure** in a community may fail. For example, the power lines may go down and electricity won't be available.

c to live through a difficult or dangerous situation

.... 4 In a strong community, many people **participate** in clubs and neighborhood events, such as cleaning up the parks.

d to change one's behavior or thinking in a new situation

B

.... 1 In many new neighborhoods, all the houses are **identical**, but where I live, the houses are all different.

a a group of people who work together

.... 2 Without a good **framework**, many projects fail because there is no organization or plan. For example, managers need to decide on the time frame and the budget.

b exactly the same

.... 3 Many schools have a **network** of interested parents who work with the teachers. Together, they make the schools better.

c a system of rules, ideas, or beliefs that is used to plan or decide something

.... 4 When people watch out for each other, they can have an **impact** on crime in their community. Crime rates typically go down.

d a strong effect on someone or something

B Academic Collocations

Collocations are words that are frequently used together. Research tells us that the academic vocabulary in Part A is commonly used in the collocations in bold below.

ACTIVITY 2.2 Focus on Meaning

Work with a partner. Circle the correct definitions.

1 Unlike my cousin's neighborhood, all the houses in my area are **nearly identical.** The only difference is color. **Nearly identical** means

   a almost exactly the same.   b not the same at all.

2 These days, many people have an online **social network**, but in past generations, relationships were always face-to-face. **Social network** means

   a a group of people that someone knows and interacts with.

   b a person that someone works closely with.

3 In the 1960s, highways had a huge **social impact** on communities. Suddenly, people could live in the suburbs but work in the city. **Social impact** means

   a a significant effect on one person.   b a significant effect on all of society.

4 A good public transportation infrastructure can **have a** positive **impact** on a neighborhood. For example, it can reduce traffic and increase safety. **Have an impact** means

   a cause change.   b cause problems.

5 After Hurricane Katrina badly damaged New Orleans in 2005, an **extensive network** of volunteers from all over the world helped to rebuild parts of the city. **Extensive network** means

   a a very large group of people.   b a small group of people.

C Writing in the Real World

The author of "Resilience Is About Relationships, Not Just Infrastructure" uses comparison and contrast to strengthen her argument.

Before you read, answer these questions: How are relationships among people in a community important? Which is more important, relationships or infrastructure?

Now read the article. Think about your answers to the questions above as you read.

RESILIENCE
Is About **RELATIONSHIPS,**
Not Just **INFRASTRUCTURE**
(adapted)

by Sarah Goodyear

1   When dealing with[1] severe weather, **infrastructure,** such as transportation services and power supplies, is important. But the social ties of a neighborhood – the kinds of relationships created by trips to the corner coffee shop and chats[2] on the sidewalk – might be equally important for saving lives.

2   In a *New Yorker* article, Eric Klinenberg looks at the **impact** that strong social **networks** can have on protecting lives when there is a natural disaster. He gives the example of the 1995 Chicago heat wave, which killed 739 people. As you might expect, the mortality rates were highest in poor neighborhoods. African-American communities were particularly badly affected.

3   Two poor Chicago neighborhoods, Englewood and Auburn Gresham, had very different death rates, yet they were demographically nearly **identical** – mostly black with high numbers of poor and elderly residents. Englewood recorded a death rate of 33 per 100,000 residents, while Auburn Gresham had a rate of only three per 100,000. Auburn Gresham's rate was better than the rate of many rich, white neighborhoods.

[1]**deal with:** take action or solve a problem
[2]**chats:** casual conversations

4 Klinenberg stated that Auburn Gresham was different from Englewood and other similar neighborhoods because that neighborhood had many sidewalks, stores, restaurants, and community organizations. People knew their neighbors. They **participated** in block clubs[3] and community groups. Because they knew each other, they helped each other when necessary. A few years before the heat wave, Englewood had lost 50 percent of its residents and most commercial businesses. As a result, social connections between people in that neighborhood were not strong.

5 After Superstorm Sandy, neighborhood networks in New York City formed quickly. Community groups were able to get help where it was needed even though government and national relief organizations were having difficulty doing so.

6 What's more, the focus on survival and recovery provided a **framework** for building new alliances among groups that didn't normally interact with each other.

In Red Hook, residents of the public housing projects worked alongside business owners. In the Rockaways, surfers and firefighters helped to clean the streets.

7 "I don't think in any way did it change the tight-knit[4] community other than to make us tighter," says one Rockaways surfer and homeowner, "because I don't know anyone who didn't help out."

8 As cities **adapt** to the consequences of climate change, they're going to need to strengthen infrastructure, change how and where buildings are built, and improve government emergency procedures. But they're also going to have to put a greater value on the human connections that exist in walkable neighborhoods where people know and support each other. It's not just about quality of life. It's about trying to **survive**.

[3]**block club:** group of neighbors who organize social events and work to keep their block safe and attractive

[4]**tight-knit:** close

2.3 Check Your Understanding

Answer the questions.

1 What is the author's main idea?

2 Why were community groups important after Superstorm Sandy?

3 Think about a neighborhood you know well. Is it tight-knit? Why or why not?

2.4 Notice the Features of Comparison and Contrast Writing

Read paragraphs 2–4 again. Notice how the writer uses comparison and contrast. Then answer the questions.

1 What does the author compare in the paragraphs?

2 How does the author compare them? In other words, what points of comparison does she use?

3 What does the comparison help to show?

In Section 1 on page 74, you saw how the writer of the Student Model essay reflected on her topic. In this section, you will analyze the final draft of her comparison and contrast essay. You will learn how to structure your ideas for your own essay.

Ⓐ Student Model

Read the writing prompt again and answer the questions.

WRITING PROMPT: Describe how your community has changed in recent years. How have the changes had an impact on the community? Explain why.

1 What do you think the essay will be about?

2 What words from the prompt do you think the writer will use in the thesis statement?

3 What are some ways that communities can change? What ways do you think the writer might mention?

Read the essay twice. The first time, think about your answers to the questions above. The second time, answer the questions in the Analyze Writing Skills boxes. This will help you notice key features of comparison and contrast essays.

Changes in My Community

1   I had always thought that Royalville, the community where I live, was kind of a boring town. While I always liked living in a multicultural community and enjoyed the music scene,[1] I did not like the town itself. There were not many businesses, so there was not a lot to see or to do. However, today it is a place that I absolutely love. The reason for this change in my town is the opening of the light rail in 2009. It had a significant **impact** on the community. Now there are many places to go and interesting things to do. Compared to before the light rail, Royalville today has a much stronger economy, more music and cultural events, and small differences in its ethnic diversity.

2   The economy is the most important difference between Royalville before the light rail and today. Before the light rail, there were not many businesses, so it was difficult to find a job. Many people had jobs outside the town. The houses were quite inexpensive and rents were affordable. Some stores were closed and left empty. The town looked unattractive and dirty. My family moved there during that time. Today, the economy has greatly improved. New apartment buildings and houses were built, and housing became more expensive. Many new types of businesses opened, like upscale[2]

> **1 Analyze Writing Skills**
>
> In paragraph 1, underline the thesis statement. Then circle the two subjects that the writer will compare.

> **2 Analyze Writing Skills**
>
> In paragraph 2, underline the topic sentence. Then circle the word that tells what the writer will discuss in the paragraph.

> **3 Analyze Writing Skills**
>
> In paragraph 2, does the writer discuss one subject or both subjects?
>
> ....

[1] **music scene:** the music and local bands in an area
[2] **upscale:** higher class, expensive

clothing shops, yoga studios, and trendier[3] places, like yogurt shops. It is easier to find a job, and the community is much more exciting.

3   Music and culture have always been important to the community, but now they are even more significant. Before the light rail, there were two clubs where local musicians played. There were also a few cultural and educational programs at the public library, such as poetry readings and English classes that my parents **participated** in. Today there are a lot more lectures and classes at the library. There are more places to hear music, such as in the park or at festivals. In addition, a blues club that had been closed for many years has reopened. There are also galleries for artists to show their work.

4   Analyze Writing Skills

In paragraph 3, underline the two sentences that introduce each subject.

4   While there have been some changes in the types of ethnic groups that live in Royalville, it is still diverse in its ethnicities. Before the light rail, the neighborhood included Somalis, Filipinos, Vietnamese, and East Africans. These ethnic communities had wonderful small family restaurants and stores that sold food and clothing for each culture. Similarly, today there are families from these same cultures. However, now there are also immigrants from Mexico, Guatemala, and El Salvador. There are still many family-owned restaurants that serve authentic foods from those countries, but there are fewer ethnic food and clothing stores.

5   Analyze Writing Skills

In paragraph 4, is the writer discussing mostly similarities or mostly differences? Circle the word that indicates this.

5   In conclusion, after the city built the light rail in Royalville, the economy improved and the number of music and cultural programs increased. However, for the most part, the diversity of the town is still similar. Some people feel that the neighborhood has become too expensive and they worry about the development and growth. For me, the neighborhood is definitely a better place today. I feel proud that my neighborhood has become desirable and that businesses are doing well. I believe communities have to **adapt** to be successful and to **survive**.

6   Analyze Writing Skills

Underline the conclusion that the writer realizes about her two subjects.

[3]**trendy:** fashionable or popular

3.1 Check Your Understanding

Answer the questions.

1 What kinds of changes has the author seen in her community?

2 Which change is the most noticeable one? Explain your answer.

3 Have you seen similar changes to the community where you live? Explain your answer.

 3.2 Outline the Writer's Ideas

Complete the outline for "Changes in My Community." Write the thesis statement.
Then use the phrases in the box.

fewer ethnic food and clothing stores	housing inexpensive	small family restaurants
galleries for artists	music and culture	today

STUDENT MODEL

ESSAY OUTLINE

I. Introductory paragraph ....

Thesis Statement ....
....
....

Body Paragraph 1   II. Economy ....

Subject A   A. Before the light rail ....

Detail   1. Not many businesses – difficult to find jobs ....

Detail   2. People worked in the city nearby ....

Detail   3. ....

Detail   4. Unattractive and dirty ....

Subject B   B. ....

Detail   1. Economy improved ....

Detail   2. New buildings and houses ....

Detail	3. Cost of housing rose
Detail	4. New types of businesses
Detail	5. Easier to find jobs
Body Paragraph 2	III.
Subject A	A. Before the light rail
Detail	1. Music clubs
Detail	2. Lectures and cultural programs at library
Subject B	B. Today
Detail	1. More places to hear music, programs at library
Detail	2. Blues club
Detail	3.
Body Paragraph 3	IV. Ethnic groups
Subject A	A. Before the light rail
Detail	1. Filipinos, Vietnamese, and East Africans
Detail	2.
Detail	3. Ethnic food and clothing stores
Subject B	B. Today
Detail	1. Same cultures, also Mexicans, Guatemalans, El Salvadorans
Detail	2. Still small ethnic restaurants
Detail	3.
	V. Concluding paragraph

B Comparison and Contrast Essays: Point-by-Point Organization

As you learned in Unit 2, writers use comparison and contrast to analyze two subjects in order to better understand the relationship between the two subjects and to reveal differences and/or similarities.

In Unit 2, you learned to organize ideas using block organization. Another way is to use **point-by-point organization**. In this type of organization, the writer compares and contrasts one **point of comparison** between the two subjects in each paragraph.

The Student Model essay on pages 80–81 is an example of an essay with point-by-point organization. Below is the organization of the writer's ideas.

CHANGES IN MY COMMUNITY

Introductory Paragraph

Body Paragraph 1: Economy (Point of Comparison 1)

    Subject A: Community before light rail

    Subject B: Community today

Body Paragraph 2: Music and Culture (Point of Comparison 2)

    Subject A: Community before light rail

    Subject B: Community today

Body Paragraph 3: Cultural diversity (Point of Comparison 3)

    Subject A: Community before light rail

    Subject B: Community today

Concluding Paragraph

 ACTIVITY **3.3** Notice

Look at the organization above. Circle the answers.

1 The writer compares two subjects in

  a body paragraph 1.   c body paragraph 3.

  b body paragraph 2.   d all body paragraphs.

2 The writer compares businesses before and after the light rail in

  a body paragraph 1.   c body paragraph 3.

  b body paragraph 2.   d all body paragraphs.

3 The writer discusses different ethnic groups before and after the light rail in

  a body paragraph 1.   c body paragraph 3.

  b body paragraph 2.   d all body paragraphs.

POINTS OF COMPARISON

As you learned in Unit 2, to compare two subjects writers choose **points of comparison**. Starting with a brainstorm list, the writer needs to choose the strongest points. Here are some things to consider when choosing those points from a brainstorm list.

- Does comparing this point reveal an interesting or unique similarity or difference between the two subjects that might surprise the reader?
- Does comparing this point reveal something surprising, unusual, or unique about one subject that is significant to point out?

Below, a writer compares and contrasts two community groups that he belongs to: a book club and a soccer team. He wrote many ideas. Then he checked three points that he thought were the strongest and crossed out points that he thought did not reveal anything interesting or new to the reader. His thoughts about his ideas are in parentheses.

WRITING PROMPT: Compare two communities or groups that are an important part of your life.

POINTS OF COMPARISON	SUBJECT A: BOOK CLUB	SUBJECT B: SOCCER TEAM
~~purpose~~ (Everyone knows this.)	- serious and fun discussions	- physical activity
members' attitudes ✓ (It might be surprising that members argue in a book club and still feel close. I could contrast the different expectations in behavior.)	- people often argue and it's OK, we don't have to agree	- team is most important; players are expected to work together and not show disagreements; we feel responsible for each other
members' commitment to the group? ✓ (This is a significant difference!)	- some members often absent; no one feels obligated to come	- we HAVE to be at practice! if members are absent, it can hurt the team
~~cost~~ (This doesn't reveal anything important.)	- no fees except books	- annual fees, a little expensive
socializing ✓ (This reveals an interesting difference!)	- we talk before each meeting about everyday events and kids; sometimes meet for coffee with individuals	- socializing after games, talking together during and after practice, more exciting - celebrating after winning, crying after losing ☹
~~achievement~~ (Obvious difference, so not interesting.)	- opportunity to read and discuss books	- winning games and tournaments

Once the writer has decided on the three points of comparison and reflected on them, he decides on a possible thesis statement.

Possible thesis statement:

My book club and soccer team offer friendship and many fun times, but they are different in the attitudes of the members, the way of socializing, and the commitment to the group.

 **3.4** Notice

Work with a partner. Look at the chart and the possible thesis statement at the bottom of page 85. Answer the questions.

1 Find the point that reveals a significant difference. Explain why it is significant in your own words.

2 Find the point that the writer thinks does not reveal anything important. Explain why the writer says that. Do you agree or disagree?

3 Find the point that the writer says is obvious. Explain why the difference is obvious in your own words. The author does not use this difference. Would you use it if you wrote the essay?

4 Read the possible thesis statement again. Notice the order of the points. Writers often order ideas from most significant to least significant or from least significant to most significant. Which order do you think the writer is using?

 3.5 Apply It to Your Writing

Look at your Venn diagram from Section 1 on page 75. Use the ideas to complete the chart below.

Points of Comparison	Subject A:	Subject B:
1	-	-
2	-	-

INTRODUCTORY PARAGRAPH

An **introductory paragraph** prepares the reader to understand the thesis and the rest of the essay. A good introductory paragraph:

• makes it clear what subjects will be compared

• gives necessary background information about the two subjects so that the reader understands the ways that the writer will compare them

• ends with a thesis statement that indicates the points of comparison

A good **thesis statement**:

• mentions the two subjects and tells the reader how the writer will compare them

• tells whether the writer will focus more on similarities or on differences

• includes the points of comparison

In Unit 2 on page 57, you learned words and phrases to help you write thesis statements that focus on similarities and differences. Below are others that you can use.

Thesis statements that focus on similarities:

***Both** team sports and individual sports teach high school students discipline, commitment, and ways to deal with failure.*

*Large families and small families may seem different, but they **have** some interesting **similarities.***

Thesis statements that focus on differences:

***Compared to** the city I grew up in, the city where I live now has much better infrastructure, more green spaces, and less crime.*

*Resilient people do better than other people after disasters because they focus **more** on positive feelings, they adapt more quickly to change, and they feel **less** anger about their circumstances.*

Thesis statement that focuses on both similarities and differences:

***Although** young learners and adult learners **are different because** of their motivation and ability to pay attention, they **both** learn from playing games.*

 3.6 Analyze Thesis Statements

Check (✓) the thesis statement that is clearest. Discuss your answer with a partner.

WRITING PROMPT: Choose two communities or neighborhoods in your city and compare them. Which is a better place for families?

- [ ] 1 South Hill is very different from Northtown in many ways.
- [ ] 2 South Hill is a neighborhood that is more desirable because of its excellent schools, beautiful parks, and community involvement.
- [ ] 3 While South Hill and Northtown are both attractive, family-friendly neighborhoods in my city, South Hill has more community involvement, better transportation, and more beautiful parks.

Read the writing prompt and complete the thesis statements.

WRITING PROMPT: Think of two neighborhoods in your town or city. Compare them.

1 Compared to my neighborhood, ...
                                     (write the name of a neighborhood)

....

2 Although my neighborhood and .... are different because ....
                                (write the name of a neighborhood)

.... ,

   they are similar because ....

BODY PARAGRAPHS: LANGUAGE OF COMPARISON

Each **body paragraph** of a point-by-point comparison essay compares the two subjects using one point of comparison. The writer describes Subject A first. Then he or she describes Subject B in comparison to Subject A. Because writers are comparing Subject B to Subject A, they sometimes use the language of comparison to show how it is different from or similar to Subject A.

Read the example body paragraph from the Student Model essay. Notice the structure and use of the language of comparison.

> The economy is the most important difference between Royalville
> before the light rail and today. Before the light rail, there were not
> many businesses, so it was difficult to find a job. Many people had
> jobs outside the town. The houses were quite inexpensive and rents
> were affordable. Some stores were closed and left empty. The town
> looked unattractive and dirty. My family moved there during that
> time. Today, the economy has greatly improved. New apartment
> buildings and houses were built and housing became **more** expensive.
> Many new types of businesses opened, like upscale clothing shops,
> yoga studios, and trendi**er** places, like yogurt shops. It is easi**er** to find
> a job, and the community is much **more** exciting.

The writer states the point of comparison.

The writer introduces Subject A (before the light rail) and explains its economy.

The writer introduces Subject B (today) and compares the economy with the light rail to Subject A.

Read the body paragraph above again. Notice the examples of the language of comparison in bold.

Below are typical words and phrases that you can use to describe differences and similarities.

Ways to explain differences:

*Today, there are **more** apartment buildings in my neighborhood.*

*The butcher shop is old**er than** the bakery.*

*Some celebrations are **not as** important **as** they used to be.*

*People are **less** concerned about crime now.*

Ways to explain similarities:

*The old movie theater and the neighborhood library are **alike** because **both** have been recently remodeled.*

*The light rail station is **similar to** the bus station because they were designed by the same person.*

*The fare for the light rail is **the same as** the fare for the bus.*

In Section 4, you will learn words and phrases that introduce similarities in sentences.

 3.8 Apply It to Your Writing

Choose one point of comparison for your writing prompt. Then write two statements that compare Subject B to Subject A in two ways. Use the examples above as a guide. Share your ideas with a partner.

1 ....

....

2 ....

....

 3.9 Practice Organizing Ideas

Read the writing prompt and the introductory paragraph. Then read the topic sentence for each body paragraph. Discuss ideas for each point of comparison with a partner. Then finish each body paragraph.

WRITING PROMPT: Compare life and personal relationships in a rural town and in an urban community. Which one do you prefer?

Some people feel lost in big cities and other people feel bored in small towns. Small towns are comfortable because family and friends are close by. Big cities can be more exciting because there is so much to do. Both have their advantages, but urban life is a better choice for people who want more options in all areas of their lives. Compared to a small town, the big city offers more opportunities to meet people, to try new things, and to be successful in a career.

The opportunities to socialize and meet others is one difference between living in a city and a small town. ....

....

Another difference is the number of opportunities to have new experiences and learn new ideas.

Finally, there are differences in opportunities to achieve success in a career.

CONCLUDING PARAGRAPH

As explained in Unit 2, the **concluding paragraph** reminds the reader of the writer's purpose for writing. The first sentence can restate the two subjects and whether the focus was on similarities, differences, or both. The second one restates the points of comparison. It ends with a final comment, usually one or two sentences, such as a realization or an opinion.

Here are some examples of final comments.

In conclusion, neighborhoods with green areas and parks are better for building a feeling of community than places without them. These neighborhoods feel safer, look nicer, and seem friendlier to everyone. <u>*In the end, it seems that it is important that people take the time to get to know their neighbors.*</u> (realization)

In sum, when there is a disaster, communities that have strong social networks, good infrastructure, and residents who can adapt to changing situations are more likely to have survivors than communities without those factors. <u>*Good infrastructure is the government's job, but strong social networks are something that all of us can create. I think that making social connections is everyone's responsibility.*</u> (opinion)

 3.10 Notice

Read the concluding paragraph below. Discuss the questions with a partner.

In conclusion, a city provides more opportunities for people to create a community that fits their needs. Unlike a small town, it is diverse, has a lot of ways to meet people, and offers more opportunities to meet and socialize with people who share similar interests. This social network of people becomes a small community, and that is what makes city life not only exciting but also comfortable.

1 Underline the three points of comparison.
2 What kind of comment is it?

Ⓐ Writing Skill 1: Words and Phrases That Show Comparison

You have learned that words and phrases showing comparison are important when you write thesis statements and when you compare subjects in the body paragraphs. In Unit 2 on page 62, you learned phrases to begin sentences that show contrast.

Below are examples of phrases that you can use to begin sentences that show comparison, or similarity.

Both parents *and* teachers are interested in the success of their children and students.

Similarly/Likewise, after-school groups like the Boys & Girls Clubs want children to spend their time creatively after school.

Like after-school programs, summer camps are a way for kids to learn and develop social skills.

After-school clubs, such as book clubs and science clubs, teach important goals. *Also*, these clubs teach kids about teamwork.

 **4.1** Combine Ideas

Read the first sentence. Then check (✓) the sentence that shows similarity. Connect the sentences using the word in parentheses.

1 In high school, the students who join the Drama Club enjoy acting in theater productions.

☐ Art students are often independent.

☐ Students in music groups such as band and chorus like performing in school programs.

(Similarly) ....

....

2 Recently, knitting groups have become popular with young people.

☐ Sewing circles have become popular with young people.

☐ Students usually do not have time to join groups.

(Both) ....

....

3 The girls' swim team requires many hours of practice every week.

☐ The swimmers' parents must spend many hours taking the girls to practice.

☐ The girls must be at every practice.

(Similarly) ....

....

4 Members of the Hiking Club should have their own equipment.

☐ Photography Club members should have their own equipment.

☐ Members will need boots and a backpack.

(Both) ....

....

B Writing Skill 2: Avoiding Sentence Fragments

A fragment is an incomplete sentence. Sometimes it is only part of a sentence. For example, the subject might be missing. You always want to avoid fragments in your writing.

Below are ways to avoid sentence fragments in writing.

HOW TO AVOID SENTENCE FRAGMENTS	
1 Every sentence must have a subject and a verb. A sentence fragment is a sentence that is missing a subject or a verb.	**It is** ~~Is~~ important to be a good member of your community. **are** Neighborhoods with parks ^ better.
2 Clauses that start with words such as *because* or *since* introduce a dependent clause. They cannot stand alone. They must join with an independent clause. Do not use a comma when you join them.	Communities are important during a crisis. **because** ~~Because~~ people need to support each other.
3 Join noun phrases with *for example* and *such as* to the sentence. Use a comma before these phrases.	People from other cities offered a lot of **, such as** different things. ~~Such as~~ warm clothes, building supplies, and even food.
4 Relative pronouns, such as *which*, *who*, and *that*, introduce dependent clauses. A dependent clause cannot stand alone. It must join with the independent clause. Remember to use commas before nonidentifying relative clauses (clauses that give extra information).	**, which** Many people sent donations. ~~Which~~ the town appreciated.

ACTIVITY 4.2 Identify Fragments

Look at the items below. If it is a complete sentence, write *S*. If it is a fragment, write *F*.

_F_ 1 Such as earthquakes and tornadoes.

_S_ 2 Communities with residents who work together are better prepared for emergency situations. *essential*

_S_ 3 Communities that remain positive can survive difficult times.

_F_ 4 Which was closed after the storm.

_S_ 5 People needed a lot of things, such as shelter and food.

_F_ 6 Because all of the roads were flooded.

_F_ 7 Is true that people who have positive attitudes survive more often than people with negative attitudes.

Find and correct five more mistakes in the paragraph below.

One factor is the warning time. With earthquakes, communities do not have any warning. Therefore, ~~it~~ is difficult to help others during the earthquake. People only have time to help themselves and react by doing the simple drills that they were taught. Such as getting under a desk or standing in a doorway. People in earthquake-prone areas should have emergency kits. Because they do not know how long they might be without water or power. These items need to be stored in a convenient location so that people can grab them quickly. For example, under the bed. Unlike earthquakes, tornadoes can be tracked through satellite and radar technology. TV and radio stations provide tornado path reports. Which are updated regularly. People in those communities have time to get into a shelter below ground. They may also have time to drive away from the path of the tornado. In both cases, they may be able to help others in their community. Since there is a little time before the disaster strikes.

C Grammar for Writing: Identifying Relative Clauses

In academic writing, nouns are often combined with relative clauses and other phrases. Understanding how to use relative clauses can help make your writing more sophisticated.

A relative clause starts with a relative pronoun: *who, when, where, which, that,* or *whom.*

Below are rules for forming **identifying relative clauses**. An identifying relative clause gives essential information about the noun. It is never separated from the rest of the sentence by commas.

IDENTIFYING RELATIVE CLAUSES	
1 In **subject relative clauses**, the relative pronoun (*who, that, which*) is the subject of the clause.	*The committee gave an award to the students **that volunteered**.* (The relative clause tells us which students).
Use *who* to describe people in academic writing.	*The people **who were on the committee** were pleased.*
Use *which* and *that* to describe everything else.	*The tsunami **that hit Fukushima** was very destructive.*
Note: In academic English, *that* is almost always used for identifying relative clauses.	

home work ✓

2 Use *whose* + noun to show possession. *Whose* can be used with people or things.	*Atlantic City is one of the cities **whose people suffered** the most during Hurricane Sandy.*
3 In **object relative clauses**, the relative pronoun is the object of the clause.	*The couple **whom he rescued** was sitting on their roof.* (The relative clause tells us which couple.) *The agency provides supplies **that** people need to survive.* (The relative clauses tells us which supplies.)

ACTIVITY **4.4** Combine Ideas

Combine the sentence pairs with relative clauses.

1 Many homes were badly damaged and could not be saved. Those homes sat under eight feet of water.

Many homes that sat under eight feet of water were badly damaged and could not be saved.

2 Earthquakes can be extremely damaging. These earthquakes last for several minutes.

Earth quakes that last for several minutes can be extremely damaging

3 Many doctors helped out, too. These doctors had special skills in emergency medicine.

Many doctors who had special skills in emergency medicine helped out, too.

4 Many months after a disaster, people may feel anxiety. These people did not expect to feel that stress.

Many months after a disaster, people may feel anxietypect that they did notexpect to feelxiety.

5 Certain public buildings are used for temporary housing for survivors. The government identifies these buildings.

which

Certain public buildings that government identifies are used for temporary housing for survivors.

6 Communities often recover more quickly from a natural disaster. Their residents have experienced a natural disaster before.

Communities whose residents have exp. a natural disaster before often recover more quickly from a n.d.

7 After a disaster, the water must be purified. People drink this water.

After a disaster, the water that people drink, must be purified.

Avoiding Common Mistakes

Research tells us that these are the most common mistakes that students make when using relative clauses in academic writing.

1 Use *who* with people. Do not use *which*.

        who
People ~~which~~ are prepared for an emergency are more likely to survive.

2 **Remember to include a relative pronoun.**

                                                                      who
In communities all over the country, many people attend these events, even people ⌃ do not often see their neighbors.

3 **When the relative pronoun is the subject, do not add another subject, such as *it*.**

Neighborhood groups can request an organization kit which ~~it~~ explains how to organize a Night Out event.

 4.5 Editing Task

Find and correct five more mistakes in the paragraph below.

    Neighborhood watch groups are one important difference. In my neighborhood we have a good neighborhood watch group that ~~it~~ has made the area a lot safer. Neighbors which are concerned about crime work together. They watch the neighborhood for any unusual activity which it might be suspicious. Our neighborhood group has a block captain which organizes meetings in the community. About once a year, the police ask an officer watches the neighborhood to speak to the group about safety. Unlike my neighborhood, my friend's neighborhood does not have a neighborhood watch group. They have a lot of street crime. A few people put up signs tell the criminals that they are being watched, but that is the only action they have taken. It is not very effective.

D Avoiding Plagiarism

When you use ideas and information that come from other people in your writing, you must say where you found the information. However, there is some information that is commonly known by everyone. You do not need to tell where you found this information. It is important to distinguish between the two types of information.

My instructor returned my paper, and he said I had plagiarized it. He underlined some sentences and wrote "needs citation" next to them. I don't really know what he means. I asked my instructor about these sentences, and he said I had to mention the person who first wrote about the ideas. I didn't think the information was so special. I'm confused! When do I need to mention the person?

Joao

Dear Joao,

First, your instructor wants you to say where you got your information. We call that a source. Details about the source, such as the author and title of the article, are the citation. You want to include citations in your paper. You don't need a citation for everything, though. Some information is known by many people. For example, most people know that Nelson Mandela was the first black president of South Africa and that diamonds are the hardest substance in the world. These are examples of common knowledge. You don't need to cite these facts. In your paper, though, it sounds as if you were writing about something that not everyone knows or accepts. In that case, you need to cite the source. If you're not sure, you should add a citation.

Best,

Professor Wright

WHAT IS COMMON KNOWLEDGE?

Common knowledge is a fact that is widely known and accepted by most people. You don't need to cite this type of information.

Common Knowledge Is:	Common Knowledge Is Not:
commonly known facts about science, history, and famous people: If you answer *yes* to these questions, the information is probably common knowledge: • Is this information widely known or believed by many people? • Did you know this information before you started your research? • Can you easily find this information on at least five websites?	other people's data, statistics, opinions, or theories.
You do not need to cite this information.	**You must cite this information.**

 4.6 Practice

Check (✓) the sentences that are common knowledge. Use the questions above to help you.

☐ 1 The fall of the Berlin Wall in 1989 led to German reunification.

☐ 2 Unemployment was around 12 percent in the Euro zone for much of 2013.

☐ 3 Bill Gates, co-founder of Microsoft, remains one of the wealthiest people in the world.

☐ 4 Some people believe that the extinction of dinosaurs was based on a sudden catastrophic event.

 4.7 Practice

Check (✓) the situations when the student needs to use citations. Discuss your answers with a partner.

☐ 1 Memo's teacher mentions Martin Luther King, Jr. and his march on Washington in 1963. As Memo is preparing his paper on civil rights, he sees that date on many websites, so he decides not to include a citation.

☐ 2 Luanda is doing research on hospital safety for her nursing studies. She includes some data from a well-known study. She can't decide if she should cite that data or not.

☐ 3 Daisuke is writing a paper on forest biology. He wants to include some information about cedar trees that he learned when he was an undergraduate. All of his professors and classmates also know this information. He decides not to cite it.

☐ 4 Anya is working on a project about public transportation in her city. She includes the mayor's opinion, which she read in a newspaper article. She doesn't cite it because it is only an opinion, not research or data.

In this section, you will follow the writing process to complete the final draft of your essay.

STEP 1: BRAINSTORM

Work with a partner. Follow the steps below to brainstorm ideas for your essay.

1 Before you start, notice how the writer of the Student Model essay brainstormed. She wrote many ideas but did not use all of them in her essay. She chose the strongest points of comparison.

WRITING PROMPT: Describe how your community has changed in recent years. How have the changes impacted the community?

Subject A:
My Neighborhood Before the Light Rail

Subject B:
My Neighborhood Now

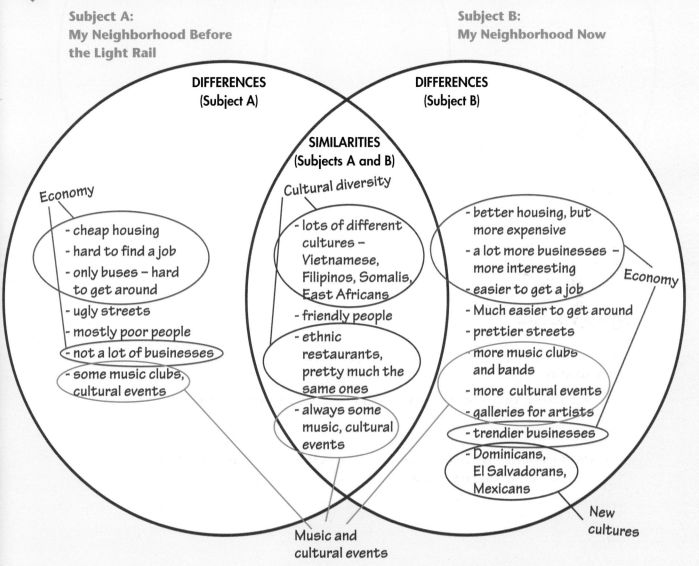

DIFFERENCES
(Subject A)

DIFFERENCES
(Subject B)

SIMILARITIES
(Subjects A and B)

Economy
- cheap housing
- hard to find a job
- only buses – hard to get around
- ugly streets
- mostly poor people
- not a lot of businesses
- some music clubs, cultural events

Cultural diversity
- lots of different cultures – Vietnamese, Filipinos, Somalis, East Africans
- friendly people
- ethnic restaurants, pretty much the same ones
- always some music, cultural events

- better housing, but more expensive
- a lot more businesses – more interesting
- easier to get a job
- Much easier to get around
- prettier streets
- more music clubs and bands
- more cultural events
- galleries for artists
- trendier businesses
- Dominicans, El Salvadorans, Mexicans

Economy

New cultures

Music and cultural events

2 Write the ideas that you wrote in Section 1 on page 75 in the Venn diagram below. Include ideas from the Your Turns throughout this unit. Brainstorm other ideas.

Subject A: ....

Subject B: ....

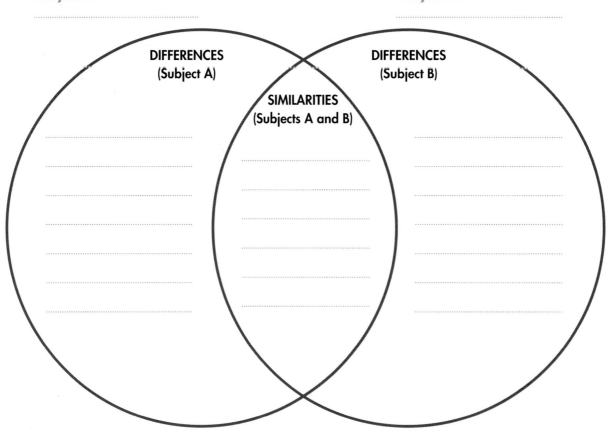

DIFFERENCES
(Subject A)

SIMILARITIES
(Subjects A and B)

DIFFERENCES
(Subject B)

When you finish, circle the three strongest points and write them below.

1 ....

2 ....

3 ....

STEP 2: DO RESEARCH

If your topic requires research, see page 261 for advice on how to find information.

STEP 3: MAKE AN OUTLINE

Complete the outline below with your ideas from the previous steps.

ESSAY OUTLINE

I. Introductory paragraph ....

Thesis Statement
....
....
....

Body Paragraph 1 II. ....

Subject A A. ....

Detail 1. ....

Detail 2. ....

Subject B B. ....

Detail 1. ....

Detail 2. ....

Body Paragraph 2 III. ....

Subject A A. ....

Detail 1. ....

Detail 2. ....

Subject B B. ....

Detail 1. ....

Detail 2. ....

(CONTINUED)

Body Paragraph 3	IV. ....
Subject A	A. ....
Detail	1. ....
Detail	2. ....
Subject B	B. ....
Detail	1. ....
Detail	2. ....
	V. Concluding paragraph ....
	....

STEP 4: WRITE YOUR FIRST DRAFT

Now it is time to write your first draft. Here are some suggestions on how to get started.

1 Use your outline, notes, and the sentences you wrote in the Your Turns and in Step 3 above.

2 Focus on making your ideas as clear as possible.

3 Remember to add a title.

After you finish, read your essay and check for basic errors.

1 Make sure that all sentences have subjects and verbs. Check to be sure there are no fragments.

2 Look at your relative clauses. Make sure that you didn't make any common mistakes.

3 Make sure that your thesis statement and topic sentences are clear.

STEP 5: WRITE YOUR FINAL DRAFT

Before you write your final draft, do the following:

1 After you receive feedback on your first draft, review it carefully. Fix any errors.

2 Make a note of errors that were most frequent (misspellings, wrong verb tense, errors in using commas). Try to avoid them as you write.

3 Review the Academic Vocabulary and Collocations from this unit. Are there any that you can add to your essay?

4 Turn to page 264 and use the Self-Editing Review to check your work one more time.

5 Write your final draft and hand it in.

4 CAUSE AND EFFECT ESSAYS

TECHNOLOGY: SHARING ONLINE

> *"Behind the need to communicate is the need to share. Behind the need to share is the need to be understood."*
>
> Leo Rosten (1908–1997)

About the Author:

Leo Rosten was a social scientist and writer of many books, including humorous ones on Jewish language and culture. He was born in Poland but spent most of his life in the United States.

Work with a partner. Read the quotation about sharing information online. Then answer the questions.

1 Do you agree that the reason people communicate is to share our thoughts, feelings, and ideas? Why or why not? Explain.

2 Do you agree that the deeper reason that people communicate is to be understood? Why or why not? Explain.

3 Do you agree or disagree that sharing online increases our understanding of each other? Explain.

A Connect to Academic Writing

In this unit, you will learn skills to help you write a cause and effect essay. While some of the skills may be new to you, others are not. In your everyday life, you think about causes and effects. For example, you might ask yourself, *Why is there so much traffic today?* (cause, or reason). You could also wonder, *If I work more hours, will it affect my grades?* (effect, or result).

B Reflect on the Topic

In this section, you will choose a writing prompt and reflect on it. You will develop these ideas throughout the unit and use them to practice skills that are necessary to write your essay.

Read the writing prompt below for the Student Model essay on pages 110–111. The student reflected on the topic and decided to focus on the benefits of sharing online. This became his thesis statement. He used a cause-effect graphic organizer to think about the benefits, or positive effects, of sharing online.

WRITING PROMPT: Explain the positive effects and benefits or the negative effects and dangers of sharing information online.

Cause

Sharing information online

Effects

Quick news after a disaster

Share pictures

Find a job

Find people who share my interests

Easy to help others anywhere

Lots of reviews and recommendations

Possible thesis statement: Sharing information online offers people important benefits.

 1.1 Notice

Work with a partner. Think of two more effects of sharing information online and add them to the graphic organizer. Share them with the class.

1.2 Apply It to Your Writing

Follow the directions to reflect on your topic.

A Choose a prompt:

- People can access their social media sites anytime, anywhere. Discuss how smartphones have affected people and their ways of communicating. In your opinion, are these effects positive or negative?

- Since their beginnings, social media sites have been popular. However, the popularity of individual sites, such as Myspace and Facebook, has risen and fallen. What are the reasons that a site might become less popular?

- Explain how technology is changing the way children learn and play.

- A topic approved by your instructor

B Complete the following tasks:

1 Think about your prompt. Decide whether your essay will focus on the causes or on the effects of something. Choose the appropriate cause-effect graphic organizer below.

2 Complete the organizer. Write down as many ideas as you can.

3 Write a possible thesis statement.

4 Compare graphic organizers and possible thesis statements with a partner.

Causes

Effect

Cause

Effects

Possible thesis statement: ....

....

2 EXPAND YOUR KNOWLEDGE

In this section, you will learn academic language that you can use in your cause and effect essay. You will also notice how a professional writer uses the language and features of cause and effect.

Academic Vocabulary

The words below appear throughout the unit. Many are from the Academic Word List. Using these words in your writing will make your ideas clearer and your writing more academic.

aware (adj)	generation (n)	ongoing (adj)	promote (v)
enable (v)	inherent (adj)	perspective (n)	scenario (n)

ACTIVITY 2.1 Focus on Meaning

Work with a partner. Circle the correct definitions.

1 For today's digital **generation**, online dating is a common thing. Many young people look for dates on dating websites. **Generation** means

   a a romantic relationship.   b people who are about the same age.

2 Although dating sites are meant to **promote** online relationships, they also encourage cybercrimes such as phishing (a crime in which thieves try to trick people into sharing personal information online in order to steal their money). **Promote** means

   a to support or actively encourage.   b to search for something.

3 Dating sites also **enable** criminals to find dates. These criminals ask their dates for money or personal information. When they get it, they disappear. **Enable** means

a to make it possible for someone to do something.

b to steal from someone.

4 One man had **ongoing** relationships with over 30 women at the same time. Over time he persuaded all of them to give him money or gifts. **Ongoing** means

a continuing.

b unusual or odd.

5 A common phishing **scenario** is for a criminal to meet a woman online and start a relationship. The woman falls in love. The criminal asks her for money and she happily gives it to him. **Scenario** means

a situation or story.

b robbery or theft.

6 It is important to be **aware** of these sites when dating online. According to the FBI, 5,600 online dating crimes were reported in 2011. **Aware** means

a afraid or concerned about a situation.

b knowledgeable about a situation.

7 There are **inherent** risks in online dating. There is always the possibility that someone could meet a criminal. **Inherent** means

a few or not frequent.

b necessary or natural.

8 A smart **perspective** on online dating is to be friendly but cautious. This viewpoint will keep you safe. **Perspective** means

a a way of looking at something or an attitude.

b a priority or seriousness.

B Academic Phrases

Research tells us that the phrases in bold below are commonly used in academic writing.

ACTIVITY 2.2 Focus on Meaning

Underline the effect in each sentence, and write the letter *E* above it. Then rewrite the sentence giving another effect.

1 One positive **effect of** the Internet on society is that <u>it makes people more aware of the world</u>.
One positive effect of the Internet on society is that people can get information instantly.

2 **As a result of** online communities, teenagers have a place to share their ideas.

....

....

3 **The** main **impact of** social media on young people is that it promotes social skills.

....

....

C Writing in the Real World

The author of "Generation Overshare" uses cause and effect to make his claims about oversharing information more convincing and sometimes startling to the reader.

Before you read, answer these questions: Have you ever heard of the expression "too much information" or "TMI"? TMI is another way of saying "oversharing." What does the expression mean?

Now read the article. Think about your answers to the questions above as you read.

GENERATION OVERSHARE
(adapted)

by Marc Savlov

What happens when the line blurs[1] between our online and offline lives?

1 The Internet has forever changed the way we work, live, and love – both online and off. Not long ago, when we met our family, friends, and colleagues, we did it face to face. Today, we are linked to millions of people all over the world through the Internet. Because of this, we are redefining the lines between our online and offline lives. Transparency[2] is the new privacy. We live our lives online, texting our triumphs and tragedies for the entire world to see and share. This sharing is making our lives more transparent. But it also raises questions of privacy. Is there such a thing as sharing too much information? Does privacy still have any meaning for today's Digital **Generation**? Oversharing can have negative effects, but it can also make us happier and freer.

2 As a longtime blogger, Stephanie Klein is keenly aware of the impact of sharing online: "In January of 2004, I was working full-time designing websites, and by night I was posting online, frustrated that I didn't know how to make myself happy. Having a blog **enabled** me to create an online scrapbook of my life (www.stephanieklein.blogs.com)." Stephanie's blog gave her a new sense of identity. Sharing her life online made her feel more content offline.

3 But blogging the private details of daily life raises questions of "oversharing." Sharing random[3] comments on Facebook or Twitter (with or without pictures) may be just another way to lose a job. Klein suggests, however, that online transparency isn't necessarily the same as oversharing. It can also be a defensive weapon against haters and make us feel freer: "I absolutely believe it's freeing, and it allows us to 'live out loud,' without the fear of someone exposing us."

[1]**the line blurs between:** the difference between two things becomes less clear
[2]**transparency:** the quality of being easily understood and clear
[3]**random:** done by chance and not planned

4   Klein also believes that sharing online makes us feel safer. One reporter asked how she could put so many graphic[4] details online for everyone to see. She answered, "It's simple. I don't care who's looking. That is, I believe all the things that embarrass us should be exposed by us. We're so scared of what people will think, how they'll judge us. But with my blog, I don't believe in holding back.[5] Is there such a thing as too much information? Not for me."

5   That said, Klein is well aware that going online can become dangerous for young people whose personality is not yet fully formed: "You're still learning right from wrong, do things to become popular, to feel liked and loved. I think one of the greatest dangers **inherent** in an entire generation being born 'linked in' is the blurred line between self-expression and exploitation."[6] If we share our thoughts and feelings online, it helps us express ourselves. At the same time, we risk others using our personal information against us when we expose ourselves online.

6   Author Bruce Sterling agrees: privacy no longer has any meaning in these changing times. From his **perspective**, the online nightmare **scenario** of being exploited or exposed has nothing to do with posting your life for the whole world to see. Oversharing is a plus: "I do think there's a lot to be said for being 'out.' Of course the kids share too much. Every generation overdoes communications by the previous generation's standards. Kids in the 1920s listened to too much radio. It's not a new story."

7   If sharing online makes us feel freer and better about ourselves, then how can that be a bad thing? It turns out, the more we share, the more secure we may become as a result. The **ongoing** chatter of a generation of bloggers texting their fingers off isn't the problem we thought it was. Change the world? Through sharing every aspect of ourselves online? Why not?

[4]**graphic:** very clear and detailed
[5]**hold back:** not do or say something
[6]**exploitation:** use of something for one's own advantage

2.3 Check Your Understanding

Answer the questions.

1   Does the author believe that oversharing is a problem? Why or why not?

2   What are two effects of sharing online that the author mentions? Are they positive or negative?

3   Do you agree or disagree that oversharing is a problem? Explain.

2.4 Notice the Features of Cause and Effect Writing

Answer the questions.

1   Does the writer's main idea explain a cause or an effect?

2   Which words in paragraph 1 help identify the main idea as a cause or an effect?

3   What is the cause and effect stated in paragraph 2? What is the purpose of this paragraph?

In Section 1, you saw how the writer of the Student Model essay reflected on his topic. In this section, you will analyze the final draft of his academic essay. You will learn how to structure your ideas for your own essay.

Ⓐ Student Model

Read the writing prompt again and answer the questions.

WRITING PROMPT: Explain the positive effects and benefits or the negative effects and dangers of sharing information online.

1 Is the writing prompt asking the writer to describe causes or effects? Circle the words in the essay prompt above that you expect the writer to use in his thesis statement.

2 What are some of the positive and negative effects of sharing information online that you think the writer might mention?

Read the Student Model essay twice. The first time, think about your answers to the questions above. The second time, answer the questions in the Analyze Writing Skills boxes. This will help you notice key features of cause and effect essays.

STUDENT MODEL

The Positive Side of Online Sharing

1   The web is over 25 years old. People have argued for some time about the benefits and drawbacks [negative] of it. Some argue that it has had negative effects on people, such as the way they interact in society or the risks of oversharing online. However, others argue that the Internet, especially social media sites, has been good for society in a number of important ways. [thesis statement] Through these sites, people are able to communicate with each other in an emergency, share information about events with everyone in the entire world, and collaborate with others to help make the world better.

2   One positive effect of online sharing is the ability to communicate with people during and after a disaster. When a disaster happens, people use social media to share information and pictures. They can find out important information about the status of the rescue efforts, aid, and the victims. In 2014, a huge landslide[1] covered many houses in the small town of Oso, Washington. Because of social media sites, organizations were able to get volunteers to help rescue survivors.[2] People found out on Twitter about the **ongoing** rescue efforts and shared their own experiences. As a result, people had several ways to help during this terrible crisis (Sleter). [source refference]

[1]**landslide:** when rocks and mud slide down a mountain
[2]**survivor:** someone who lives through a disaster

---

1 Analyze Writing Skills

In paragraph 1, draw a box around the thesis statement. Will the writer focus on causes or effects?

....

2 Analyze Writing Skills

In paragraph 1, underline the points the writer will discuss. Then find them in the essay. Do they follow the same order?

....

3   Another positive impact is the ability of citizen journalists to take photos and write about events that are happening in the world and share them using Twitter and blogs. Pictures about events are communicated instantly. During recent protests about the economy, for example, citizen journalists tweeted photos of the protesters and police. Even the TV news programs and newspapers used the information. In addition, citizen journalists write about news events and give their own **perspectives** on the issues. The blogs help viewers become aware of the issues and form their own opinions.

3 Analyze Writing Skills

In paragraph 3, circle the words in the topic sentence that are the same as or similar to the second point in the thesis statement.

4   The primary effect of social media is that people can become involved in organizations that are trying to make the world better. First, the Internet makes it easier for people to find and volunteer for issues that they are interested in. For example, they can volunteer for Habitat for Humanity and build houses in developing countries. Second, people can fund projects for organizations. When an organization needs money, it can crowdfund[3] its project through social media websites. For example, people helped PencilsofPromise.org build over 150 schools around the world through online donations (Shawbel). On websites like change.com, readers add their name to an online petition[4] to support an idea, such as asking companies to keep our food safe. On dosomething.org, people share their creative ideas to **promote** causes,[5] such as better education or a clean environment.

reference)

4 Analyze Writing Skills

In paragraph 4, what phrase does the writer use to introduce cause and effect?

....

5   In conclusion, online sharing is a valuable tool that has changed our society for the better. Because of social media, people are able to find out information during an emergency, share news instantly, and learn about ways they can make a difference in the world. The world is a lot closer because of online sharing, and that makes me feel hopeful about the future.

5 Analyze Writing Skills

In paragraph 5, underline the writer's comment.

Works Cited

Shawbel, Dan. "Adam Braun: How He Started Pencils of Promise." *Forbes.* Forbes.com, 18 Mar. 2014. Web. 24 Apr. 2015.
Sleter, Greg. "Social Media Analysis Aids in Washington Mudslide Response." *Government Technology.* e.Republic, 7 Apr. 2014. Web. 29 Apr. 2015.
[3]**crowdfund:** collect money through small donations for a special project
[4]**petition:** a document that a lot of people sign and that asks a company or government to change something
[5]**cause:** important idea or belief that a group supports

kickstarter website

3.1 Check Your Understanding

Answer the questions.

1 Do you agree or disagree with the author's thesis? Explain why.

2 What is one other example of a positive effect of online sharing?

3 Do you think there are more benefits or more dangers to sharing online? Why?

 3.2 Learn How Writers Organize Ideas

Complete the outline for "The Positive Side of Online Sharing." Write the thesis statement. Then use the phrases in the box.

ability to communicate in disasters	people used Twitter
crowdfund projects	TV news programs and newspapers used them
help people become aware of the issues	

ESSAY OUTLINE

	I. Introductory paragraph
Thesis Statement	
Body Paragraph 1 Effect 1	II.
Supporting idea 1	A. Share information
Detail	1. Can find out about rescue efforts and victims
Detail	2. 2014 landslide
Sub-detail	a. Social media helped organize volunteers
Sub-detail	b.

Body Paragraph 2 Effect 2	III. Citizen journalists
Supporting idea 1	A. Take photos and video of events
Detail	1.
Sub-detail	a. Recent protests
Sub-detail	b. News programs used the information
Detail	2. Lectures and cultural programs at library
Supporting Idea 2	B. Write about events
Detail	1. Give their own perspectives
Detail	2.
Body Paragraph 3 Effect 3	IV. Become involved in organizations
Supporting idea 1	A. Easier to volunteer
Detail	1. Habitat for Humanity
Supporting idea 2	B.
Detail	1. PencilsofPromise.org
Detail	2. Change.com
Detail	3. Dosomething.org
	V. Concluding paragraph

B Cause and Effect Essays

Writers write about the causes and effects of an action or event to understand why it happened (the cause) and what happened as a result of it (the effect). Understanding these relationships is essential in many kinds of academic writing.

There are several ways to organize ideas in cause and effect essays. It depends on your thesis. Below are two possible ways. Organization A focuses on the causes of an event, and Organization B focuses on the effects of an event.

ORGANIZATION A: FOCUS ON CAUSES

Essay prompt: What are reasons that some people stop using a social media site?

Introductory Paragraph

Thesis statement: *Some people stop using a social media site because they dislike the advertising, they think that the site is not popular anymore, and they want to protect their privacy.*

Body Paragraph 1 (Cause 1): *Dislike advertising*

    Supporting Idea: *Do not like the pressure to buy*

Body Paragraph 2 (Cause 2): *Think site is not popular anymore*

    Supporting Idea 1: *Friends use other sites*

    Supporting Idea 2: *People complain about the site's policies*

Body Paragraph 3 (Cause 3): *Want to protect their privacy*

    Supporting Idea 1: *Advertisers*

    Supporting Idea 2: *Cybercriminals*

Conclusion

ORGANIZATION B: FOCUS ON EFFECTS

Essay prompt: Explain the positive effects and benefits OR the negative effects and dangers of sharing information online.

Introductory Paragraph

Thesis statement: *Through these sites, people are able to communicate with each other in an emergency, share information about political events with everyone in the entire world, and collaborate with others to help make the world better.*

Body Paragraph 1 (Effect 1): *Ability to communicate in disasters*

    Supporting Idea: *Share information*

Body Paragraph 2 (Effect 2): *Citizen journalism*

    Supporting Idea 1: *Take videos and photos*

    Supporting Idea 2: *Write about events*

Body Paragraph 3 (Effect 3): *Help organizations*

    Supporting Idea 1: *Volunteer with organizations*

    Supporting Idea 2: *Fund projects*

Conclusion

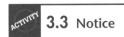 **3.3** Notice

Work with a partner. Look at the two charts on page 114. Answer the questions.

1 Look at Organization A.

   a How many causes will the writer write about?

   b Writers sometimes arrange the body paragraphs so that the strongest idea is last. Review the body paragraphs. Do you think that this writer arranged them this way? Why or why not?

2 Look at Organization B.

   a How many effects will the writer write about?

   b Do you think that this writer arranged the body paragraphs so that the strongest idea is last? Why or why not?

INTRODUCTORY PARAGRAPH

The **introductory paragraph** in a cause and effect essay includes:

- a **hook**, such as a surprising statistic, story, or fact, that makes the reader interested in the topic
- **background information** about the topic that will help the reader understand the causes and effects that you will discuss
- the **thesis statement**, which gives the causes or effects that will be explained in the essay

The **thesis statement** makes it clear to the reader what the essay will focus on – causes or effects – and what the writer's opinion is.

The words and phrases in bold in the chart below help alert the reader to the focus of the essay.

THESIS STATEMENTS	
Focus on Causes	**Focus on Effects**
Social media can **cause** anxiety and depression because it makes people compare themselves to others.	Spending too much time online can **lead to** lower grades at school, anxiety, and problems with friendships.
Taking selfies is popular **because** it is a great way to share important experiences and get quick feedback.	Social networking sites can have a **positive impact** on people's lives by giving them more ways to help each other.
There are two main **reasons that/why** people decide not to share online: They do not want a lot of companies to know their personal information and they want to avoid identity theft.	**If** parents do not control the amount of time that their children spend online, **then** their children will likely be poor students and feel lonely.

Work with a partner. Circle the cause and effect words or phrases in the sentences below. Write *C* if the writer will focus on cause. Write *E* if the focus is on effect.

............1 Smartphones are having a negative impact on our close relationships.

............2 The use of social media is causing problems in relationships.

............3 If teenagers socialize mainly through social media, then they become less comfortable about making new friends face-to-face and they have fewer close friendships.

............4 There are three reasons that social media is more effective than other advertising for making brands successful.

3.5 Apply It to Your Writing

Look at the ideas in your cause-effect graphic organizer in Section 1 on page 105. Revise your thesis statement if needed and share it with a partner. What information do you think your partner will include in his or her essay?

....

....

BODY PARAGRAPHS

Your **body paragraphs** are the main part of your essay. Each paragraph includes the following:

- one **topic sentence** that states a point in the thesis
- four or more **supporting sentences and details** that explain the cause or effect in the topic sentence and make it seem logical and believable

Each topic sentence clearly links to the thesis.

Below is the thesis statement for Organization A (which focuses on causes) from page 114. Notice how the underlined phrases in the three topic sentences focus on the causes.

ORGANIZATION A THESIS STATEMENT: *Some people stop using a social media site because they dislike the advertising, they think that the site is not popular anymore, and they want to protect their personal information.*

Topic Sentence 1: <u>One reason that/why</u> people stop using a social media site <u>is that</u> they do not like all the advertising that they see.

Topic Sentence 2: <u>Another reason that/why</u> they stop using a site <u>is that</u> they think that the site is no longer the site that most of their friends are on.

Topic Sentence 3: <u>The primary reason that/why</u> people no longer use a social media site <u>is that</u> they want to keep their personal information private.

Below is the thesis statement for Organization B (which focuses on effects) from page 116. Notice how the underlined phrases in the three topic sentences focus on the effects.

ORGANIZATION B THESIS STATEMENT: *Through these sites, people are able to communicate with each other in an emergency, share information about political events with everyone in the entire world, and collaborate with others to help make the world better.*

Topic Sentence 1: <u>One</u> positive <u>effect of</u> online sharing <u>is</u> the ability to communicate with people during and after a disaster.

Topic Sentence 2: <u>Another</u> positive <u>impact is</u> the ability of citizen journalists to take photos and write about events that are happening in the world and share them using Twitter and blogs.

Topic Sentence 3: <u>The primary effect of</u> social media <u>is that</u> people can become involved in organizations that are trying to make the world better.

 3.6 Practice Topic Sentences

Rewrite the topic sentences using the underlined phrases in the chart at the bottom of page 116.

Thesis Statement: *Children become bullies when they are mistreated by parents, when they do not have any discipline at home, or when they are unable to feel empathy for others.*

1 **Topic Sentence 1:** Children become bullies when they are abused at home.
   One reason that children become bullies is that they were abused at home.

2 **Topic Sentence 2:** Children become bullies when their parents do not discipline them at home. ....
   ....

3 **Topic Sentence 3:** Children become bullies when they are unable to feel compassion for others. ....
   ....

 3.7 Apply It to Your Writing

Look at the graphic organizer you created for your writing prompt in Section 1 on page 105 and your thesis statement from Activity 3.5. Write topic sentences using the language that you learned. Share them with a partner.

....

....

....

....

SUPPORTING SENTENCES

In a cause and effect essay, the supporting sentences and details explain your topic sentence. They sometimes show cause and effect, too. Read the example from the Student Model essay on page pages 110–111.

One positive effect of online sharing is the ability to communicate with people during and after a disaster. When a disaster happens, people use social media to share information and pictures. They can find out important information about the status of the rescue efforts, aid, and the victims. In 2014, a huge landslide covered many houses in the small town of Oso, Washington. Because of social media sites, organizations were able to get volunteers to help rescue survivors. People found out on Twitter about the ongoing rescue efforts and shared their own experiences. As a result, people had several ways to help during this terrible crisis (Sleter).

> The writer introduces the first positive effect of communication: "people use social media to share information and pictures." The line that follows explains the importance of sharing information.

> The writer gives an example of a disaster.

> The writer introduces a positive effect of communication: "organizations were able to coordinate volunteers."

 3.8 Practice Supporting Sentences

Read each topic sentence. Write a supporting sentence and an example to support it. Use the body paragraph from the Student Model essay above to help you.

1 **Topic Sentence:** One positive effect of social media is that more young people know what is going on in the world.

....

....

....

....

2 **Topic Sentence:** A second positive effect of using social media is that it enables people to feel more empathy for others.

....

....

....

....

ACTIVITY **3.9** Apply It to Your Writing

YOUR TURN

Look at your topic sentences from Activity 3.7 on page 117. Choose one and write two or three supporting sentences. Then share them with a partner.

....

....

....

....

ACTIVITY **3.10** Practice Organizing Ideas

Work with a partner. Read the writing prompt. Decide if the answer will focus on causes or effects. Then complete the body paragraphs of the essay with supporting sentences.

WRITING PROMPT: Discuss how social media has affected the way we travel and whether the effects are positive or negative.

How Social Media Has Made Travel Easier

Jennifer stands outside the gate to Topkapi Palace in Istanbul, takes a photo of the garden, and posts it on social media. Her friend Amy sees it and calls Jennifer. They talk for a half an hour as Jennifer describes her day at the palace. Traveling and using social media make the experience so much better. Social media has made traveling more fun because people can be in constant contact, travelers can find important information about their trip from others, and travelers can make or change plans much more easily.

One positive benefit of social media on traveling is that it allows tourists to stay in touch with their friends and family easily. ....

....

....

....

....

Finding recommendations from other travelers is another positive effect of using social media while traveling. ....

....

....

....

....

A third impact of social media is that tourists are able to make or change travel plans with others quickly. ....

....

....

....

In conclusion, the use of social media has had a positive effect on the way that people travel. As a result of these websites, when people go abroad, they can communicate with people back home, get ideas from other travelers, or change plans easily. Overall, it is a positive change and it has resulted in more people traveling and learning more about the world. Social media makes travelers feel like the world is very close and familiar.

CONCLUDING PARAGRAPHS

The **concluding paragraph** in a cause and effect essay has the same parts as in other essays. A concluding paragraph:

- restates the thesis
- reminds the reader of the importance of the topic
- ends with a comment or suggestion

ACTIVITY **3.11** Notice

Work with a partner. Look at the concluding paragraph of the Student Model essay on pages 110–111. Answer the questions.

1 Does the writer include the effects discussed in all of the body paragraphs? ....

2 Check (✓) the type of comment the writer gives in this conclusion.

   ☐ an explanation of why the topic is important

   ☐ an opinion

   ☐ a prediction

   ☐ encouragement to do something

3 Does the essay seem finished? Why or why not? ....

Ⓐ Writing Skill 1: Phrases That Show Cause and Effect

In this section, you will learn the writing and grammar skills that will make your writing more sophisticated and accurate.

PHRASES THAT SHOW CAUSE

Use the phrases below before nouns that show cause. These phrases must be part of a main clause. They can go in the beginning or middle of a sentence:

due to

as a result of

because of

Note: When the phrases come first, they are followed by a comma.

> NOUN   SUBJ   VERB
> **Due to** her blog, Stephanie's bakery became more popular.

> NOUN   SUBJ   VERB
> **As a result of** the Internet, we are linked to millions of people all over the world.

> SUBJ   VERB   NOUN
> Our lives are more transparent **because of** online sharing.

PHRASES THAT SHOW EFFECT

Use the phrases below to introduce an effect or reason:

As a result,

For this reason,

That is why

Note: *As a result* and *For this reason* are followed by a comma and a clause. *That is why* is **not** followed by a comma because it is part of the clause.

> SUBJ   VERB
> **As a result,** they were able to keep up with events.

> SUBJ   VERB
> **For this reason,** they could share their own experience.

> SUBJ   VERB
> **That is why** they were able to find out how to help.

 4.1 Focus on Use

Complete each sentence with the correct phrase in parentheses.

1 Online sharing allows users to communicate at a very low cost with anyone anywhere

anytime; ....**for this reason,**............ many people use the Internet to keep in touch with
  (for this reason, / because of)
family and friends.

2 People who live far from a college can now get an education ....
                                                                                              (as a result, / due to)
the development of online courses.

3 .... online predators, people need to be careful about who they
   (Because of / That is why)
meet online.

4 The Internet makes it possible to reach thousands in an instant. ....
                                                (For this reason, / Due to)
   people can be informed immediately about an emergency or police news.

5 .... computers, today's children may have more flexible brains than
      (As a result, / As a result of)
   their parents.

 4.2 Write About Ideas

Add a cause or an effect to complete each sentence below. Write C above the causes and E above the effects.

                                    C   E

1 Because an email address is valuable personal information, ...*I never put it on my*......
   Facebook page...

2 I don't like to receive texts during class. For this reason, ...
   ....

3 My generation knows a lot more about social media than our parents. As a result, ...
   ....

4 Sharing news and photos with family and friends is really important to me. That is why ....
   ....

5 Due to ....
   people enjoy shopping online.

B Writing Skill 2: Parallel Structure

In writing, you will often use lists with several words or phrases to support your point. In cause and effect writing, lists can show that there is more than one cause or effect. As you learned in Unit 3, parallel structure means that all the ideas in the list are written with the same part of speech or form – for example, nouns, adjectives, prepositional phrases, or gerund phrases.

Below are examples of lists using parallel structure.

ADJECTIVE   ADJECTIVE   ADJECTIVE
Because of video game communities, some players do not feel as <u>awkward</u>, <u>shy</u>, or <u>lonely</u>.

ADVERB   ADVERB
As a result of online sharing, important information can be sent <u>quickly</u> and <u>easily</u>.

VERB   VERB   VERB
Due to social media, colleges are able to <u>attract</u>, <u>support</u>, and <u>keep</u> top students.

NOUN   NOUN   NOUN
<u>Musicians</u>, <u>singers</u>, and <u>artists</u> often post their work on that website.

We also use parallel structure with longer phrases and clauses. To make it easier to read, the phrases or clauses in each sentence should be a similar length. Below are some examples.

GERUND PHRASE
Colleges communicate with high school students by <u>maintaining a Facebook page</u>,

GERUND PHRASE   GERUND PHRASE
<u>uploading videos on YouTube</u>, and <u>hosting concerts by pop stars</u>.

PREPOSITIONAL PHRASE   PREPOSITIONAL PHRASE
The most common online relationships are <u>between family members</u> or <u>among friends</u>.

NOUN CLAUSE   NOUN CLAUSE
People who are phishing want to know <u>where you bank</u> and <u>what your account number is</u>.

INDEPENDENT CLAUSE   INDEPENDENT CLAUSE   INDEPENDENT CLAUSE
<u>My grandmother calls me</u>, <u>my mom emails me</u>, and <u>my friends text</u> me.

 4.3 Editing Task

Read the sentences below. Correct the word or phrase that does not have parallel structure.

1 In the United States most people get their news from newspapers, social networking sites, and ~~listen to~~ the radio.

2 Local businesswomen use Twitter to support each other, get knowledge from others, and growth of their business.

3 For political protests, social networking sites are a quick way to spread information, move people, and for the organization of events.

4 Teachers use social media for teaching, communicating with students, and they interact with other teachers.

5 Teens report that social networking makes them feel less shy, more outgoing, and have more confidence.

6 Most children use digital devices easily, confidently, and they are enthusiastic.

Complete the sentences below with your own ideas. Use parallel structure.

1 Teens report that social media helps them <u>stay in touch</u> with old friends, <u>get to know</u> their classmates better, and ....

2 The reasons why social media can be bad for people are that they can get addicted to it, they can feel stressed by the posts, or ....

3 Text messages can be sent <u>quietly</u>, ..., and ....

4 The Internet has provided access to more <u>educational</u>, <u>cultural</u>, and .... information than ever before.

5 Many people check the Internet every morning for information, such as <u>traffic updates</u>, ..., and ....

 ## Writing Skill 3: Paragraph Unity

Unity in a paragraph means that everything in a paragraph is about one topic. In other words, all of the sentences support the topic sentence. A sentence should not be included if it is not related to the main idea of the paragraph. It might be true or interesting, but if it's off-topic, do not include it. Read the example below.

In the United States, a lot of people get their news from social media. For example, most of my friends use Facebook more than any other site for news information. I have read that a lot of people also get their news from YouTube. <u>Many people also use YouTube for watching videos or listening to music.</u> I like reading news stories on reddit.com, although very few of my friends are aware of that site.

The topic of the paragraph is getting news from social media. It is not about watching videos or listening to music. Even though the underlined sentence is true, it is not related to news on social media. That sentence is off-topic.

Work with a partner. Cross out three sentences that don't support the topic sentence.

Another serious effect of online bullying is that it can affect students' studies and academic performance. When students are bullied online, they may not pay attention in class. They also often stop participating in class, or taking part in class discussions. They worry that if they talk in class, they may be bullied more. Teachers should stop this. Next, bullied students may start to neglect their schoolwork. As a result, their grades start to drop. Colleges are not interested in people with bad grades. Many bullied students begin to skip classes because they feel uncomfortable at school. Some of these students finally quit school altogether and never graduate. Children who bully usually do not have loving parents.

D Grammar for Writing: Real Conditionals

Sentences with real conditional clauses can show cause and effect. In a real conditional, there are two clauses. The *if* clause describes a possible situation, condition, or cause. The main clause describes the result, or effect.

PRESENT REAL CONDITIONALS	
1 Use the simple present in the *if* clause and also in the main clause.	[CAUSE] [EFFECT] *If people **text** while driving, they **put** themselves and others in danger.*
2 Put *if* clauses first or last. If the *if* clause is first, a comma comes after it. If the *if* clause is last, there is no comma.	[EFFECT] [CAUSE] *People can lose their jobs if they share inappropriate images online.* [CAUSE] [EFFECT] *If people share inappropriate images online, they can lose their jobs.*
3 You can use *when* instead of *if*. The meaning is the same.	[CAUSE] *When/If people share negative comments about their workplace,* [EFFECT] *they often regret it.*

FUTURE REAL CONDITIONALS	
1 Use *will* in the main clause to describe future results.	[CAUSE] *If Facebook users see that their friends have voted,* [EFFECT] *they will probably vote, too.*
2 When the *if* clause has several effects, do not repeat the *if* clause.	[CAUSE] [EFFECT] *If a musician signs up for a Twitter account, she will be able to communicate* She *with her fans very quickly. ~~If she signs up for a Twitter account, she~~ will also* *be able to follow other music industry tweets.*

4.6 Combine Ideas

Read the two sentences. One is the cause, and the other is the effect. Join the two sentences into one sentence that starts with an *if/when* **clause.**

1 People use professional social media sites like LinkedIn.
   Potential employers contact those people about jobs in their field.
   When people use professional social media sites like LinkedIn, potential employers contact them about jobs in their field.

2 People start a Twitter feed about an important environmental issue, such as clean air.
   Followers spread the word to promote positive change.

3 People share political messages about an event with others through social networks.
   There is more news coverage.

4 Schools offer programs about bullying.
   Fewer children are bullied.

5 A child feels no empathy for others.
   The child probably becomes a bully.

Avoiding Common Mistakes

Research tells us that these are the most common mistakes that students make when using real conditionals in academic writing.

1 Use a comma after the *if/when* clause when it is the first part of the sentence. Do not use a comma when the *if/when* clause is the second part of the sentence.

If someone shares something online‚ it will always be there.

Parents should pay attention to their children's ~~activities, when~~ they are online.
activities when

2 Be sure that the verb and subject agree in the *if/when* clause.

goes
When a child ~~go~~ online, the parents are responsible for the child's safety.

3 In real conditionals, use *will* in the main clause. Do not use *will* in the *if/when* clause.

If teens ~~will~~ avoid posting personal details, they will be a little safer online.

 4.7 Editing Task

Find and correct six more mistakes in the paragraph below.

Many problems can result from sharing the wrong information on social media sites. First, if
shares
someone ~~will share~~ personal information, such as a cell phone number or an email address, that

person may become a victim of cybercrime. Many teens share their email addresses online and

do not realize the danger. If a cybercriminal get access to someone's personal site, they can use

that information for identity theft or fraud. Another problem that some social media users can

face is posting photos that are later embarrassing. For example, a college student might post

a photo from a party at spring break. Later, if she will apply for a job the employer may see

the photo and decide not to hire her. Furthermore, when someone posts something on the

web, it do not disappear. Users should always remember that fact, and be careful in what they

post. The third problem with sharing inappropriate information online relates to work. If an

employee will make rude comments about a boss, a co-worker, or a client online, they could

lose their job. There can also be problems, if an employee shares company secrets.

E Avoiding Plagiarism

Writers follow certain rules when they use information from sources. Following these rules makes it easier for their readers to recognize and locate the sources.

I know I need to cite my sources, but I'm not sure how to do it. Do I cite online sources and printed books the same way? What if I can't find an author's name? Can I still use the source? It seems so complicated. I'd love some advice. Thanks!

Ani

Dear Ani,

I'm glad you know that you should cite your sources. You don't want to plagiarize. Your questions are good ones, and you will be happy to know that the answers are fairly simple. Print and web sources are cited a little differently, but the rules are quite easy to learn. The first thing to find out is which style of citation your school uses, because each style has different rules. This book teaches MLA style, but APA is often used, too. Ask your instructor which style you should use. One tricky part about citing is having all the important information about the source available when you need it, so make sure you note important information, such as the author's name, title of the article or book, and publication date for each source. It's easier than you think to cite, though, so don't worry!

Best,

Professor Wright

CITING SOURCES

Citing sources in texts refers to mentioning them in two places:

- in the text, also called **in-text citations**

- at the end of the paper in an alphabetical **Works Cited** list

In-text Citations

An in-text citation is a short reference to a source that tells the reader where the information or quotation comes from. In MLA style, the citation is often just the name of an author and a page number where the information appeared. A more detailed description of the source appears in a Works Cited list at the end of the paper. Following are general rules for creating in-text citations for some print sources (books and articles in magazines, newspapers, or journals) and web sources (online magazines, newspapers, and journals, and websites).

Below are general rules for creating in-text citations for some print sources (books and articles in magazines, newspapers, or journals) and web sources (online magazines, newspapers, and journals, and websites).

HOW TO CREATE IN-TEXT CITATIONS

1 **Print Sources**

For print sources, always include the author's name (or names, if there is more than one author) and the page number where you found the information. The name can appear in the sentence or at the end of the sentence with the page number in parentheses.

AUTHOR'S NAME

Agger argues that people tell lies when they overshare to

PAGE NUMBER

appear more interesting (4).

People tell lies when they overshare to make themselves more

AUTHOR'S NAME AND PAGE NUMBER

interesting (Agger 4).

MULTIPLE AUTHORS NAMES

Baum and Vincent note that in some states, schools cannot have access to students' social media accounts.

In some states, schools cannot have access to students' social media accounts

MULTIPLE AUTHORS NAMES

(Baum and Vincent).

Note: The information in parentheses always comes before the period.

2 **Web Sources**

Web articles often do not have page numbers. As in print sources, include the author's name in either the sentence or in parentheses at the end of the sentence.

Golbeck states that some people create a distinctive online persona that is a new identity.

Some people create a distinctive online persona that is a new identity (Goldbeck).

Works Cited

A Works Cited lists all the sources used in your article.

Below are general guidelines for creating entries for a Works Cited list:

1 There should be one entry for each in-text citation by a different author. In other words, the number of in-text citations by different authors should match the number of entries in your Works Cited list.

2 The list should be in alphabetical order. Notice that for long entries the second line is indented.

Agger, Ben. *Oversharing: Presentation of Self in the Internet Age.* New York: Routledge, 2012. Print.

Grant, Adam. "Why Some People Have No Boundaries Online." *Psychology Today.* Sussex Publishers, 11 Sept. 2013. Web. 16 Mar. 2014.

Follow the guidelines below for creating entries in a Works Cited list.

For a book:

LAST NAME FIRST NAME   TITLE OF BOOK   CITY OF PUBLICATION PUBLISHER

Agger, Ben. *Oversharing: Presentation of Self in the Internet Age.* New York: Routledge,

YEAR MEDIUM

2012. Print.

For a web article:

AUTHOR   TITLE OF ARTICLE   TITLE OF MAGAZINE

Grant, Adam. "Why Some People Have No Boundaries Online." *Psychology Today.*

PUBLISHER DAY MONTH YEAR MEDIUM DATE ACCESSED

Sussex Publishers, 11 Sept. 2013. Web. 16 Mar. 2014.

For a scholarly journal:

LAST NAME FIRST NAME   TITLE OF ARTICLE

Washington, Edwina Thomas. "An Overview of Cyberbullying in Higher Education."

JOURNAL VOLUME DATE PAGES   DATA BASE   MEDIUM DATE OF ACCESS

Adult Learning 26.1 (2015): 21–27. *Academic Search Complete.* Web. 3 Mar. 2015.

 4.8 Practice

Write the in-text citations for the sources and information below.

1 From a web newspaper article titled "Temptation to Share Online Can Come Back to Haunt Teens," published on March 10, 2012, on SeattleTimes.com (published by Seattle Times), written by Julie Weed, accessed on February 12, 2013.

It surprises teens to find out that when they behave badly, that behavior might appear on the web.

In-text citation: Weed reports that it surprises teens to find out that when they behave badly, that behavior might appear on the web. OR
It surprises teens to find out that when they behave badly, that behavior might appear on the web (Weed).

2 From a web journal article written by Charisse L. Nixon, titled "Current Perspectives: The Impact of Cyberbullying on Adolescent Health," in *Adolescent Health, Medicine, and Therapeutics* (in the *Dove Press* database), dated August 2014, Vol. 123, Issue 1, pp. 143–158, accessed on February 28, 2015.

(page 149) Adolescents who bullied others also had other negative behaviors.

In-text citation:

3   From a book written by Randi Zuckerberg called *Dot Complicated: Untangling Our Wired Lives*. Published by Harper in New York in 2013.

    (page 50) "Tech can fill our lives with meaning, rather than fear."

    In-text citation: ....

    ....

ACTIVITY **4.9** Practice

Create a Works Cited list for the sources in Activity 4.8. Be sure to put them in alphabetical order.

....

....

....

....

....

....

....

....

In this section, you will follow the writing process to complete the final draft of your essay.

STEP 1: BRAINSTORM

Work with a partner. Follow the steps below to brainstorm ideas for your essay.

1 Before you start, notice how the writer of the Student Model essay brainstormed. He wrote many ideas but did not use all of them in his essay.

WRITING PROMPT: Explain the positive effects and benefits or the negative effects and dangers of online sharing.

Cause

Effects

Sharing online

→ Quick news after a disaster

→ Share pictures

→ Find a job

→ Find people who share my interests

→ Easy to help others – give money

→ Lots of reviews and recommendations

→ Find out things quickly about political events

→ Citizen journalists – take photos and videos of events and post them

→ Find people who share my interests

→ Help organizations – money, volunteer

2 Write the ideas that you wrote in Section 1 on page 105 in the appropriate cause-effect graphic organizer below. Include ideas from the Your Turns throughout this unit. Brainstorm other ideas.

Causes   **Effect**

Causes	Effect
☐ →	☐
☐ →	
☐ →	
☐ →	

Cause   **Effects**

Cause	Effects
☐	→ ☐
	→ ☐
	→ ☐
	→ ☐

3 Circle the three strongest points that support your thesis and write them below.

1 ....

2 ....

3 ....

STEP 2: DO RESEARCH

If your topic requires research, see page 261 for advice on how to find information.

STEP 3: MAKE AN OUTLINE

Complete the outline below with your ideas from the previous steps.

ESSAY OUTLINE

I. Introductory paragraph

Thesis Statement

Body Paragraph 1
Cause/Effect 1

II.

Supporting Idea 1

A.

Detail

1.

Detail

2.

Supporting Idea 2

B.

Detail

1.

Detail

2.

Body Paragraph 2
Cause/Effect 2

III.

Supporting Idea 1

A.

Detail

1.

Detail

2.

Supporting Idea 2

B.

Detail

1.

Detail

2.

Body Paragraph 3	IV. ....
Cause/Effect 3	
Supporting Idea 1	A. ....
Detail	1. ....
Detail	2. ....
Supporting Idea 2	B. ....
Detail	1. ....
Detail	2. ....
	V. Concluding paragraph ....
	....

STEP 4: WRITE YOUR FIRST DRAFT

Now it is time to write your first draft. Here are some suggestions on how to get started.

1 Use your outline, notes, and the sentences you wrote in the Your Turns.

2 Focus on making your ideas as clear as possible.

3 Add a title.

After you finish, read your essay and check for basic errors.

1 Check that all sentences have subjects and verbs.

2 Make sure that your subjects and verbs agree.

3 Check that you have used a comma after an *if/when* clause, but not before.

4 Make sure your thesis statement, topic sentences, and concluding statement are clear.

STEP 5: WRITE YOUR FINAL DRAFT

1 After you receive feedback on your first draft, review it carefully. Fix any errors.

2 Make a note of errors that were most frequent. Try to avoid them as you write.

3 Review the Academic Vocabulary and Phrases from this unit. Are there any that you can add to your essay?

4 Turn to page 265 and use the Self-Editing Review to check your work one more time.

5 Write your final draft and hand it in.

5 SUMMARY ESSAYS

HEALTH: BALANCED LIFESTYLES

"Don't confuse having a career with having a life."

Hillary Clinton (1947–)

About the Author:

Hillary Clinton is a former U.S. First Lady, Secretary of State, U.S. senator, and presidential candidate.

Work with a partner. Read the quotation about work-life balance. Then answer the questions.

1   What do you think "having a life" means?

2   What do you think Clinton means when she says not to confuse having a career with having a life?

3   Why do you think that Clinton says this?

Ⓐ Connect to Academic Writing

In this unit, you will learn the skills to help you write summary essays. While some of the writing skills that you will use may be new to you, others are not. In your everyday life, you use summarizing when you tell a friend about a book you are reading, a movie you saw recently, or a lecture you attended.

Ⓑ Reflect on the Topic

In this section, you will read an article and reflect on it. You will learn how to summarize the ideas in an article throughout the unit, and you will practice skills that are necessary to write your summary essay.

The writing prompt below was used for the Student Model essay on pages 146–147. The student read an article and used the chart to list important ideas in the article. This helped him figure out the main idea of the article, or what the article is about.

WRITING PROMPT: Summarize the article "A Tax on Unhealthy Foods" by Michelle Embrich.

Title of the Article: A Tax on Unhealthy Foods

Author's Name: Michelle Embrich

THE AUTHOR'S IDEAS
"Too many people are overweight, and the impact on the economy could be disastrous."
"Put a tax on foods that are high in fat and high in sugar. This tax would reduce the number of unhealthily overweight people and keep health care costs from rising."
"Would tax on unhealthy foods be effective? Absolutely."
"The bigger question is whether a tax like this one would be politically acceptable. Probably not – because Americans traditionally don't like the government to interfere in their private lives."
"They might agree to a tax if they had to pay high income taxes."

The author's main idea: A tax on unhealthy foods would save people's lives and help the economy.

 1.1 Notice

Work with a partner. Read the ideas in the chart above. What do you think the article is about?

1.2 Apply It to Your Writing

Follow the directions to reflect on your topic.

A Choose a prompt:

- Read the article "More Than Job Satisfaction" on page pages 161–162 and write a summary essay.

- Read a text approved by your instructor and write a summary essay.

B Complete the following tasks:

1 Write the title of the article and the name of the author in the chart.

2 Read the article a few times and underline what you think the author's most important ideas are.

3 List the ideas from the article in the chart. Write a statement that you think gives the main idea of the article.

4 Compare charts with a partner.

Title of the Article: ....

Author's Name: ....

THE AUTHOR'S IDEAS

The author's main idea: ....

In this section, you will learn academic language that you can use in your summary essay. You will also notice how a professional writer uses the language and features of academic essays.

Ⓐ Academic Vocabulary

The words below appear throughout the unit. Many are from the Academic Word List. Using these words in your writing will make your ideas clearer and your writing more academic.

conscious (adj)	ensure (v)	focus (v)	sense (n)
consume (v)	experiment (n)	global (adj)	urge (n)

 2.1 Focus on Meaning

Work with a partner. Match the words in bold to the letters of their meanings.

A

.... 1 In a recent *Psychology Today* article entitled "Working Our Lives Away," author Steve Taylor, PhD, claims that it is not healthy to **focus** our lives on work.

      a relating to the whole world

.... 2 Taylor argues that the **global** trend toward working "forty hours a week, 48 weeks a year, for up to 50 years" is harmful to people.

      b to eat or drink

.... 3 The author suggests that our jobs do not define who we are and should not be used to measure our **sense** of happiness.

      c to give a lot of attention to something

.... 4 Taylor says that a few thousand years ago humans spent only about four hours each day looking for food to **consume**, and this was their major work.

      d feeling or understanding

B

.... 1 Taylor encourages readers to fight the **urge** to work too much because it is not good for our well-being.

      a to make certain that something happens

.... 2 Companies do not always **ensure** that their workers get enough rest and relaxation.

      b a strong desire or need

.... 3 People must be **conscious** of the fact that being financially successful may not lead to happiness.

      c tests to discover something

.... 4 Researchers do **experiments** to understand how eating habits impact job performance.

      d aware

B Academic Collocations

Collocations are words that are frequently used together. Research tells us that the academic vocabulary in Part A is commonly used in the collocations below.

conduct an experiment	make a conscious decision	a strong urge
the main focus of	make sense	

 2.2 Focus on Meaning

Work with a partner. Circle the correct meanings.

1 Psychologists **conduct experiments** to discover answers to their questions about human behavior. The phrase **conduct an experiment** is a more academic way of saying

   a experience on one's own.　　　　b do a scientific test.

2 The company Expedia does a global report each year on vacations. **The main focus of** the report is to find out what people's perceptions of vacations are around the world. The phrase **the main focus of** is used to introduce

   a a detail.　　　　b an objective.

3 While it **makes sense** to take paid vacations, often Americans do not use their vacation days. They work instead. The phrase **make sense** is used when something seems

   a logical or reasonable.　　　　b clear or clever.

4 While on vacation, many people feel **a strong urge** to check their email and do some work. The phrase **a strong urge** explains

   a something that is hard to control.　　　　b something that is fun to do.

5 People in some cultures make **a conscious decision** to take all their paid vacation days because they feel that taking vacations is necessary. The phrase **a conscious decision** is a decision that someone makes

   a after a lot of careful thinking.　　　　b without thinking a lot about it.

C Writing in the Real World

The author of "Mindful Eating: How to Think More and Eat Less" uses features of summary writing to explain research in order to support his main idea.

Before you read, answer these questions: What does it mean to eat "mindfully"? How can thinking about what you are eating help you eat less?

Now read the article. Think about your answers to the questions above as you read.

MINDFUL EATING:
HOW TO THINK MORE AND EAT LESS
(adapted)

BY SIMON USBORNE

1 "Mindful[1] eating" is a meditative[2] approach to consumption for those who want to give more thought to their food. I'm about to try it by taking 10 minutes to eat a single raisin.

2 "Letting the raisin rest on your palm, become aware of its pattern, color, and shape," explains mindfulness trainer Michael Chaskalson. His main focus isn't eating – he instructs people how to be more in tune with[3] themselves and their surroundings[4] – but he uses the raisin exercise to start his courses.

3 "Taking your other hand, feeling the movement of your muscles as you do it, pick up the raisin and get a sense of its texture," he tells me. I obey, trying to fight the urge to gobble the raisin.

4 Mindful eating isn't a diet. Practitioners[5] don't care what you eat, but how, and how quickly. Just as Buddhists expand their consciousness by thinking about breathing, they think about eating.

5 Academics, too, are interested. Harvard nutritionist Dr. L. Cheung reports mindless eating is one cause of the global obesity epidemic.[6] "Being aware of what we eat and drink ensures we don't overconsume," she says.

[1]**mindful:** giving attention to
[2]**meditative:** thinking calmly and slowly
[3]**be in tune with:** understand what someone wants or needs
[4]**surroundings:** place and conditions in which you are
[5]**practitioner:** someone who does something regularly

[6]**epidemic:** when a large number of people have the same illness

6   Studies have shown that thinking about the way we eat food means we consume less. *Mindless Eating* author Brian Wansink conducted an experiment to show this. He gave stale popcorn to cinemagoers in different sizes. When he weighed the buckets after the film, he found those with bigger buckets ate 53 percent more. When we don't make a conscious decision to think about food, we'll eat anything and we eat more of it and get fatter.

7   As food containers grow along with distractions and demands on our time, it's bad news for our hearts and waistlines. Other research has shown that those who eat quickly get fatter because the chemicals that tell our brain we're full take time to reach it.

8   "Slowly begin moving the raisin toward your lip. Now, just let the raisin rest on your tongue, exploring any faint flavors," the trainer continues. Five minutes after picking up the raisin, it has finally made contact with my face.

9   Mindful eaters are also conscious of the origins of food. When you eat a chocolate bar, says Dr. Cheung, "give thanks to all those who made the chocolate bar possible, including nature, the cocoa plant, and farmers. You would not have the chocolate bar in your hand if these elements were not present."

10 Right. The raisin has been resting on my tongue long enough. Chaskalson announces: "Move the raisin between your back teeth, letting it just rest there." Oh, come on!

11 "Now, take a bite slowly chewing until there's almost nothing left," he adds. "Focus on the sound, and texture. Then, swallow and track the raisin down your throat until you lose sight of it."

12 After 10 minutes, the raisin is no more. I have never eaten so slowly. Chaskalson asked me what I had noticed. I said I had felt the raisin squish between my teeth, and almost heard the popping as I bit it. Weirdly, I notice my voice is quieter and calmer. I put the phone down. Do I eat the rest of the packet more slowly? Perhaps not, but I certainly think about doing it.

 2.3 Check Your Understanding

Answer the questions.

1   What does "mindful eating" mean?

2   According to the article, why is "mindless eating" harmful to people's health?

3   Are you a "mindful" or "mindless" eater? Give an example.

 2.4 Notice the Features of Summary Writing

Answer the questions.

1   Paragraph 6 is an example of a summary. It briefly explains an experiment and its results. What is the experiment, and what are its results?

2   What is the writer's purpose in including the experiment?

In Section 1, you saw how the writer of the Student Model essay reflected on his article. In this section, you will analyze the final draft of his academic essay. You will learn how to structure your ideas for your own essay.

Ⓐ Student Model

A student read the article "A Tax on Unhealthy Foods" and made notes. Then he wrote a summary essay of the article.

Read the article. The first time you read, think about these questions.

1 What is the article about?
2 How does the author try to convince the reader of her ideas?

Read the article again. Notice how the student annotated, or marked up, the article to prepare to write a summary essay. Then answer the questions below.

A Tax on Unhealthy Foods
by Michelle Embrich

There is a crisis[1] today in the United States. It is not a political crisis. It is not an economic crisis. It is a health care crisis. Simply put: Too many people are overweight, and the impact on the economy could be disastrous.

The overweight American, fairly rare when I was growing up in the 1970s, is now the norm. In fact, according to the results of a 2014 study cited in the Harvard School of Public Health Obesity Prevention Source, over two-thirds of adults are overweight or obese. Overweight and obese people are not only a danger to themselves, living shorter, unhealthy lives; but they also put a strain[2] on the country's health care system and make health care costs and health insurance higher for everyone. I propose a simple solution: Put a tax on foods that are high in fat and high in sugar. This tax on unhealthy foods would reduce the number of unhealthily overweight people and keep health care costs from rising.

A tax on unhealthy foods could solve the problem of obesity.

Would a tax on unhealthy foods be effective? Absolutely. First, we have a history of successfully discouraging unhealthy habits by putting a high price tag on them. For instance, high taxes on tobacco worked to reduce the number of smokers in the United States. People were less likely to buy

[1]**crisis:** extremely dangerous or difficult situation
[2]**strain:** something that causes problems or makes a situation more difficult

cigarettes – or simply bought fewer than usual – because they did not want to spend more money on them. It seems likely that our food habits would change just as our cigarette habits did. Second, research shows that if a tax of 18 percent were put on soda and pizza alone, the average American could lose five pounds (*Archives of Internal Medicine*). Imagine how much more weight could be lost if hamburgers and fries were taxed, too.

The bigger question is whether a tax like this one would be politically acceptable. Probably not – because Americans traditionally don't like the government to interfere in their private lives. One example is the unsuccessful attempt to ban[3] oversized sodas in New York City restaurants. The public was outraged.[4] "We don't like being bossed around by the government," residents said. "This is becoming a nanny state,"[5] they argued. In fact, a poll by NBC found that as many as 6 in 10 New Yorkers felt that the ban was a bad idea. Similarly, an April 2012 national survey on a related topic found that only 28 percent of Americans said that they would support taxing high-fat and high-sugar food. It is also likely true that the companies that make those foods would not want that, either.

However, while Americans dislike government interference in their private lives, they might agree to a tax if they had to pay higher taxes. Today, the annual cost of obesity-related health care in the United States is estimated by some researchers to be $190 billion, or 20 percent of the total health care costs in the country. It is expected to almost double by 2030. It won't be long before there are more and more people saying: "Why didn't the government do more to combat this economic crisis?"

A tax on unhealthy foods, combined with subsidizing[6] the cost of healthy foods, is inevitably[7] in America's future. It will save lives and reduce the rising cost of health care. We must admit that for this crisis, the freedom to eat fast foods is not worth fighting for because many of us will not live long lives if we win it.

[3]**ban:** forbid someone to do something
[4]**outraged:** very angry or shocked
[5]**nanny state**: a view that government has too much control over people's choices
[6]**subsidize:** give money as part of the cost to encourage something
[7]**inevitably:** in a way that cannot be avoided

Work with a partner. Match the two parts of the sentences to explain how the student writer took notes on the article on pages 144–145.

.... 1 In paragraphs 1–2, the underlined phrases

.... 2 In paragraph 2, the circled sentences

.... 3 In paragraphs 3–5, the double underlined sentences

.... 4 In paragraphs 3–5, the underlined phrases with stars next to them

a explain the author's thesis.

b are the main points that support the thesis.

c are convincing details.

d explain the topic of the article.

Now read the final draft of the Student Model summary essay. Read the essay twice. The first time, compare the ideas with those in the original article. The second time, answer the questions in the Analyze Writing Skills boxes. This will help you notice which information the student writer used in his summary essay.

Summary of "A Tax on Unhealthy Foods"

1   In "A Tax on Unhealthy Foods," Michelle Embrich claims that the growing number of obese Americans is causing a serious health crisis in the United States, and that a tax on unhealthy foods can help solve the obesity crisis. According to the author, over two-thirds of the population is overweight or obese. This growing issue is not only dangerous for people's health, but also for the country's health care system.

2   The author claims that a tax on unhealthy foods would solve the problem of obesity for several reasons. She starts by saying that this tax would be effective because it has worked for other unhealthy habits. She gives the example of cigarettes and smoking. Higher prices reduced the number of smokers, so a tax on unhealthy foods would reduce the number of overweight people. The author mentions that Americans might not accept the tax because they do not like taxes, and they do not like the government to tell them what to do. She quotes New York City residents who say, "We don't like being bossed around by the government." In fact, she states that a poll in 2012 found that almost three-quarters of Americans would oppose the tax. The author also argues that even though Americans dislike taxes, they would vote for the tax if they realized that health care costs were high because of obesity. She mentions a study that

1 Analyze Writing Skills

Circle the information that appears in the introductory paragraph.

a author's name
b title of the article
c author's main idea
d background information on the topic

2 Analyze Writing Skills

Look at the annotated article. Find the points that the writer double underlined. Underline those same points in paragraph 2 of this essay.

shows that health care costs for the obese will double in 20 years. She even thinks that the American public would tell the government to do something. The author ends by saying that fighting for the right to eat fast foods is not worth fighting for.

3 Analyze Writing Skills

Check (✓) the purpose of the last sentence.

☐ a   to restate the author's last comment in the article

☐ b   to explain the author's thesis statement

 3.2 Check Your Understanding

Answer the questions.

1   The student writer explains Michelle Embrich's main idea in paragraph 1. What is it?

2   What reasons, or points, does the student writer mention to support the author's main idea?

3   Does the student writer include his own opinions?

 3.3 Outline the Writer's Ideas

Write the main idea from the article ("A Tax on Unhealthy Foods"). Then complete the outline for the summary essay. Use the phrases in the box.

example – smoking	research from *Archives of Internal Medicine*
health care costs expected to double	tax would not be acceptable
national survey	

ESSAY OUTLINE

I. Introductory paragraph ....

Main Idea of the Article   ....

....

....

(CONTINUED)

Summary	II. Several reasons
Supporting Idea 1	A. Has worked for other unhealthy habits
Detail	1.
Sub-detail	a. Higher prices, fewer smokers
Detail	2.
Supporting Idea 2	B.
Detail	1. Americans do not like government to interfere
Sub-detail	a. Unsuccessful attempt to ban sodas in NYC
Detail	2.
Supporting Idea 3	C. Americans might agree if they had to pay higher health care costs
Detail	1.
Detail	2. They would ask government to do something

B Summary Essays

Writers use summary essays to restate the main ideas of an article in a short and concise way. A summary is always much shorter than the original article. This is because the writer only includes the thesis and the main points from the article. In this unit, you will learn to write a two-paragraph summary essay for an article. Professors often assign summary essays to check students' understanding of articles.

Summary essays can be organized in many different ways. Below is one way:

- An **introductory paragraph** that includes:
  - the author's name
  - the title of the article
  - the author's main idea
  - a little background information on the topic

- A **summary paragraph** that includes:
  - a sentence that either restates the main idea or gives a general introduction to the author's ideas
  - the author's main points with one or two examples or other details for each point

When you write a summary essay:

DO	DON'T
1 Keep it short and write only the author's ideas.	1 Do not write your opinion.
2 Write the ideas in your own words.	2 Do not use quotes from the text unless they are absolutely necessary to convey an idea.

 3.4 Notice

Circle the correct words and phrases to complete the sentences.

1 A summary essay is **longer than / shorter than / the same length as** the original text.

2 A summary essay tells the author's ideas in the **student writer's words / author's words**.

3 A summary essay **includes / does not include** the student writer's opinions.

THE INTRODUCTORY PARAGRAPH

The introductory paragraph of a summary essay tells the readers everything they need to know about the article so that they are prepared to read the summary. Below is a way to present the information:

1 The first sentence states the author, the title of the article, and the main idea. Below are two ways to include this information:

    In "(title of article)," (name of author) claims / states / argues / says / states / reports that (thesis / main idea).

    According to (name of author) in "(title of article)," (thesis / main idea).

2 The next sentence or two provides background information from the article on the topic – in other words, what the reader needs to know about the topic to understand the author's ideas.

 3.5 Practice Introductory Paragraphs

Complete the introductory paragraph. Use the phrases in the box.

> Music makes people happy by chemically changing the brain.
>
> "Is There a Link Between Music and Happiness?"
>
> Music is an important part of many people's lives. While many people say that it has a positive effect on them, there has not been research to support their claims until now.
>
> Molly Edmonds

In ...., ... claims that

....

....

....

 3.6 Apply It to Your Writing

Look at your notes on the article from Section 1 on page 139. Write sentences that you can use in the introductory paragraph of your summary essay.

....

....

....

....

THE SUMMARY PARAGRAPH

The summary paragraph explains the author's main idea and points. The student writer writes those ideas in his or her own words to avoid plagiarizing. The order of the ideas in the summary is the same as in the original article.

The order of information to use in writing the summary paragraph, as well as common phrases to include, is as follows:

1 **First sentence:** The first sentence is an introductory sentence. It introduces the summary by either restating the main idea or giving a more general introduction to the author's ideas Common phrases include:

   The author describes/discusses/states/claims/argues that …

2 **Middle sentences:** The next six or more sentences contain main points and details. Each main point usually has one or two details that briefly explain the point. Common phrases to introduce main points include:

   The author says/states that …

   The author mentions that …

   The article goes on to say that …

   The author points out/adds that …

   Note: Writers do NOT include all the details.

3 **Last sentence:** The last sentence can restate the main idea or **state the author's ending comment**.

   The author/article concludes that …

   In short, the author/article says/recommends that …

Because the summary is composed of only the points with enough explanation to understand each point, do NOT include:

- your own ideas (Use only the ideas from the article.)
- a lot of details (Choose one or two details to explain each point.)

FINDING THE MAIN IDEA

Finding the main idea is an important skill in summarizing. The main idea tells what the article is about. One way to identify the main idea correctly is to reread the title and the points that you find. These should help you in composing the main idea. The main idea is sometimes restated in the conclusion as well.

A good way to find the points is to read and keep asking yourself: Is this a new idea (a point), or is this a detail for a point? This will help you keep focused on the points and not get lost in the less important but sometimes fascinating details.

3.7 Analyze a Summary Paragraph

Match the sentences from the Student Model essay to their functions. You will use some of the items more than once.

a introductory sentence	c convincing example	e author's last comment
b point	d convincing statistics	

............1 The author claims that a tax on unhealthy foods would solve the problem of obesity for several reasons.

............2 She starts by saying that this tax would be effective because it has worked for other bad habits.

............3 She gives the example of cigarettes and smoking. Higher prices reduced the number of smokers, so a tax on unhealthy foods would reduce the number of overweight people.

............4 The author mentions that Americans might not accept the tax because they don't like taxes, and they don't like the government to tell them what to do.

............5 She quotes New York City residents who say, "We don't like being bossed around by the government."

............6 In fact, she states that a poll in 2012 found that almost three-quarters of Americans would oppose the tax.

............7 The author also argues that even though Americans dislike taxes, they would vote for the tax if they realized that health care costs were high because of obesity. She mentions a study that shows that health care costs for the obese will double in 20 years.

............8 The author ends by saying that freedom to eat fast foods is not worth fighting for.

3.8 Choose the Main Idea

Work with a partner. Read the article on pages 142–143 again. Check (✓) the best main idea and explain your answer.

☐ 1 In his article "Mindful Eating: How to Think More and Eat Less," Simon Usborne states that mindful eating helps people think about their eating.

☐ 2 In his article "Mindful Eating: How to Think More and Eat Less," Simon Usborne states that mindful eating makes people more aware of their food and can cause people to eat less.

☐ 3 In his article "Mindful Eating: How to Think More and Eat Less," Simon Usborne states that mindful eating is similar to meditation.

ANNOTATING AN ARTICLE FOR A SUMMARY

Taking good notes as you read is the best way to identify important ideas in a text. Use the steps below to help you find and annotate articles for summarizing.

How to Annotate an Article for a Summary Essay

STEP 1

Get a general idea of the article.

Read the article once or twice. As you read, think about these questions: *What is the article about? How does the author try to convince me of his or her ideas?* These first readings will help make the other steps easier.

STEP 2

Find information for the introductory paragraph.

Read the article again. As you read:

1 Circle the author's name and his or her title or credentials, if mentioned.

2 Underline a few key words or phrases in the first few paragraphs that describe the topic and would be helpful to include as background information for your reader.

3 Try to find a thesis statement in the first few paragraphs that seems to indicate the main idea of the article. If you find it, draw a box around it and use it to help write the main idea in the margin. (Remember that in longer texts, the first few paragraphs may be background information for the reader.) For additional help, use the ideas for finding the main idea on page 151. If you still cannot find the main idea, the tasks in the next step will help you.

STEP 3

Find information for the summary paragraph.

1 Read the article again and underline the author's main points. To find these, after you've read each paragraph, ask yourself the question: *Is the point of this paragraph a new one OR is it just more information about the point in the previous paragraph?* Double-underline each point. These sentences may occur at the beginning of paragraphs (similar to topic sentences) or sometimes at the end. After you find the points, check that they support the main idea that you wrote in Step 2. If you did not write a main idea, write it now. It should be clearer to you by now.

2 If there is not a match between the points and main idea, skim through the article again and double-check the points. Make necessary changes to the main idea or to the points. This time you should feel more familiar with the content and be able to match the main idea and points more easily. Make any changes and modify the main idea to match.

3 Now think about how you will explain each point. Put a star ✳ next to one or two details that are the most helpful or convincing to explain each point.

Ⓐ Writing Skill: Purpose, Audience, and Tone

Writers think about their **purpose**, **audience**, and **tone** before they write.

- The **purpose** is your reason for writing. It answers the question *Why am I writing?* In this unit, your purpose is to summarize an article.

- The **audience** is your intended reader. It answers the question *Who am I writing for?* In academic writing, you usually write for your instructor or classmates. You will make choices about what to tell your audience based on what you think they know about the topic that you are writing about.

- The **tone** is your attitude, such as informal or formal. It answers the question *How am I writing?* In academic writing, your tone is usually formal.

Purpose and audience are fairly easy to determine and to keep in mind as you write.

ACADEMIC TONE

Maintaining an academic tone can be challenging. Follow the guidelines below to maintain an academic tone.

1 **Use third person:** Use the third person (*he/she/it/they*) instead of the second person (*you*) unless it is appropriate. You can sometimes use the first person (*I/we*), depending on the prompt or assignment, but do not overuse it. Ask your instructor to be sure.

2 **Use precise language:** Use precise language and avoid overusing words that are more general in meaning. Below are other words that you should avoid using if possible and a few examples of replacements:

Instead of …	Use words such as …				
good	*beneficial*	*acceptable*	*valuable*	*convenient*	*well done*
bad	*inappropriate*	*unsatisfactory*	*serious*	*inconvenient*	*poor*
people	*consumers*	*researchers*	*society*	*employees*	*workers*

3 **Avoid abbreviations and informal expressions:** Do not use abbreviations used in texting and other informal ways of writing. Below are examples to avoid in academic writing:

Instead of …	Use …
b/c	*because*
imo	*in my opinion*
@	*at or around*
u	*you*
i	*I*

Do NOT use *lol* (laughing out loud) in academic writing.

4.1 Write Academically

Rewrite the sentences using correct academic tone and language.

1 imo laughing is good b/c it makes us feel joyful.

   In my opinion, laughter is beneficial because it makes people feel joyful.

2 People at the Mayo Clinic found that laughter can help u relieve stress and pain.

3 A recent study @ Loma Linda University showed that watching funny movies is good for people's memory.

4 Laughter can also help our learning ability b/c it exercises the brain.

5 i think that laughing while u do yoga is bad b/c yoga should be serious.

B Grammar for Writing: Reporting Verbs

Writers use reporting verbs, such as *describe*, *claim*, and *suggest*, to report ideas from their sources.

Below are some rules for using reporting verbs.

REPORTING VERBS

1 Many reporting verbs are followed by a *that* clause. Examples include: *argue, believe, conclude, explain, mention, recommend, say, show, state, suggest* Do not omit the word *that* in academic writing.	VERB · *THAT* CLAUSE The research showed that laughing has a positive effect on our health. The author states that eating mindfully can help people eat less. Bains suggests that laughing can improve our ability to learn.
2 Many reporting verbs can also be followed by a noun phrase.	VERB · NOUN PHRASE Some research has shown a relationship between **laughter and mood**. The author also **mentions the effects of obesity on health care costs**.
3 The reporting verbs below can only be followed by a noun phrase (not a noun clause): *describe, give, present*	VERB · NOUN PHRASE The author presented two reasons that she believes in the tax on unhealthy foods.
4 The reporting verbs below are used to explain the results of research: *demonstrate, find, show*	The study demonstrated the effects of mindfulness on eating. Recent research on mindfulness has shown that it has a positive impact on health.

 4.2 Practice Reporting Verbs

Work with a partner. Write sentences using the information below. Choose the correct reporting verb in parentheses and the word *that* where necessary.

1 Expedia's 2011 report on vacations / Americans have fewer vacation days than people in many other countries.

   (present / find) Expedia's 2011 report on vacations found that Americans have a smaller number of vacation days than people in many other countries.

2 Steve Taylor / the importance of work in primitive societies.

   (find / describe) ....

3 Taylor / there is too much emphasis on working.

   (argue / give) ....

   ....

4 Current research / working too much causes depression.

   (find / say) ....

   ....

5 The author / there is a link between poor health and working too much.

   (demonstrate / say) ....

   ....

Avoiding Common Mistakes

Research tells us that these are the most common mistakes that students make when using reporting verbs in academic writing.

> 1 **Do not use *that* after reporting verbs that are followed by noun phrases.**
>
>   *The article demonstrates ~~that~~ the positive benefits of laughter.*
>
> 2 **In other cases, make sure to include *that* after the verb.**
>
>   that
>   *Research shows ˄younger workers want more flexible hours.*

 4.3 Editing Task

Find and correct four more mistakes in the paragraph below.

                                        that
In "Four-Legged Support," Samantha Joel argues ˄there are health advantages in owning a pet. She describes that pet owners are less lonely, depressed, and stressed after getting a pet. The owners said they feel these benefits even when they had close relationships with other people. Joel goes on to say that pets are similar to friends because they can both make people feel better socially. In fact, one study said that pets can help people handle rejection. This study also presented owning a pet really can improve people's well-being.

C Avoiding Plagiarism

Using sources is part of successful academic writing, but it is important to use reliable and objective sources.

I'm writing a paper on the history of the pyramids in Egypt, and I found this great Internet blog. It's written by a woman who likes to travel the world and see monuments. She wrote a few posts about the pyramids and gave some interesting historical facts, and I want to use this information in my paper. My friend said our instructor might not approve of this source, but I don't understand why she wouldn't.

Xiomara

Dear Xiomara,

The Internet is a great resource for finding information for a paper. However, your friend is probably right. Your teacher may not like someone's travel blog as a source. Not all sources give information that is accurate, objective, or reliable. Sites like blogs give more personal information. They also might be biased. Biased information is based on someone's prejudices or opinions, not on facts or research. Instead, try to use sites from universities, respected newspapers and journals, or government agencies. They have expert opinions, and the information is more often credible – in other words, trustworthy.

Best,

Professor Wright

EVALUATING INTERNET SOURCES

Once you have found a source that discusses your topic, you need to evaluate the credibility of the source. A good source contains expert, unbiased information. Avoid using sources that are unreliable.

Below are examples of web sources that are not recommended because the content in them may not be objective.

UNRELIABLE INTERNET SOURCES	EXPLANATION
1 A website where people can add information about topics	There is no single known author. There is no certainty that the writer is knowledgeable or an expert on the topic. There is no certainty that the information is up-to-date.
2 A personal blog	Anyone can create a personal blog. There is no expertise needed. The writer may have a personal bias.

(CONTINUED)

3 A company website (ending in .com)	Commercial websites are usually biased. The purpose of the website is to sell a product or service; therefore, it may not present all the information accurately.
4 A political or religious website	This type of website often presents a biased point of view. Writers discuss one side of an issue and are not always interested in providing balanced information.

Below are sources that are generally reliable.

RELIABLE INTERNET SOURCES	EXPLANATION
1 An academic website (ending in .edu)	Writers on most academic websites are recognized experts in their field. They are usually professors, scientists, and researchers who write about current research.
2 A government website ending in .gov, such as dol.gov (the U.S. Department of Labor) and usa.gov	Government websites usually include reliable, factual, and up-to-date information and data from government agencies.
3 A nonprofit website ending in .org	Nonprofit websites usually provide reliable information, but be careful. Be sure to do more research about the organization if it is not familiar to you.

ACTIVITY **4.4** Practice

Check (✓) the sources that are reliable. Discuss your answers with a partner.

☐ 1 "5 Easy Steps to a Balanced Lifestyle," from a personal blog

☐ 2 "Career-Life Balance Initiative," from the National Science Foundation website

☐ 3 "Improving Emotional Health," from a nonprofit called Helpguide.org

☐ 4 "Work-Life Balance Defined," from a company that sells time-management programs

☐ 5 "Manage Your Work, Manage Your Life," from the *Harvard Business Review*

In this section, you will follow the writing process to complete the final draft of your essay.

STEP 1: READ FOR THE MAIN IDEAS

Follow these steps to find the information you need to write your summary essay.

1 Before you start, reread "How to Annotate an Article for a Summary Essay" on page 153.

2 Annotate the article you read in Section 1. Then look at the sentences from your chart on page 139. If needed, revise the author's main idea and most important ideas.

STEP 2: MAKE AN OUTLINE

Complete the outline below with your ideas from Step 1.

OUTLINE

I. Introductory Paragraph

Main Idea of the Article
....
....
....

Summary Paragraph II. ....

Supporting Idea 1 A. ....

Detail 1. ....

Detail 2. ....

Supporting Idea 2 B. ....

Detail 1. ....

Detail 2. ....

Supporting Idea 3 A. ....

Detail 1. ....

Detail 2. ....

STEP 3: WRITE YOUR FIRST DRAFT

Now it is time to write your first draft. Here are some suggestions on how to get started.

1 Use your outline and the ideas in Section 3.

2 Remember to use your own words to explain the author's ideas. Include the phrases you learned to introduce and talk about the author's ideas on page 151.

3 Remember to add a title.

After you finish, read your essay and check for basic errors.

1 Check that all sentences have subjects and verbs.

2 Check that you have used commas and periods correctly.

3 Check that you have used a comma after dependent clauses with words like *Although/While/Because* when they start a sentence.

STEP 4: WRITE YOUR FINAL DRAFT

1 After you receive feedback on your first draft, review it carefully. Fix any errors.

2 Make a note of errors that were most frequent. Try to avoid them as you write.

3 Review the Academic Vocabulary and Collocations from this unit. Are there any that you can add to your essay?

4 Turn to page 266 and use the Self-Editing Review to check your work one more time.

5 Write your final draft and hand it in.

MORE THAN JOB SATISFACTION
(adapted)
BY KIRSTEN WEIR

What do you do? That's often the first question people ask when meeting someone. This is not surprising since most adults spend most of their waking hours at work, and work can be a big part of their identity. Unfortunately, a report by Gallup Inc. shows that 70 percent of American workers are either "not engaged"[1] or "actively disengaged" in their work (2013). Disengaged employees are more likely to steal from the job, negatively influence co-workers, miss days, and drive away customers. According to Gallup, this disengagement costs U.S. companies $450 billion to $550 billion yearly.

Several recent studies have focused on one aspect of work: how much meaning people find in it. They have discovered that when workers feel their work is meaningful, it is good for both the workers and the company – and that even employees in tiresome jobs can find ways to make their work more meaningful. These studies show that there are ways to use work to increase meaning and improve people's lives.

Of course, there are different ways to find meaning in one's work, says Michael G. Pratt, PhD, a professor of management and organization at Boston College. He illustrates this through a story about three bricklayers[2] hard at work. When asked what they're doing,

[1] **engaged:** interested in or seriously involved in an activity
[2] **bricklayer:** someone whose job is to build walls with bricks

the first bricklayer responds, "I'm putting one brick on top of another." The second replies, "I'm making six pence[3] an hour." And the third says, "I'm building a cathedral — a house of God." Pratt says that all of them have created meaning out of what they've done, but the last person could say what he's done is meaningful. Meaningfulness is about why you do something. According to Douglas Lepisto and Camille Pradies in a chapter in the 2013 book *Purpose and Meaning in the Workplace*, people can find meaning through the pride of doing their job well, the ability to provide for their families, the sense of service that they feel on the job, or in the close relationships that they have with co-workers.

The people who are the most content are those who believe that their work has a higher calling.[4] Zookeepers are a good example of this. They earn less than $25,000 a year, there is little advancement, and they are not generally highly respected, says Stuart Bunderson, PhD, a professor of organizational behavior at Washington University in St. Louis (*Administrative Science Quarterly*). Yet they feel very passionate and satisfied with their jobs because they believe that they were born to do that kind of work. In other words, they feel a personal connection to their jobs, and this motivates them to do their best.

Fortunately, anyone can find meaning in their work through "job crafting," says Jane E. Dutton, PhD, a professor of business administration and psychology at the University of Michigan. Described by Dutton and colleagues in *Purpose and Meaning in the Workplace*, "job crafting" is a way of shaping a job to create meaning. Employees can shape their work experiences in three ways. First, they can spend more time and energy on tasks that are satisfying. A professor who loves interacting with students, for example, might find ways to spend more time advising students. Second, they can focus on relationships that are positive. Spending time with a colleague who respects and values you is "like taking a vitamin," Dutton says. Finally, a person can change the way he or she thinks about work. Michael F. Steger, PhD, an associate professor of counseling psychology and applied social psychology at Colorado State University, gives the example of an accountant at a community college who found her work very meaningful not because of what she did, but because she felt her work allowed others to improve themselves educationally.

Dutton does admit that there is a drawback. Organizations could use job crafting to abuse[5] their workers. In other words: "I'll give you a crappy[6] job, and it's up to you to make something good out of it," she says. Organization should still be fairer and better, but in the meantime, she sees value in empowering workers "… to craft their work in ways that will make it less depleting and more enriching."

[3] **pence:** plural of penny (British English)
[4] **higher calling:** a feeling that the your work benefits mankind and that you must do it
[5] **abuse:** to treat a person or animal badly or cruelly
[6] **crappy:** uninteresting, bad

6 SUMMARY–RESPONSE ESSAYS

BEHAVIORAL SCIENCE: LANGUAGE AND CULTURE

> "To learn a language is to have one more window from which to look at the world."
>
> Chinese proverb

Work with a partner. Read the quotation about the benefits of learning another language. Then answer the questions.

1 How is language a window to the world?

2 Has learning another language changed the way you see the world? If so, how?

3 In your opinion, is learning another language essential in today's world? Why or why not?

A Connect to Academic Writing

In this unit, you will learn the skills to help you write a summary–response essay. While some of the writing skills you will use may be new to you, others are not. You already use the skills needed to summarize and respond in your everyday life. For example, you use some of these skills when you tell a friend about an interesting magazine article you read and explain your reactions to it or when you tell a friend about a movie you saw that he or she hasn't seen yet.

B Reflect on the Topic

In this section, you will choose a writing prompt and reflect on it. You will develop these ideas throughout the unit and use them to practice skills that are necessary to write your essay.

The writing prompt below was used for the Student Model essay on pages 172–174. The student read a letter in a newspaper that explains why immigrants should not give up their cultures and languages when they come to the United States. In the chart below, the student wrote the ideas from the letter that he thought were important on the left, and he wrote his reaction to each idea on the right.

STUDENT MODEL

WRITING PROMPT: Newspaper and magazine readers sometimes write letters to the editor to give opinions on articles from the newspaper or magazine. Find a letter to the editor on the topic of immigration. Summarize the writer's ideas and respond to them.

Title of the Article: Letter to the Editor

Author's Name: Dr. Carla Banks

THE AUTHOR'S IDEAS	MY REACTIONS
1 "If we proudly consider ourselves a multicultural society, then why are we so eager for immigrants to adopt American culture at the expense of their native cultures?"	Do I have to choose? My sister and I act differently School – like Americans Home – like Mexicans
2 "Asking our immigrants to give up their cultures and languages in order to be successful is misguided and damaging."	Agree. People can be bilingual and bicultural.
3 "Furthermore, pressure to become fully integrated into another culture can have a negative effect on people."	Article from class says the opposite is true. (Grosjean)

ACTIVITY 1.1 Notice

Work with a partner. Check (✓) the reactions the student writer above has to the article.

☐ agrees   ☐ disagrees   ☐ thinks of personal examples

☐ connects to class readings   ☐ questions the author

1.2 Apply It to Your Writing

Follow the directions to reflect on your topic.

A Choose a prompt:

- Read the article "Third Culture Kids" on pages 195–196. Write a summary–response essay. Support your response through your experience and knowledge, as well as with ideas you have learned through one other article or book that you have read.

- Read a text approved by your instructor and write a summary–response essay.

B Complete the following tasks:

1 Write the title of the article and the name of the author in the chart.

2 Read the title and the first two paragraphs of the article. Predict what the article will be about. This will help you prepare to read.

3 Read the rest of the article. Were your predictions correct?

4 Fill in the chart below. In the left column, write ideas from the article that you think are important. In the right column, write your reactions: for example, points with which you agree or disagree, a personal experience, or a question. Use the Student Model chart on page 164 to help you.

5 Compare charts with a partner.

Title of the Article: ....

Author's Name: ....

THE AUTHOR'S IDEAS	MY REACTIONS

In this section, you will learn academic language that you can use in your summary–response essay. You will also notice how a professional writer uses this language and the features of summary–response essays.

Ⓐ Academic Vocabulary

The words below appear throughout the unit. Many are from the Academic Word List. Using these words in your writing will make your ideas clearer and your writing more academic.

appropriate (adj)	ignore (v)	instance (n)	shift (v)
emphasize (v)	immigrant (n)	interact (v)	various (adj)

 2.1 Focus on Meaning

Work with a partner. Match the words in bold to the letters of their meanings.

A

.... 1 Bilingual people often **shift** from one language to another in the same conversation. First, they might speak English, and then Spanish.

    a to not pay attention to something

.... 2 When bilingual people **interact** with others from their culture, they may talk in both languages.

    b to change

.... 3 Sometimes when people use both languages in a conversation, they **ignore** the grammar rules. They do not focus on them.

    c someone who moves to live in another country

.... 4 When an **immigrant** first arrives in a country, he or she often has a difficult time adjusting to the new culture.

    d to talk and do things with other people

B

.... 1 Some cultures **emphasize** the importance of family. Their focus is on the family.

    a right for the situation

.... 2 **Appropriate** behavior in school is different in different cultures, so immigrants should learn what is acceptable and unacceptable.

    b an example

.... 3 Every culture has its own rules of politeness. For **instance**, in Ecuador it is important to always say hello.

    c to show that something is important

.... 4 There are **various** ways to show respect in Chinese culture. One is to always be on time.

    d many different

B Academic Phrases

Research tells us that the phrases in bold below are commonly used in academic writing.

1 Use **the fact that** to introduce a <u>fact</u>. It is followed by a *that* clause.	*In "Raising Bilingual Children," the authors emphasize* **the fact that** *parents do not need to teach their children to become bilingual.*
2 Use **for this/that reason** to introduce a <u>result</u>. It refers back to an earlier sentence. This is a good way to link sentences together.	*Kids learn new languages naturally.* **For this reason***, parents don't need to teach language to children.*
3 Use **in part** when you are explaining just <u>one part of a reason</u>. It means there are other reasons, too, but you don't mention them.	*Kids become bilingual* **in part** *because their parents introduce them to many different people and situations.*

ACTIVITY 2.2 Focus on Meaning and Use

Complete the sentences with the academic phrases in the chart above.

1 In the article "Lost in Translation," the author points out that in the Piranha language, speakers prefer words like *few* and *many* rather than numbers. ...., it is hard for them to keep track of exact amounts.

2 Russians have many words for both light and dark blue. These findings explain .... Russians are better able to see small differences in shades of blue.

3 The author also states that people of different cultures see the world differently .... because of the languages they speak.

Xie Xie

Terima kasih

Kiitos

Toda Raba

Arigato

Dank je

Thank you

Gracias

C Writing in the Real World

The author of the article "Bilingualism Good for the Brain, Researchers Say" uses features of summary and response to strengthen her argument.

Before you read, answer these questions: Some people believe bilingualism has many benefits. Would you agree that people who speak two languages are smarter or better in some way than people who only speak one language? Why or why not?

Now read the article. Think about your answers to the questions above as you read.

Bilingualism Good for the Brain, Researchers Say

(adapted)

by Amina Khan

1 Does bilingualism give children an advantage? It depends on who you ask.

2 Some see bilingual education as an imperfect way of teaching students whose native language is not English. However, many researchers agree that bilingualism has many positive effects on the brain.

Several such researchers presented their findings at a meeting of the American Association for the Advancement of Science. Among them:

- Bilingual children multitask[1] more effectively.

- Bilingual adults are better at prioritizing[2] information. This is especially true in confusing situations.

- Bilingualism helps ward off symptoms of Alzheimer's disease.

[1]**multitask:** do more than one thing at one time
[2]**prioritize:** decide what is most important so you can do it first

3 These benefits come from having a brain that juggles[3] two languages, said Ellen Bialystok, a professor at York University. For **instance**, a person who speaks both Hindi and Tamil can't turn Tamil off when he's speaking Hindi. Why not? Because the brain must decide which language is most **appropriate** for the situation.

4 This constant shifting between two linguistic[4] systems means frequent exercise for the brain. When bilinguals **interact**, their brains seem to inhibit one language, said Pennsylvania State University professor Judith Kroll. This effect is more noticeable when the speaker chooses the weaker language.

5 Juggling two languages in the brain probably leads to advantages for bilinguals. Still, researchers **emphasize**, this doesn't mean they learn better than monolinguals. However, it does keep the brain more nimble.[5] **For that reason**, bilinguals usually multitask better.

6 Yet many schools are moving away from bilingual education. In fact, this movement has been going on for some time. **In part**, this **shift** has been due to political beliefs. The children who speak more than one language typically come from **immigrant** families.

7 Schools are focused on teaching children English. Therefore, parents who want their children to be bilingual should continue speaking their native language. Further, they must insist on use of the native language in the only setting they can control: the home.

8 "You're basically in a society in which English is the language of power," Kenji Hakuta, a professor at Stanford University and proponent of bilingualism, said. If parents use both English and another language, they're "likely to raise a monolingual English speaker."

---

[3]**juggle:** try to do several things at one time
[4]**linguistic:** related to languages
[5]**nimble:** able to think quickly and easily

2.3 Check Your Understanding

Answer the questions.

1 According to the article, how does bilingualism help the brain?

2 What is the current state of bilingual education? Why?

3 What is the author's opinion of the state of bilingual education?

2.4 Notice the Features of Summary–Response Writing

Answer the questions.

1 What is the purpose of paragraph 2?

2 In paragraphs 2–5, is the author explaining her ideas or other people's ideas?

3 In paragraph 7, what is the author's purpose?

In Section 1, you saw how the writer of the Student Model essay used a chart to list the important ideas in an article and to respond to them. In this section, you will analyze the final draft of his summary–response essay. You will learn how to structure your ideas for your own summary.

Ⓐ Student Model

A student read a letter to an editor in a newspaper and made notes. Then he wrote a summary–response essay about the letter.

Read the letter twice. The first time, think about these questions.

1 What is the letter about?
2 How does its author try to convince you of her ideas?

The second time, notice how the student annotated, or marked up, the letter to prepare to write a summary–response essay.

To the Editor:

Last week's article "Success!" by Carol Smith (Op-Ed, June 1) was a well-deserved tribute[1] to this year's graduating seniors. Many of these students belong to "Generation 1.5," a term often used for **immigrants** who moved to the United States from other countries as children or young teens. At the beginning, the author notes the "incredible multiculturalism" of the graduates. However, in the rest of the article, the writer **emphasizes** the benefits of becoming "fully American" and "blending in." This assimilation is a striking contradiction.[2] If we proudly consider ourselves a multicultural society, then why are we so eager for immigrants to adopt American culture at the expense of their native cultures?

The United States has always been a country of immigrants. In fact, only one percent of us are actually Native Americans. The very strength of our nation comes from the rich diversity of ideas, traditions, and languages that people from all over the world have brought. Asking our immigrants to give up their cultures and languages in order to be successful is misguided and damaging.

The message that achieving success requires blending into American culture and shedding[3] one's home culture is not only inconsistent with our history; it is also not **appropriate** as a message for our times. A huge part of our proud history is the waves of immigrants that have come to this country and have shaped our values and traditions. While we hope that immigrants share our values of freedom and individual rights, is it necessary for them to give up their cultures and languages, which bring with them fresh

[1]**tribute:** something that expresses respect or admiration for someone
[2]**contradiction:** difference between two ideas or facts, both of which cannot be true at the same time
[3]**shed:** get rid of something you do not want

perspectives and innovative ideas? I think not. In addition, in today's global world, being familiar with more than one language and culture is important for development in every area – from education and the arts to science and business. We need other languages and cultures to be competitive in the world.

Furthermore, pressure to become fully integrated into another culture can have a negative effect on people. And I have seen this up close.

[margin note: Good example · But not my experience]

One of my daughter's good friends at school is an immigrant from Thailand. Sarai speaks Thai at home with her parents and English elsewhere. However, she still struggles a bit with the language, especially when she **interacts** with people she doesn't know well. She worries about speaking correctly and fitting in with her American classmates. I wish she could appreciate **the fact that** she is enriching our lives. It's fascinating to listen to her stories about Thailand. I value the opportunity to hear points of view on world events and social issues from someone who isn't "fully American." She helps our family see things from a different perspective and stay open to new ideas. I have told her this many times, but in the outside world, she doesn't get the sense that her difference is valued. Consequently, Sarai feels torn. "It's not fun to be caught between two cultures," she says, "and not really belong to either one."

[margin note: why does author focus only on negatives? Grosjean would disagree]

[margin note: I don't feel this way – I have 2 cultures!]

A friend of mine, Min-jun, immigrated to the United States from Korea. Following his parents' advice, he immersed[4] himself in the new culture and tried to speak only English. He studied hard, did well in school, and graduated with a degree in business. Today he is a respected employee whose fresh ideas help us solve problems in creative ways. Min-jun enjoys his work and is grateful for the opportunities he has had. However, he regrets that much of his native culture has been lost. He can no longer speak Korean well and has difficulty relating to family back home. What a shame (and how unnecessary) that this talented young man was pressured[5] to choose between cultures. He has contributed much to ours, but this has resulted in an unfortunate **shift** in focus away from his own.

[margin note: 2nd example]

[margin note: very sad]

According to recent data collected by the U.S. Census Bureau, there are over 40 million immigrants like Sarai and Min-jun in the country today. This is about 13 percent of the total population (or 1 in every 8 people). These people are crucial to our country's development in an increasingly interconnected world. We need to honor and support their biculturalism and send them the right message. As public policy expert Jacob Vigor says, "You can retain[6] a cultural identity and still be an assimilated[7] person." I couldn't agree more. Vigor points the way toward the true road to success, both for our immigrants and our country.

[margin note: AGREE! We need to respect biculturalism]

[margin note: Confusing! This contradicts author's definition of assimilation in introduction]

Dr. Carla Banks
Professor of History
Two Peaks College

[4]**immerse:** be completely involved in or part of something
[5]**pressured:** forced to do something
[6]**retain:** keep
[7]**assimilate:** change to become part of a group or society

A Work with a partner. Look at the letter on pages 170–171 and check (✓) the correct answers. Some questions may have more than one correct answer.

1 What information did the writer circle?

☐ a the author's name

☐ b the author's title

☐ c background information on the topic

2 Read the sentence that is in a box. Why do you think the writer put a box around the sentence?

☐ a The sentence helped him write the main idea of the article.

☐ b The sentence is important background information.

3 What information did the writer double-underline in the paragraphs?

☐ a details

☐ b important points that support the main idea

4 What do you notice about the information that the writer underlined?

☐ a The information is details.

☐ b The information is surprising or interesting.

B Answer the questions.

1 Which ideas did the writer agree with? Why?

2 Which ideas did the writer disagree with? Why?

Read the Student Model summary–response essay twice. The first time, notice how the writer used the information that he marked up in the article. The second time, answer the questions in the Analyze Writing Skills boxes. This will help you learn how the writer organized his ideas in the essay.

Assimilation Does Not Mean Losing Culture

1   In her letter to the editor in the *Brownsville Times*, Dr. Carla Banks, a history professor at Two Peaks College, argues that immigrants should not have to assimilate and shed one's culture to be successful in America. Although I agree with Dr. Banks that immigrants should not lose their cultures, I do not agree that assimilation to a new culture always has negative effects. Immigrants can enjoy the many advantages of living in two cultures.

2   The author describes several points that emphasize the difficulties of assimilation. She starts her argument by saying that the pressure to assimilate goes against U.S. history and that it is poor advice because today people need to understand different cultures in a global world.

1 Analyze Writing Skills

What information does the student writer include in paragraph 1?

Check (✓) all that apply.

☐ a author's name

☐ b title of article or way of identifying the article

☐ c author's main idea

☐ d student writer's general reaction to the article

☐ e examples from the article

Allowing immigrants to keep their cultures and languages would keep the country competitive. She goes on to say that pressure to blend in with a new culture has negative effects on immigrants. She mentions a young woman she knows who often feels torn[1] between two cultures, not fully fitting in with either. Banks provides a contrasting example of a very successful friend who felt pressured to choose between two cultures and now has lost his own culture and regrets that loss. In both situations, Banks blames the problems on the pressure to assimilate that immigrants feel. The author ends by saying that these people and their biculturalism are important to this country and we should respect their culture and encourage people to keep their cultural identity.

3   In response to Banks' letter, I do not feel that the reasons that she gave to support her argument matched my own experience. The author suggests that when a person assimilates and becomes more American, one cannot also keep one's culture. In my opinion, that is not necessarily true. Just as people can be bilingual, they can also be bicultural, or live in two cultures. For example, my siblings and I speak and behave like Americans at school, but when we are with our relatives, we easily go back to our first language and the social customs of our native culture. The author also **emphasizes** the negative effects of assimilating, but I wonder if there is research to support this. In class we read an article by Francois Grosjean that claims that the opposite is true. He argues that people who are bicultural actually have **various** social advantages: These people have larger social networks, and they are more aware of cultural differences. In fact, it is possible that contrary[2] to Banks' view, her daughter's friend is uncomfortable because she has not really assimilated yet. Studies show that those who are bicultural are more creative, flexible, and successful (Grosjean). It is possible that Banks' colleague was successful because he is bicultural.

4   One thing that confused me about Banks' argument is that she defines assimilation in two different ways. First, she states that assimilation means that a person loses their own culture. However, at the end of her letter, she suggests that someone can both assimilate and keep their culture. This makes her argument weaker because we are not sure of her ideas.

[1]**torn:** unable to decide between two things
[2]**contrary:** opposite to what someone said or thought

2 Analyze Writing Skills

What is the purpose of paragraph 2?

a to explain the student writer's opinions of Dr. Banks' ideas

b to explain Dr. Banks' ideas

3 Analyze Writing Skills

What is the purpose of paragraph 3?

a to explain the student writer's opinions of Dr. Banks' ideas

b to explain Dr. Banks' ideas

4 Analyze Writing Skills

How does the student writer support his opinion in paragraph 3? Check (✓) all that apply.

☐ a fact

☐ b personal example

☐ c quotation

☐ d research

5 Analyze Writing Skills

What is the purpose of paragraph 4?

....

(CONTINUED)

5   Banks maintains that assimilation has serious negative effects on immigrants, including losing one's culture or having to choose between two cultures. It is my view that when someone assimilates, they do not lose one culture, but they gain a second culture. Being comfortable in two cultures is both possible and valuable.

Works Cited

Banks, Carla. Letter. *Brownsville Times*. 3 Oct. 2014: C5. Print.

Grosjean, Francois. "Advantages of Being Bicultural." *Psychology Today*. Sussex Publishers, 19 Apr. 2013. Web. 28 Sept. 2014.

 3.2 Check Your Understanding

Answer the questions.

1 According to the student writer, what is the author's main idea?

2 According to the student writer, what three main points does Banks make?

3 The student writer did not think that Banks should have focused on the negative effects of assimilation. What are his reasons? What do you think Banks would think of his reasons?

 3.3 Outline the Writer's Ideas

Complete the outline for the Student Model summary–response essay. Use the phrases in the box.

Grosjean – social advantages
biculturalism – important, should respect
not my experience

one confusion – definition of assimilation
pressure to blend in – negative effects

ESSAY OUTLINE

I. Introductory paragraph

Main Idea of the Article

In her letter to the editor in the Brownsville Times, Dr. Carla Banks, a history professor at Two Peaks College, argues that immigrants should not have to assimilate and "shed one's culture" in order to be successful in America.

Student Writer's Thesis

Although I agree with Dr. Banks that immigrants should not lose their cultures, I do not agree that assimilation to a new culture always has negative effects. Immigrants can enjoy the many advantages of living in two cultures.

Body Paragraph 1 Summary	II. Immigrants – should not have to assimilate
Point 1	A. Pressure to assimilate – against U.S. history and poor advice
Detail	1. People need to understand different cultures in global world
Detail	2. Keeping cultures and languages keeps the country competitive
Point 2	B.
Detail	1. Ex: daughter's friend – torn between two cultures
Detail	2. Ex: friend – lost culture
Point 3	C.
Body Paragraph 2 Response	III.
Point 1	A. People cannot keep one's culture – disagree
Detail	1. They can be bilingual
Detail	2. Ex: my siblings and I
Point 2	B. Author emphasizes assimilation's negative effects – disagree
Detail	1.
Detail	2. Banks' friend – not assimilated yet
Detail	3. Grosjean – bilinguals more creative, flexible, successful
Sub-detail	a. Banks' friend
Body Paragraph 3 Response	IV.
Point 1	A. Two definitions of assimilation
Detail	1. Makes argument weaker
	V. Concluding paragraph

B Summary–Response Essay

A summary–response essay gives writers the opportunity to evaluate and express opinions about an author's ideas. The summary paragraph explains the writer's main idea and main points. The response paragraph or paragraphs respond to the ideas using personal experiences, facts, and examples.

Summary–response essays can have different structures. Below is one common way of organizing this type of essay.

SUMMARY–RESPONSE ESSAY ORGANIZATION	
Paragraph	**Purpose**
Introductory Paragraph	To give the reader basic information about the article that the writer is responding to: the author's name, the author's main idea, the title of the article, and the student writer's thesis
Summary Paragraph	To briefly summarize the main points in the original article
Response Paragraph(s)	To evaluate and respond to the author's ideas
Concluding Paragraph	To remind the reader of the author's main idea, to point out the student writer's thesis, and to make a comment

ACTIVITY **3.4** Notice

Read the information on the left side of the chart. Check (✓) the paragraph where each piece of information appears.

	Introductory Paragraph	Summary Paragraph	Response Paragraph(s)
1 First mention of the author's name			
2 Your thesis statement			
3 The main idea of the original article			
4 The title of the article			
5 A summary of the author's points			
6 Your personal experiences, facts, and knowledge from other sources to support your responses			
7 Your personal ideas, opinions, and reactions related to the writer's ideas			

INTRODUCTORY PARAGRAPH

The **introductory paragraph** is brief. Writers include the following information to make the source of the text clear to the reader.

What To Include:	Why It Is Important:
the author's name	You must cite your source.
the title of the article	Readers must be able to search for the original article online or in a library.
information about the author, if it is available	The reader should know if the person is an expert (for example, a professor, a researcher, or a specialist in a field).
the author's main idea, or thesis, in your own words	The reader needs to know the point of view of the original author.
your own thesis statement	The reader wants to know your response to the original article from the start.

Below are words and phrases that writers use to introduce key information in the first sentence.

> *According to* Amina Khan, *in her article* "Bilingualism Good for the Brain, Researchers Say," *even though research shows that bilingualism has many positive effects on the brain, bilingual education is becoming less popular.*

> *In her article* "Bilingualism Good for the Brain, Researchers Say," *Amina Khan, science writer for the* Los Angeles Times, *states/argues/claims that even though research shows that bilingualism has many positive effects on the brain, bilingual education is becoming less popular.*

The thesis statement should say how the student writer responds to the ideas in the original article. Below are examples of thesis statements. Notice that the author's name is included in these statements.

> *I agree strongly with* Khan's theories that there are many positive effects on the brain from being bilingual and that bilingual education programs should be maintained.

> *While I agree with* Khan *that* bilingual education is important, I do not believe that the reasons for the decline are political, but rather are based on economic factors and availability of trained educators.

> *In general, I do not agree with* Khan *that* it is important for immigrants to grow up bilingual because it is more important to learn English to be successful.

 3.5 Notice

Read the introductory paragraph. Check (✓) the items that are missing.

Sarah McCuskee, a research officer at the London School of Economics, claims that health care professionals must understand an immigrant group's cultural beliefs about health in order to treat people effectively.

☐ a author's name

☐ b details about the author

☐ c main idea of article

☐ d student writer's thesis statement

☐ e title of article

 3.6 Practice

Use the information below to write the first sentence for an introductory paragraph. See page 177 for examples.

Author's name: Richard McCoy

Author's credentials: Social worker, California Department of Social Services

Name of article: "Why Culture Matters"

Main idea: Maintaining cultural traditions is important for the mental health of immigrant children.

....

....

....

ACTIVITY **3.7** Apply It to Your Writing

YOUR TURN

Look at the article for your essay on pages 195–196. What information do you need for your introductory paragraph? Write it below.

....

....

....

....

SUMMARY PARAGRAPH

In Unit 5, you learned that a summary paragraph contains the parts below.

1 **First sentence:** A sentence that introduces the summary by either restating the main idea or giving a more general introduction to the idea. Common phrases to use in the summary include:

> *The author gives/describes/discusses/states/argues that …*

2 **Next few sentences:** The next few sentences state the points in order and briefly explain each one using one detail, such as an example or explanation from the article. Common phrases to introduce the points include:

> *The author starts by saying/stating that …*
>
> *The article goes on to say that …*
>
> *The author points out/adds that …*
>
> *The author also mentions that …*

3 **Last sentence:** The last sentence can restate the main idea or state the author's ending comment:

> *The author/article concludes that …*
>
> *In short, the author/article says/recommends that …*

Below are important points to remember.

- Write the author's ideas in your own words.
- Be accurate when reporting someone else's ideas. You should not change the meaning of what the author has said.
- Use a short quotation only if the quotation describes or explains an idea well.
- Include one or two examples that make the author's ideas clear.
- Keep the summary short and in only one or two paragraphs. The summary should be much shorter than the original author's article.

A good summary paragraph does NOT include:

- unnecessary details, such as statistics, explanations, or all examples
- your opinion or experience, or sentences with the word *I*
- long quotes from the text
- exact words from the author unless they are in quotes

3.8 Analyze a Summary Paragraph

Below is a student writer's summary paragraph for the letter to the editor on pages 170–171. The writer has made several mistakes, which are underlined and numbered. Match the numbers of the mistakes with the descriptions below. Then discuss your answers with a partner.

The author discusses several problems with assimilation. She starts by saying that <u>blending into American culture and shedding one's home culture is not only inconsistent with our history; it is also not appropriate as a message for our times</u>. The United States has always been
(1)
an immigrant nation, and this fact will keep it competitive. The author goes on to say that the pressure to assimilate has negative effects on people. Banks gives several examples of friends who struggle with fitting in to the culture or regret losing their native culture. One example she gives is her daughter's friend Sarai, who says that she does not feel a part of either culture. <u>The writer says that she enjoys the stories that Sarai tells them because they are so interesting. She also mentions how interesting it is to hear Sarai talk about world events.</u> <u>I know that this</u>
(2)
<u>period of difficulty will pass for her because I had a similar experience</u>. She ends by saying that
(3)
<u>"these people are crucial to our country's development in an increasingly interconnected world.</u>
(4)
<u>We need to honor and support their biculturalism and send them the right message."</u>

.... a Includes his own experience and uses the word *I*

.... b Gives too many unnecessary details

.... c Uses long quotes from the text

.... d Uses the words of the original author and not his own words

 3.9 Apply It to Your Writing

Reread the article for your essay. Find one point and write in your own words. Then share it with a partner.

....

....

....

....

RESPONSE PARAGRAPHS

In response paragraph(s), as the writer you respond to the author's ideas. Make sure you understand what kind of response your instructor expects. Some instructors may ask you to respond to every point in separate paragraphs, while others may ask you to choose one idea to respond to. A response paragraph is like imagining that you are talking to the author.

You want to tell him or her what you think of particular ideas in the article and give specific reasons why. You may need more than one paragraph for the response.

Below are ways that you can respond to the author's ideas. The language that you can use is in bold.

Ways to Respond to an Author's Ideas

1 Agree or disagree with the ideas.

   I agree with the author that bilingual programs should be eliminated because it is too costly and they do not help students succeed.

   I disagree with the author that bilingual programs should be eliminated *because* many immigrant children need that extra support.

2 Find strengths or weaknesses in the author's writing.

   The author makes a strong/weak argument when she says that parents know that speaking English is essential. It doesn't mean students shouldn't also learn in their own language.

3 Consider the quality of the author's support.

   The thing that confused me was that she referred to "our national language," but the United States doesn't have a national language.

4 Connect the ideas to your personal experiences.

   In my experience, students in bilingual programs do well when the teacher pushes the students to communicate in both English and Spanish.

   For instance, I know students who dropped out because they did not do well in English.

5 Connect ideas to other ideas in articles and other sources that you discussed.

   That reminds me of a report by the Pew Research Center that we discussed in class. It said that 95 percent of Hispanics think that their children should speak Spanish.

6 Question the author's ideas.

   Why can't a person learn English and also learn in their own native language?

 3.10 Practice

Reread "Bilingualism Good for the Brain, Researchers Say" on pages 168–169. Write three sentences about the ideas in the article using what you learned above.

....

....

....

....

....

CONCLUDING PARAGRAPH

The concluding paragraph is very short. It restates the author's main idea and your thesis, and ends in a final comment. The comment can express your opinion on the topic, give a recommendation, or state a call to action.

 3.11 Write

Write a final comment for "Bilingualism Good for the Brain, Researchers Say" on pages 168–169.

....

....

HOW TO ANNOTATE AN ARTICLE FOR A SUMMARY–RESPONSE ESSAY

Good writers read a text a few times and annotate – or mark up – the text as they read. Below is an approach to annotating an article that will help you find the information and respond to the necessary information.

How to Annotate an Article for a Summary–Response Essay

STEP 1

Get a general idea of the article.

Read the article once or twice, and as you read, think about these questions: *What is the article about? How does the author try to convince me of his or her ideas?* These first readings will help make the other steps easier.

STEP 2

Find information for the introductory paragraph.

Read the article again. As you read:

- Circle the author's name and his or her title or credentials.

- Underline a few key words or phrases in the first few paragraphs that describe the topic and would be helpful to include as background information for your reader.

- Try to find a thesis statement in the first few paragraphs that seems to indicate the main idea for the whole article. If you find it, draw a box around it and use it to help write the main idea in the margin. (Remember that in longer texts, the first few paragraphs may be background information for the reader.)

Find information for the summary paragraph.

1 Read the article again and underline the author's main points. To find these, after you have read each paragraph, ask yourself the question: *Is the point of this paragraph a new one OR is it just more information about the point in the previous paragraph?* Double-underline each point. These sentences may occur at the beginning of paragraphs (similar to topic sentences) or sometimes at the end. After you find the points, check that they support the main idea that you wrote in Step 2. If you did not write a main idea, write it now. It should be clearer to you by now.

2 If there is not a match between the points and main idea, skim through the article again and double-check the points. Make necessary changes to the main idea or the points. This time you should feel more familiar with the content and match the main idea and points more easily. Make any changes and modify the main idea to match.

3 Now think about how you will explain each point. Put a star ✦ next to one or two details that are the most helpful or convincing to explain each one.

Choose information to respond to in your response paragraphs.

1 Make sure you understand how your instructor wants you to respond to the original article. Your instructor may want you to respond to the main idea or many points in an article.

2 Evaluate ideas and make notes in the margins next to them by asking yourself questions such as:

- Is the idea clear and logical to me? Sample responses:

  *confusing   very clear!   well said!   true in my experience!
  disagree – this is not true in my experience*

- Is the idea weak or strong? Sample responses:

  *great example! – weak example – not convincing – convincing statistics –
  scary!   good historical support   facts – old, is this true today?*

3 Reflect further on the ideas and ask yourself questions such as:

- Did the author omit anything? Sample responses:

  *did not talk about cultural differences
  wish she had mentioned prejudice against immigrants*

- Are there any connections that I can make between this author's ideas and the ideas in other articles that I have read? Sample responses:

  *idea contradicts what Hakuta says
  idea supports Khan's point that bilingualism has advantages*

Ⓐ Writing Skill 1: Coherence 1

Good writers make sure that their readers can understand their ideas. Linking ideas in sentences is called coherence. One way of creating coherence is to use **transition words and phrases**. Below are ways to connect ideas using these words and phrases.

TRANSITION WORDS AND PHRASES

1 To show chronological order / sequence: *first, second, then, after that, next, finally, last*	*In a new country, culture shock does not happen right away. There are several stages.* **First**, *a person is often very happy and excited.* **Then** *that person may start to feel frustrated or worried.* **After that**, *an immigrant usually makes friends and becomes more comfortable.* **Finally**, *the person starts to accept the new culture and enjoy it.*
2 To give additional information: *in addition, furthermore, also, too*	*The author explains that during the frustration stage, a person may have trouble sleeping.* **In addition**, *they may cry for no reason. At this stage, they may begin to experience being homesick,* **too**.
3 To give examples: *for example, for instance, such as*	*I have read that women adjust to changes more easily than men. I noticed that in my own family.* **For instance/example**, *my brother was not comfortable at school for a while, but it was easier for my sisters and me after a short time.* *In adjusting to a new country, there were many things we all had to get used to,* **such as** *language, food, cultural norms, and even weather.*
4 To show differences: *however, on the other hand, in contrast*	*The author explains that people who are confident learn the new language quickly and adapt easily.* **In contrast**, *those who are less confident avoid social situations and adapt more slowly.*
5 To show similarities: *both .... and ....,* *likewise, similarly*	**Both** *immigrants and international students experience similar stages of culture shock.* **Similarly**, *they adapt to the new environment over a period of time.*
6 To conclude: *in conclusion, in short, in summary*	**In conclusion**, *culture shock is a part of living in a new place.* **In short**, *I agree that, with time, people can get through the difficult stages of culture shock and feel more at home in a new country.*

4.1 Use Transition Words

Complete the sentences below. Use your own ideas.

1 In my experience, there are many benefits to knowing more than one language. First, ...

....

Second, ...

On the other hand, being a nonnative speaker can sometimes be frustrating. For example, ...

....

2 Sometimes I enjoy having "a secret language" when speaking my native language in public.

However, ...

....

3 There are certain times when I only speak my native language, such as at family gatherings.

In addition, ...

....

4 The author makes a good point when she says that our native language influences how we

see the world. Similarly, ...

....

Ⓑ Writing Skill 2: Coherence 2

Another way to connect ideas between sentences and create coherence is to use words such as *this*, *that*, *these*, and *those* with nouns, articles, and pronouns. Follow the guidelines below to create coherence using these words.

WAYS TO CONNECT IDEAS ACROSS SENTENCES

1 Use *this/that/these/those* before a noun from the previous sentence to refer to it without repeating its modifiers, such as adjectives.	*The author points out that <u>many cultural traditions</u> are not easily practiced. As a result, many of **these traditions** are being lost.*
2 Use *this/that/these/those* to refer to an idea or groups of words from the previous sentence.	*She says that as children assimilate, <u>they may be embarrassed by their traditional customs</u>. **This** can be hard for immigrant parents to understand.*
3 The first time you mention a common count noun, use *a/an*. The second time you mention the same noun, use *the*.	*In one of my classes, we watched <u>**a** movie</u> about the loss of culture after people immigrate. **The** movie showed the importance of keeping traditions in the modern world.*
4 Replace a noun with a pronoun after it is mentioned. Be sure the pronoun is the correct one.	*The author goes on to say that <u>some couples</u> may have a <u>traditional wedding ceremony</u> for **their** families, but **they** really want a <u>modern **one**</u>.*

4.2 Practice Linking Ideas

Connect each pair of sentences. Use one of the ways in the chart on page 185.

1 The author describes a school that wanted the immigrant students to feel welcome. A school gave the students opportunities to share the students' cultures and countries.

....

....

2 Every spring, all of the international students organized a special cultural festival. All of the international students spent a lot of time preparing for the cultural festival.

....

....

3 The authors point out that the success of the program was partly due to the support of the faculty. The authors go on to say that the success of the program was also due to students' enthusiasm and cooperation.

....

....

4 In my opinion, this kind of program is a valuable experience for everyone because this kind of program allows all students to socialize naturally. Also, this kind of program helps all students to create new friendships.

....

....

C Grammar for Writing Skill: Passive Voice

The passive voice is often used in academic writing to explain studies (the process and the results). The focus of the passive is on the action and what happened rather than on the subject, or who did the action. The passive voice helps writers communicate ideas in a neutral or objective manner. Below are some examples of passive voice.

> *Both bilingual and monolingual students were given the same test.*

> *The results of the study were published in* Nature, *a scientific journal.*

This grammar structure can only be used with transitive verbs, or verbs that take objects. Read the examples below. Notice that when a sentence changes from active to passive, two things happen:

1 The object becomes the subject, and the subject is omitted or becomes part of a *by* phrase at the end of the sentence.

   Active: *Educators are debating the future of bilingual education.*

   Passive: *The future of bilingual education is being debated **by educators**.*

2 The verb changes to the corresponding form of *be* and the past participle form of the verb.

SUBJECT   VERB   OBJECT

Simple Present Active: *Researchers **know** some effects of bilingualism.*

OBJECT   PRESENT OF *BE*
AS SUBJECT   + PAST PARTICIPLE

Simple Present Passive: *Some effects of bilingualism **are known**.*

SUBJECT   VERB   OBJECT

Present Perfect Active: *Scientists **have used** English to share research.*

OBJECT   PRESENT PERFECT OF *BE*
AS SUBJECT   + PAST PARTICIPLE

Present Perfect Passive: *English **has been used** to share research.*

Below are some rules for when writers choose the passive.

RULES FOR USING THE PASSIVE FORM OF SENTENCES	
1 Use the passive to focus on the action.	**Active:** *Someone donated English books and computers to the bilingual education program.* **Passive:** *English books and computers **were donated** to the bilingual education program.*
2 Use the passive to focus on the object of the active sentence.	**Active:** *Teachers are teaching classes in both English and Spanish.* **Passive:** *Classes **are being taught** in both English and Spanish.*
3 Include the *by* phrase only when it is necessary information for the reader.	*The students **were given** an orientation to the school **by the Student Affairs Assistant Director.***

ACTIVITY **4.3** Use the Passive

Rewrite the sentences in passive voice. Use the *by* phrase only if necessary.

1 The Senate approved a bill to fund bilingual education.

....

2 Immigrant students in the Seattle Public Schools speak 129 languages.

....

3 Researchers have discovered important benefits of being bilingual.

....

4 People have debated the benefits of bilingual education for years.

....

5 Many people recognize the importance of bilingual education.

....

Avoiding Common Mistakes

Research tells us that these are the common mistakes that students make when using passive voice in academic writing.

---

1 Use *being,* not *been,* in progressive forms of passives.

           being
Millions of children are ~~been~~ raised in bilingual homes.

2 Make sure that the subject and verb agree.

           are
Common vocabulary words ~~is~~ learned naturally from parents' conversations.

3 Do not use the passive if the subject of the sentence does the action.

        take
Bilingual students ~~be taken~~ standardized tests in either their native language or English.

ACTIVITY 4.4 Editing Task

Find and correct five more mistakes in the paragraphs below.

    The article states that multinational corporations often have communication problems because of the different languages that ~~is~~ *are* spoken by their partners or clients. The author's solution is to hire multilingual employees who can communicate in those languages. However, it can be difficult to find qualified multilingual workers. Even when a qualified worker who speaks the languages are found, it is not always practical to hire the person. Corporations must decide which languages are mostly been used and hire people who speak those languages.

    Another solution could be to hire translators through a translation company. These translators are translated documents, phone calls, or meetings, although they may work for several places at the same time. But can the company trust these translators? One solution is translation software, which is been developed to translate conversations. Unfortunately, at this time idioms and slang are being caused inaccurate translations. Further advances in technology will undoubtedly solve this problem.

Ⓓ Avoiding Plagiarism

It's important to organize notes in the research stage of writing a paper. Otherwise, using sources correctly in your final essay can be difficult.

I'm so upset! My instructor returned my essay, and she said she was really disappointed in me because I plagiarized some of my ideas. I guess the notes I took were the words of experts, and I thought they were MY words! I couldn't believe it! I would never plagiarize, and I worked so hard on my paper. I apologized to my teacher, and she is letting me resubmit my paper. How can I prevent this from happening again?!

Ayşe

Dear Ayşe,

The problem is that you probably mixed your ideas with the ideas from your sources. To avoid this in the future, you need a better system of note taking. First, take the time to read and understand the information from your sources. Then organize your notes so that you can see clearly which ideas are from your sources and need to be cited, and which ideas are your own. This will save you time and make your writing task easier. It will also help you avoid plagiarizing.

Best of luck!

Professor Wright

TAKING EFFECTIVE NOTES

Good note taking involves understanding the information from your sources and organizing your notes. Follow the steps below to take effective notes.

Steps in Effective Note-Taking

STEP 1 **Write source information on a piece of paper, in an electronic document, or on a notecard.**

Be sure to include the author's name, title of the source, date that you accessed the source, and any other information that you might need for your Works Cited list. Include the URL if from the web in case you need it in the future.

STEP 2 **Read to get a general understanding of the main ideas.**

Underline words and terms that the writer repeats and that appear to be important. This will help you understand the main idea and key points. DO NOT underline everything.

STEP 3

Read again for the main idea and key points, and begin to make notes.

Underline sentences that help you understand the key points and that you think you could use in your paper. Copy them word for word and use quotation marks so that you remember that they are the author's words. Add the page numbers where you found them if they are available. You may choose to rewrite these ideas in your own words, but having the quotations will help you rewrite them accurately.

STEP 4

Color-code the information on your cards to avoid plagiarizing as you write.

Use different-colored highlighters or pens to label the different types of notes:
- quotes (in quotation marks)
- paraphrases of the author's ideas
- your own ideas and comments

STEP 5

Organize your notes well.

Alphabetize the sources by the last name of the author or by title of the source.

 4.5 Analyze Notes

Read the original text from Amina Khan's article on bilingualism. Label the quote, the paraphrase, and Ayşe's own ideas by using a different-colored pen or highlighter for each one.

Original text

Yet many schools are moving away from bilingual education. In fact, this movement has been going on for some time. In part, this shift has been due to political beliefs. The children who speak more than one language typically come from immigrant families.

Schools are focused on teaching children English. Therefore, parents who want their children to be bilingual should continue speaking their native language. Further, they must insist on use of the native language in the only setting they can control: the home.

Ayşe's notes

Amina Khan. Bilingualism *Good for the Brain, Researchers Say*. <u>LA Times</u>. 2/26/2011.
Schools = less bilingual ed. Due to political beliefs because it is mostly immigrants. So parents should speak native language.
"They must insist on use of the native language in the only setting they can control: the home."
I agree. My cousins don't speak our native language well. Their parents always try to speak English in the house.

 4.6 Reflect

How do you take and organize notes? What ideas from this lesson will you use in your next assignment? Share ideas with a partner.

5 WRITE YOUR ESSAY

In this section, you will follow the writing process to complete the final draft of your summary–response essay.

STEP 1: READ FOR THE MAIN IDEAS

1 Before you start, reread How to Annotate an Article for a Summary–Response Essay on pages 182–183.

2 Read the article you chose in Section 1 again. Review the sentences from your chart on page 165, and decide which ones express important ideas. Find the ideas in the article and follow the directions for annotating the text. Also, use the Student Model annotation on pages 170–171 as a guide.

STEP 2: DO RESEARCH

If your topic requires research, see page 261 for advice on how find information.

STEP 3: MAKE AN OUTLINE

Complete the outline below with your ideas from Step 1.

ESSAY OUTLINE

I. Introductory paragraph

Main Idea of the Article	
Student's Thesis	
Body Paragraph 1 Summary	II.
Point 1	A.
Detail	1.
Detail	2.

Point 2	B.
Detail	1.
Detail	2.
Point 3	C.
Detail	1.
Detail	2.
Body Paragraph 2 Response	III.
Point 1	A.
Detail	1.
Detail	2.
Point 2	B.
Detail	1.
Detail	2.
Body Paragraph 3 Response	IV.
Point 1	A.
Detail	1.
Detail	2.
Point 2	B.
Detail	1.
Detail	2.
	V. Concluding paragraph

STEP 4: WRITE YOUR FIRST DRAFT

Now it is time to write your first draft. Here are some suggestions on how to get started.

1 Reread your article to make sure that your summary will include the key points.
2 Use your outline as you write to stay focused, but put the original article away to avoid accidentally plagiarizing.
3 Make sure to paraphrase the author's ideas so that you do not plagiarize.

After you finish, read your essay and check for basic errors.

1 Check that all sentences have subjects and verbs.
2 Check that you have used commas and periods correctly.
3 Make sure that your thesis statement and topic sentences are clear.

Finally, compare your essay against the article and make sure that you did not plagiarize.

STEP 5: WRITE YOUR FINAL DRAFT

1 After you receive feedback on your first draft, review it carefully. Fix any errors.
2 Make a note of errors that were most frequent. Try to avoid them as you write.
3 Review the Academic Vocabulary and Phrases from this unit. Are there any that you can add to your essay?
4 Turn to page 267 and use the Self-Editing Review to check your work one more time.
5 Write your final draft and hand it in.

Third Culture Kids (adapted)

by Bilal Ahmed

I am a "Third Culture Kid" (TCK) who attempts to push existing definitions of what that means. The term was originally invented by sociologist and anthropologist Ruth Hill Useem in the 1950s to refer to children who accompany their parents into a new society and adjust their identities to reflect that society. Recently, sociologist David C. Pollock developed a more substantial definition, classifying a TCK as:

"A person who has spent a significant part of his or her developmental years outside the parents' culture. The TCK frequently builds relationships to all of the cultures, while not having full ownership in any. Although elements from each culture may be assimilated into the TCK's life experience, the sense of belonging is in relationship to others of similar background."

I am a TCK because I grew up in the United Arab Emirates, Canada, and the United States. While living in the UAE, I was part of the South Asian middle class. We were able to rely on my father's income to move and live in Saskatoon (Canada), London, and North Brunswick, New Jersey (U.S.A). I have spent most of my childhood outside Pakistani monoculture, and continue to mature in a cosmopolitan, multicultural environment.

While popular discussions on TCKs focus on the issues of identity, these issues are not unique to TCKs. They affect a lot of immigrants and others with cross-cultural experiences. So what makes TCKs - military brats,[1] foreign service children,[2] missionary kids,[3] and other people who grew up in expatriate[4] contexts- different from others? And why is it necessary to have a separate classification for them? TCKs are different because of their class and the global economy in which they live.

TCKs almost always come from middle class[5] households. Like immigrants and refugees, TCKs blend their original culture and the foreign culture in which they live to create a personal third culture, but they differ in their wealth. TCKs lead comfortable lives and are likely to become wealthy professionals.

They are also comfortable with change, for example, traveling here and there because of sudden relocations of a parent's job. In fact, we are often praised for our adaptability. In truth, most of us are able to adjust well and deal with diverse situations because we have no financial worries. We have the money and support from people around us to deal with the changes. These circumstances help us turn our skill of adaptability into an asset.

[1]**military brats:** children of military personnel
[2]**foreign service children:** children of parents who work in the government departments
    staffed by diplomats and consular personnel
[3]**missionary kids:** children of parents who are sent on a religious mission
[4]**expatriate:** someone who does not live in his or her native country
[5]**middle class:** a social group that consists of well-educated people who have good jobs

But TCKs are more than just rich kids. Our ability to live in a constantly changing society makes us ideal citizens of this modern world, according to some sociologists. Zygmunt Bauman asserts that in the modern world with its market-driven economies people cannot have fixed identities when it comes to culture and language. Rather, they must adapt to changing circumstances. This sounds like a TCK to me. Also, our worldliness and flexibility make us ideal citizens because we feel secure in this risky international economy. Most parents of TCK kids worked in professions that relocated constantly and the crucial source of their identity was financial. In my case, I grew up in the Gulf monarchies. These oil selling states and the global economy created a luxurious life style and my parents took the opportunities that were available to them. The opportunities created this Third Culture Family, so to speak. Our values as kids reflect our upbringing. We love flexibility, not predictability. We love relocation, not rootedness.[6]

While people from traditional backgrounds may feel that our freedom might inspire nonconformist behavior, it does not at all. We need to rely on our families for personal grounding in some ways more strongly than others because standards for personal happiness, for social life, for setting personal and professional goals can seem confusing and unclear. If the family structure is not strong, TCKs can suffer. Lack of purpose can cause them to behave in a destructive manner.

According to the experts, TCKs will be able to find happiness only if they accept their unique identities. I agree. In my opinion, TCKs also need a strong sense of direction in order to truly decide whether or not they have found happiness. If they fail to do so, their loss of direction can become a prison.

[6]**rootedness:** the state of living in one place for a long time

ARGUMENTATIVE ESSAYS 1

ECONOMICS: DEMOGRAPHICS AND THE ECONOMY

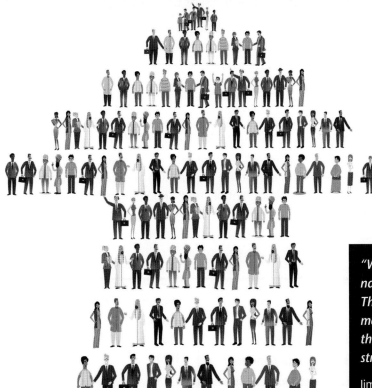

"We are of course a nation of differences. Those differences don't make us weak. They're the source of our strength."

Jimmy Carter (1924–)

About the Author:

Jimmy Carter (1924–) is a former U.S. president (1977–1981), Nobel Peace Prize recipient (2002), diplomat, and human rights advocate.

Work with a partner. Read the quotation about diversity. Then answer the questions.

1 What does Carter mean by saying that the United States is "a nation of differences"? What are some examples?

2 Do you agree with Carter that these differences are "the source of our strength"? Explain.

Ⓐ Connect to Academic Writing

In this unit, you will learn how to state and argue your point of view convincingly. While some of the skills you will learn may be new to you, the skill of arguing is not new. In your everyday life, you use the skill of argumentation when you try to convince a friend to quit smoking or explain why the book version of a story is much better than the movie version.

Ⓑ Reflect on the Topic

In this section, you will choose a writing prompt and reflect on it. You will develop these ideas throughout the unit and use them to practice skills that are necessary to write your essay.

The writing prompt below was used for the Student Model essay on pages 204–205. The student reflected on her prompt and used a chart to help her think of reasons why companies should and should not have to hire more women. This helped her choose a side and think of a possible thesis statement.

WRITING PROMPT: According to recent information on diversity in the workforce of the largest tech companies, over 70 percent of employees were male. Some people say that these companies should hire more women. Others say that it is not necessary for there to be more women in that industry. What is your point of view? Should tech companies hire more women?

YES	NO
- Women need these jobs for their families. - Women can learn these skills, too. - Women are just as smart as men. - Women have different ideas than men. - There's prejudice against women, and that's not right.	- Men have better skills for the jobs. - Women are not attracted to those kinds of jobs. - No one should tell a company who to hire.

Possible thesis statement: *Tech companies should hire women because women need the jobs, they have unique opinions, and they can learn the skills, too.*

 1.1 Notice

Work with a partner. Look at the chart above. Which side do you think is more convincing? Explain why.

1.2 Apply It to Your Writing

Follow the directions to reflect on your topic.

A Choose a prompt:

- Do you agree or disagree with the following statement? Living in a multicultural city (a city with people from different cultures) is better than living in a monocultural city (a city with people from mostly one culture). Explain why.

- Is the diversity of a country – diversity of cultures, political and social ideas, etc. – always good for a country? Explain why or why not.

- Does the gender of a leader matter in terms of how successful or effective he or she is?

- A topic approved by your instructor

B Complete the following tasks:

1 Think about your prompt. What two sides is the prompt asking you to consider?

2 Complete the chart below. Write as many reasons as you can to support each side.

3 Decide on the side that you will write about. Then write a possible thesis statement.

4 Compare charts and possible thesis statements with a partner.

WRITING PROMPT:	
YES	NO

Possible thesis statement:

2 EXPAND YOUR KNOWLEDGE

In this section, you will learn academic language that you can use in your argumentative essay. You will also notice how a professional writer uses the language and features of argumentation.

A Academic Vocabulary

The words below appear throughout the unit. All are from the Academic Word List. Using these words in your writing will make your ideas clearer and your writing more academic.

accumulate (v)	diminish (v)	evolve (v)	motive (n)
acknowledge (v)	diversity (n)	isolation (n)	norm (n)

 2.1 Focus on Meaning

Work with a partner. Circle the correct definitions.

1 People need to accumulate skills in their jobs in order to be competitive and become successful. **Accumulate** means

   a to be successful at something.   b to increase over a period of time.

2 Some employers think that older people have more difficulty acquiring new skills, but according to some studies, the ability to learn new skills does not **diminish** as people get older. **Diminish** means

   a to reduce.   b to grow.

3 A few decades ago, American society did not think that women should be in the workforce, but this thinking has **evolved**. Now most of society believes that women belong in the workforce, too. **Evolve** means

   a to rotate slowly.   b to change gradually.

4 The United States is known for its **diversity** of cultures, which comes from a history of immigration. **Diversity** means

   a a variety.   b a type.

5 Learning a foreign language is optional in most American schools. It is not the **norm**.
   Norm means

   a choice among items.   b rule or standard.

6 Some islands in the Pacific are not well known. Few people travel to them. The people of
   the islands do not interact much with other people. This **isolation** keeps their culture from
   changing. **Isolation** means

   a separation.   b growth.

7 The **motive** for companies to offer better maternity and paternity leave policies is to attract
   young workers who want to have families. **Motive** means

   a motion.   b reason.

8 Some large technology companies **acknowledge** that there are very few women employees.
   In one company over 90 percent of its employees are male. **Acknowledge** means

   a to disagree.   b to admit.

B Academic Collocations

Collocations are words that are frequently used together. Research tells us that the academic
vocabulary in Part A is commonly used in the collocations in bold below.

accumulate wealth	geographical isolation	social norm
cultural diversity	primary motive	

 2.2 Focus on Meaning

Work with a partner. Circle the correct meanings.

1 Because many large companies today are global, managing the **cultural diversity** in their
   workforce is a priority. A company with **cultural diversity** expects employees to have

   a different points of view on issues.   b similar points of view on issues.

2 Many global companies provide cultural training to employees. The **primary motive** of
   management is to help their employees avoid conflicts that occur from cultural differences.
   A **primary motive** is

   a one of several reasons.   b the most important reason.

3 Every culture has **social norms** that are learned in early childhood. These behaviors can be
   very different in different cultures. **Social norms** means

   a rules of acceptable ways of interacting. b behaviors that are not acceptable.

4 The **geographical isolation** of a country can affect its economic growth because it has less
   trade and less connection to the rest of the world. **Geographical isolation** means

   a the separation by a barrier or border.   b the social differences in a country.

5 Many people's dreams include finding ways to **accumulate wealth** so that they have
   enough money to enjoy their lives when they become elderly. **Accumulate wealth** means

   a to collect money and possessions.   b to share money and possessions.

C Writing in the Real World

The author of "Diversity Leads to Economic Growth" uses features of academic essays to strengthen his argument.

Before you read, answer these questions: What do you think the author means by diversity? What are some ideas that the writer will argue?

Now read the article. Think about the answers to the questions as you read.

DIVERSITY LEADS TO ECONOMIC GROWTH
(adapted)
by Richard Florida

1 For many scientists, economic growth has always been tied to natural resources[1], technology, and skilled workers. However, recent studies suggest that geography and culture also play major roles in a country's development. They claim that it is cultural **diversity,** or openness to other people and cultures, that makes economic progress possible. Skeptics[2] counter that diversity is not the cause of economic growth. It is the result of a strong economy. They argue that people move to other places because they have already **accumulated** wealth or are hoping to get rich.

2 Economists Quarmrul Ashraf and Oded Galor examined the link between diversity and the economy. Their important new study "Cultural Diversity, Geographical Isolation, and the Origin of the Wealth of Nations" focuses on economic differences from preindustrial[3] times to the modern era. The researchers looked at how geographical **isolation** has affected culture and the economy around the world. They found that countries with more diverse cultures developed more quickly. Those that were less diverse grew more slowly. In other words, places open to other people had a stronger economy. Ones closed to other cultures were weaker. According to their research, Europe and the New World **evolved** much faster than other areas during this period. They report, "The gap between the richest regions of the world and the poorest increased from a modest 3 to 1 ratio in 1820 to an astounding 18 to 1 ratio in 2000." The authors conclude that this was because of the many different people that emigrated there.

3 Many scientists have searched for the cause of the West's rapid economic expansion. Max Weber credited the "Protestant work ethic."[4] He claimed that saving money and working hard made this expansion possible. Others thought it was due

[1]**natural resources:** oil, minerals, forests, etc,. that have economic value
[2]**skeptics:** people who doubt an idea or a belief

[3]**preindustrial:** before the economy was based on the production of goods from large companies and factories
[4]**Protestant work ethic:** the belief that work is valuable as an activity

to the unique social **norms** in these places. They believed Western values such as individual effort, freedom, and the spirit of enterprise[5] favored economic growth there. In *The Rise of the Western World*, the authors Douglass C. North and Robert Paul Thomas affirm that institutions were the reason for this development. They argue that democracy, capitalism, and individual rights encouraged technology in these countries. In short, technology accelerated their economic progress. On the other hand, in Jared Diamond's *Guns, Germs, and Steel*, geography is at the center of the West's advance. For the author, a better climate, more natural resources, and less disease gave them a definite advantage.

4 Ashraf and Galor affirm that what really drove progress in Europe and the New World was their relative openness to other people and cultures. The findings clearly show that diversity was the main source of their economic strength. The authors draw three major conclusions in their study.

First, geographical isolation played a positive role in preindustrial times. Being isolated and less diverse helped these early societies gain skilled workers. This helped them to develop agriculturally in the beginning. However, their lack of diversity **diminished** their ability to adapt to new technologies later. Second, societies isolated in preindustrial times still tend to be less diverse and economically weaker today. Third, throughout history, diversity has always had a positive impact on industrial and economic growth.

5 It is time for skeptics to **acknowledge** the importance of diversity. Hard work and freedom were certainly important factors in the West's speedy development. However, openness and tolerance were the key engines of its economic prosperity.[6] The rich cultures that people brought with them contributed greatly to its progress. This is no less true today. Achieving diversity should be the primary **motive** of any country that values a strong economy. As the study suggests, people will always be the true wealth of nations.

[5]**enterprise:** the will or energy to do something new

[6]**prosperity:** success, especially financial

 2.3 Check Your Understanding

Answer the questions.

1 What did economists Ashraf and Galor study? What did they find?

2 What are two other possible causes of the West's rapid expansion?

3 Think about your country and culture. How well do the ideas in the article explain your country's economy? Is diversity a factor in your economy?

 2.4 Notice How the Writer Uses Argumentative Writing

Answer the questions.

1 Look at paragraph 1. The author includes an opposing argument in the last three sentences starting with "Skeptics counter that …" Why do you think he does this?

2 Look at paragraph 2. The author gives statistics concerning the gap between the richest and poorest regions of the world. What is the purpose of the statistics? What do they prove?

3 Look at paragraph 3. What does the writer talk about? Why do you think he included this paragraph?

In Section 1, you saw how the writer of the Student Model essay reflected on her topic. In this section, you will analyze the final draft of her academic essay. You will learn how to structure your ideas for your own essay.

(A) Student Model

Read the writing prompt again and answer the questions.

WRITING PROMPT: According to recent information on diversity in the workforce of the largest tech companies, over 70 percent of employees were male. Some people say that these companies should hire more women. Others say that it is not necessary for there to be more women in that industry. What is your point of view? Should tech companies hire more women?

1 What is the essay prompt asking the writer to write about?

2 Look at the title of her essay. What will she argue?

Read the essay twice. The first time, think about your answers to the questions above. The second time, answer the questions in the Analyze Writing Skills boxes. This will help you notice key features of argumentative essays.

Why We Need More Women in Technology Jobs

1 Women have 52 percent of professional jobs in the United States (Warner), but they have only about 12 percent of tech jobs at technology "start-ups" (Gilpin). Some people believe it is not important to have more women working in technology companies. They feel it should not matter if employees are men or women. In fact, companies should hire more women in technology because they would be more innovative and competitive, and society would be much stronger.

2 If tech companies hired more women, they would increase their innovation. First, everyone knows that diversity of ideas is important for innovation, so hiring more women, including women of different cultures, would give new perspectives on

1 Analyze Writing Skills
Underline the hook in paragraph 1 that gets your attention. What kind of hook is it? Circle the correct word.
observation   statistic question   story quotation   visualization

2 Analyze Writing Skills
In paragraph 1, underline the three main points that the writer will discuss in her body paragraphs.

ideas. The discussions about products will be different because these women will challenge the men's ideas. Secondly, women could help to design products for women. Since women make 85 percent of consumer purchases ("Marketing to Women"), their preferences are important. Women engineers could help companies design products that really address their needs. For example, one app was easily activated by tapping a phone in a pocket. However, a female engineer pointed out that women often keep phones in purses. As a result, the design of the phone was changed. It is clear that women in technology would give a new perspective on ideas.

3   If there were more women as leaders, technology companies would be more successful. According to a study by the *Harvard Business Review* (Zenger and Folkman), women were given higher ratings in their leadership abilities. They were better at leading employees and achieving results. Some examples of successful women leaders who have shown strong leadership are Sheryl Sandberg of Facebook and Marissa Mayer of Yahoo. Also, since there are not many women in technology, women do not feel comfortable and they work harder. Men feel comfortable in technology, so they may not work as hard as women. It is possible that women leaders could make companies achieve more.

4   Most importantly, our society will benefit from more women in technology companies. First, these jobs will help women take care of their families. There are many single mothers who are raising children in this country. Since technology jobs pay well, the single mother will be able to live well and not worry about her finances. In addition, these jobs will also benefit mothers who must work to help their husbands make enough money to raise a family. Second, if women get these jobs, they can be role models for younger girls and encourage them to study for jobs in technology. It is clear that hiring women for tech jobs will make families stronger and society more stable.

5   In sum, hiring more women in tech jobs would benefit companies by making them more creative and successful, and this change would benefit society. This will happen only if companies change their ideas about hiring women, and this may not be easy for them to do. Also, teachers must encourage girls to consider careers in tech jobs. In my case, I plan to work in a tech job and will be proud to be a role model for young girls.

Works Cited

Gilpin, Lyndsey. "The State of Women in Technology: 15 Data Points You Should Know." *TechRepublic*. CBS Interactive, 8 July 2014. Web. 11 Nov 2014.

"Marketing to Women – Quick Facts." *She-conomy: A Guy's Guide to Marketing to Women*. WordPress.com, n.d. Web. 6 Nov. 2014.

Warner, Judith. "Fact Sheet: The Women's Leadership Gap." *Center for American Progress*. Center for American Progress, 7 Mar. 2014. Web. 4 May 2014.

Zenger, Jack, and Joseph Folkman. "Are Women Better Leaders Than Men?" *Harvard Business Review*. Harvard Business School Publishing, 15 Mar. 2012. Web. 2 Feb. 2015.

---

3 Analyze Writing Skills

In paragraph 2, what kind of information does the writer give to support the topic sentence? Circle all that apply.

example
fact
personal experience
quotation
statistic

4 Analyze Writing Skills

In paragraph 3, how many supporting sentences does the writer include to support her topic sentence? ....
Underline them.

5 Analyze Writing Skills

In paragraph 4, how many supporting sentences does the writer include to support her point? ....
Circle the words that she uses to introduce them.

3.1 Check Your Understanding

Answer the questions about the Student Model essay on pages 204–205.

1 What is the purpose of the essay?

2 Which point do you think is strongest? Explain.

3 What is your opinion of the writer's ideas? Do you agree or disagree? Explain.

 3.2 Outline the Writer's Ideas

Complete the outline for "Why We Need More Women in Technology Jobs." Write the thesis statement. Then use the phrases in the box.

help design products for women	men may not work as hard
higher ratings in leadership abilities	women can be role models for young girls
increase their innovation	

ESSAY OUTLINE

I. Introductory paragraph

Thesis Statement
....

....

Body Paragraph 1 Point 1   II. ....

Supporting Idea 1   A. Give new perspectives on ideas

Detail   1. Will challenge men's ideas

Supporting Idea 2   B. ....

Detail   1. Women – 85% of consumer purchases

Detail   2. Avoid wrong decisions

Body Paragraph 2 Point 2	III. Help companies be more successful
Supporting Idea 1	A.
Detail	1. Better at leading and achieving
Detail	2. Ex: Sandberg and Mayer
Supporting Idea 2	B. Women work harder – less comfortable
Detail	1.
Body Paragraph 3 Point 3	IV. Society will benefit
Supporting Idea 1	A. Jobs will help women take care of their families
Detail	1. Help single mothers
Detail	2. Help mothers who help support their families
Supporting Idea 2	B.
Detail	1. They can encourage girls to study for jobs in technology
	V. Concluding paragraph

B Argumentative Essays

The ability to write argumentative essays is essential in academic writing. You will often be asked to give your point of view on a topic that you have discussed in class. Stating your point of view clearly and supporting it using information from texts and your experience is a key skill in both speaking and writing. This skill will help you be successful both in school and in your career.

WHAT IS AN ARGUMENT?

An **argument** is an opinion, or a point of view, with reasons and evidence to prove that the point of view is valid. An argument tells the reader, "I believe that my point of view is a good one, and I have persuasive reasons supported by facts and research to prove it." A successful argument makes your reader understand and recognize that your point of view has some value; however, it does not mean that your reader will in the end change their opinion and agree with you.

The Student Model writer's argument is summarized below.

Student Model Writer's Argument: Companies should hire more women in technology because they would be more innovative, they would be more competitive, and society would be much stronger.

Reasons and Evidence for Argument: Increasing the number of women in tech positions would make companies more innovative since the diversity of women from different cultures would make the workplace more creative. Women would challenge ideas and bring new ones. It would make the companies more competitive since women have a lot of power as consumers and they are good leaders. Finally, it will benefit society because more women will be able to take care of their families, especially single mothers, and these women will be role models to young girls and encourage them to choose careers in technology.

DEBATABLE TOPICS

When writers choose a topic for an argumentative essay, they must make sure that they choose a debatable topic. Debatable topics are those that people have serious disagreements about, such as women's rights, freedom of religion, animal rights, free higher education, and the death penalty.

On the issue of "Should higher education be free?," three points of view are:

Point of view 1: Higher education should be free because if a country's citizens are all educated, there will be more skilled workers. More skilled workers means that companies will produce more and sell more.

Point of view 2: Higher education should be free because it is a citizen's basic right. It should not matter if a person is rich or poor. Everyone should get a good education.

Point of view 3: Higher education should not be free because if it is free people will not work hard or care about their studies. People will not be educated or competitive. As a result, the economy will suffer.

Other debatable topics include "Should governments control the Internet?," "Is marriage necessary?," "Should men and women receive equal pay for the same job?," and "Is a job a human right?"

ARGUMENTS VS. FACTS

Do not confuse arguments with facts. Facts are not debatable because they have been proven. They are scientific facts or the results of current research.

Below is a list that includes debatable arguments, as well as facts. Which of the following are facts and which are arguments?

1　According to a study by Quarmrul Ashraf of Williams College and Oded Galor of Brown University, immigration is good for an economy.

2　Almost half of the labor workforce in the United States is made up of women.

3　Children of single parents are more likely to have psychological problems and live in poverty.

4　Imagination is more important than knowledge because it is imagination that has been responsible for the major innovations of humankind.

Sentences 1 and 2 are facts because they state the results of current studies or are widely known and accepted to be true. Sentences 3 and 4 are arguments because they are debatable. Writers of these arguments will have to prove that there is evidence to show that their argument is valid.

 3.3 Notice

Write *A* if the statement is an argument and *F* if the statement is a fact. Explain your choices to a partner.

............1　According to a 2011 report by the U.S. Department of Commerce, 14 percent of engineers were women.

............2　There are more women in certain jobs such as teaching and nursing because women have natural skills for those jobs.

............3　It is necessary to have laws that require companies to hire the disabled because every person should be able to have a job.

............4　The majority of legislators, or lawmakers, in the United States are over the age of 55.

ARGUMENTS VS. OPINIONS

Do not confuse arguments with opinions. An opinion is a belief that is stated without logical reasons to support it. The following are opinions: "It is wrong to kill animals." "Celebrities get paid too much money." "Parents should be able to choose the sex of their children."

Read the following statements. Which are arguments and which are opinions?

Statement 1: Parental leave laws, laws that allow parents to stay home and care for their newborns and still get paid, have clear benefits to their families because they allow families to bond and allow the parents to recover from childbirth.

Statement 2: When co-workers of different cultures, sexual orientations, and religions work together to solve problems, they are more likely to find innovative solutions because they bring new perspectives on the problems.

Statement 3: Children of working mothers get into trouble a lot.

Statement 4: Education can change a person's life.

Statements 1 and 2 are arguments because they contain clear reasons that the writer can prove by evidence. Statements 3 and 4 are opinions because there are no clear reasons that the writer can prove by evidence. It is possible to turn opinions into arguments by providing reasons that could be proven. Notice how adding the underlined reasons to Statement 4 changes it from an opinion to an argument.

Statement 4 (revised): Education can change a person's life <u>because it can give him or her more employment opportunities, more personal satisfaction, and a higher income.</u>

 3.4 Identify Arguments

Write *A* if the statement is an argument and *O* if the statement is an opinion.
Explain your answers to a partner.

.... 1 A person's gender should not matter in the workplace.

.... 2 Companies should have parental-leave policies.

.... 3 Immigrants help an economy by paying taxes, starting new businesses, and increasing innovation.

.... 4 The economy of a country where the cost of education is high will suffer from an unskilled workforce and less innovation.

 3.5 Write Arguments

A Circle your answers to give your opinion.

1 In my opinion, women with young children **should / should not** work.

2 The Olympic Games **are / are not** good for creating goodwill in the world.

B On a separate sheet of paper, write arguments for your opinions in Part A. Add two logical reasons to each one.

 3.6 Apply It to Your Writing

With a partner, read the possible thesis statements that you wrote in Section 1 on page 199. Are they opinions or arguments? If needed, make changes so that they are arguments.

THE STRUCTURE OF AN ARGUMENTATIVE ESSAY

Writers carefully construct each part of their essay because each part has a specific purpose.

1 The **introductory paragraph** gets the reader's attention, convinces the reader that the topic or issue is important, and leads the reader to the thesis statement. It consists of:

- a **hook**, such as a famous quote, a story, a surprising or alarming fact, or a statistic about the issue
- **background information**, which explains the issue, its importance, the different sides of the debate, and information that introduces the thesis
- the **thesis statement**, which usually contains the points that the writer will prove in the body paragraphs

2 The **body paragraphs** build the argument by explaining each reason and giving clear evidence – such as facts, examples, personal experiences, and research – to convince the reader that the reason is valid.

3 The **concluding paragraph** summarizes the argument and reminds the reader why the topic is important. It ends with a memorable closing statement, quotation, or call to action.

ACTIVITY 3.7 Notice

Check (✓) the correct answers. In some cases, there may be more than one answer.

1 In which paragraph(s) does the writer tell the reader why the topic is important?

☐ a introductory paragraph ☐ b body paragraphs ☐ c concluding paragraph

2 How do writers use facts in an argumentative essay?

☐ a as a hook ☐ b to prove a reason in a body paragraph ☐ c as part of the thesis statement

3 In which paragraph(s) do writers give support for the reasons in an argument?

☐ a introductory paragraph ☐ b body paragraphs ☐ c concluding paragraph

4 In which paragraph does the writer comment on the issue or tell the reader to do something?

☐ a introductory paragraph ☐ b body paragraphs ☐ c concluding paragraph

WRITING AN INTRODUCTORY PARAGRAPH

The introductory paragraph in an argumentative essay has a lot to accomplish. As mentioned earlier, it:

- gets the reader's attention and interest using a hook
- explains a little bit about the issue and the different sides of the debate so that the reader understands what the issue is, what people are saying about the issue, and why the thesis statement makes sense
- ends in the thesis statement

If the introductory paragraph is uninteresting or vague, the reader will have difficulty reading and understanding the rest of the essay.

 **3.8** Notice

Look at the introductory paragraph of the Student Model essay on pages 204–205. Answer the questions.

1 The writer chooses a statistic as her hook. Why is it effective?

2 How does the writer help you understand the issue?

 3.9 Apply It to Your Writing

Look at your chart from Section 1 on page 199. Think about the essay prompt and ask yourself these questions.

1 What background information should the reader know about the topic in order to understand why it is an important issue?

....

....

2 Write a possible way to get your reader's attention (e.g., an interesting or surprising statement, a quote, a story, a fact, or a statistic).

....

....

STRONG AND WEAK THESIS STATEMENTS

In an argumentative essay, the **thesis statement**, also called a **claim**, states the writer's point of view. A strong thesis statement:

- Answers the prompt with a clear point of view. The prompt may ask you to agree or disagree, to say whether something is or is not a problem, or to say whether something is or is not true. It contains the word *should* if necessary.
- Uses key words from the prompt that are part of the question and the issue.
- Gives specific reasons that are clear and could be supported by evidence.

Read the writing prompt and the weak and strong thesis statements that follow. Notice the differences between the two.

WRITING PROMPT: Tech companies are not known for the diversity of their workforce. In fact, in some of the largest tech companies, almost three-quarters of their workforce is made up of young males, mostly Caucasian. There has been a lot of debates about whether these companies should be more diverse and include more diversity in gender and ethnicity. What is your point of view? Should tech companies hire people with more diverse backgrounds?

Strong Thesis Statement: *Tech companies should hire more people of diverse backgrounds because companies with a diverse workforce are more innovative, the workforce should reflect the people in the society, and someone's gender or ethnicity should not determine who gets a job.*

This thesis statement is strong because:

1 The point of view is clear. The writing prompt has *should* in it, and the thesis statement does, too. The writer thinks that the lack of diversity is a problem and that tech companies should hire more women and people of different ethnicities.

2 The writer includes key words such as *tech companies*, *gender*, and *hire*.

3 The reasons are clear, support the point of view, and could be supported by evidence.

Weak Thesis Statement: *There are not many women or different kinds of people in technology jobs, but this is how our society is.*

This thesis statement is weak because:

1 The point of view is not clear. The writing prompt has *should* in it, but the thesis statement does not, so it does not answer the prompt.

2 The thesis does not contain key words from the question or about the topic.

3 The reasons are not clearly stated, and it is not apparent what the reasons will be.

 3.10 Evaluate Thesis Statements

Read the thesis statements for each writing prompt. Write *W* for weak and *S* for strong. Discuss your answers with a partner.

WRITING PROMPT 1: Is a high-paying job necessary to have a happy life?

.... 1 A high-paying job is not necessary for a happy life because a happy life depends on things that do not need money, such as having good friends and a loving family, being a good person, and enjoying life.

.... 2 A high-paying job is necessary for a happy life because you can take care of your family, enjoy participating in things that cost money, and help others.

.... 3 When people make a lot of money, it can sometimes make them happy, but often it is a problem because money can make people greedy and they do not make good decisions.

WRITING PROMPT 2: Should the Internet be controlled by governments?

.... 1 The Internet is a human right and there is a lot of important information that companies, scientists, and all people need.

.... 2 The Internet should not be controlled by governments because access to information is a right and countries without control are more innovative.

.... 3 The Internet should be controlled by governments because governments must protect its citizens from illegal activities, false information, and hateful people.

MORE ABOUT THESIS STATEMENTS

Thesis statements do not have to list the reasons or points. Read the thesis statements below. One thesis statement does not give the specific reasons for the reader, but they both clearly indicate what the writer will discuss in the body paragraphs that will follow.

> **Thesis Statement 1:** *Living in a multicultural society is challenging because you have to adjust to different social norms, deal with feelings of isolation, and change your habits.* (The writer includes three specific reasons for the point of view.)

> **Thesis Statement 2:** *Living in a multicultural society is challenging because people must always make adjustments and these adjustments can be difficult.* (The reasons are not specific, but the reader knows that the writer will discuss adjustments and why they are sometimes difficult.)

 3.11 Analyze Thesis Statements

Work with a partner. Read the thesis statements and discuss the points the writer might discuss.

1 Money is not the most motivating factor in choosing a job.

2 People can peacefully live together in a multicultural society if they work together to respect each other's customs and values.

BUILDING AN ARGUMENT IN THE BODY PARAGRAPHS

Each **body paragraph** in an argumentative essay has a clear goal. The goal is to make the reader, especially the reader who disagrees with you, say, "I may not totally agree with your argument, but this paragraph sure is convincing!"

Each **body paragraph** consists of:

- a **topic sentence** that links to the thesis statement by repeating important words from the thesis statement in it

- **evidence**, such as facts or statistics, quotations or examples, logical reasons, or personal experiences, and an explanation that shows how the paragraph supports the topic sentence

Below are examples of the types of evidence that writers use.

1 **Facts:** Facts are ideas that can be proven or are accepted as true. They make your arguments seem valid.

   Today, Russia and the United States are two of the top destinations for immigrants.

2 **Statistics:** Figures are numbers, data, or statistics that come from research, surveys, or polls. They make your arguments more credible.

   Over 800,000 immigrants arrived in the United States in 2013.

3 **Quotations:** Quotations are relevant phrases and sentences that are copied from another source, put in quotation marks, and properly credited.

In a study by Harvard Business Review, *researchers found that women were rated as "better overall leaders than their male counterparts" (Zenger and Folkman).*

Zenger, Jack and Joseph Folkman. "Are Women Better Leaders Than Men?" *Harvard Business Review*, 15 Mar 2012. Web. 2 Feb 2015.

4 **Examples:** Examples are specific stories or cases that illustrate a point. They help the reader imagine and understand what you mean.

Imagine a Saudi man, a U.S. woman, a Dominican man, and an Egyptian woman all discussing ways that the company can improve its sales in the global market. Each person will have a unique perspective on the various markets. This conversation will be much more valuable than one between four people of the same gender and culture.

5 **Personal Experiences:** Personal experiences are stories that happened to you or someone you know. They make your arguments more real and believable.

In 2007, my family immigrated to Manitoba, Canada. That same year, my parents opened a Filipino restaurant in a small town in Manitoba. After working hard for many years, my father has become a respected leader of the community.

Whichever you choose, strong evidence is key. To find strong **evidence**, ask yourself these questions:

- What facts or statistics would most likely convince my reader?
- What quotations or examples clearly support my opinion?
- What personal experiences would make my opinion more believable and persuasive?

 3.12 Identify Evidence

Work with a partner. Read the underlined sentences in the paragraph. Identify the type of evidence in each sentence.

A job is not supposed to make people happy. First, a job is a paycheck and not a place to have fun. Many people in the world would agree with this. <u>In a global survey on jobs by Gallup (qtd. in Gallo), over 80 percent of people in the world did not care about their jobs.</u> <u>In my family, three of my uncles work in construction.</u> <u>They all complain about their job, but they have very good salaries, so they go to work every day.</u> Also, the supply and demand of goods controls the kinds of jobs that exist. <u>If people want to work, they have to take the jobs that are available.</u>

 **3.13** Choose Evidence

Work with a partner. Check (✓) the evidence that would best support the body paragraphs.

WRITING PROMPT: Are women better leaders than men?

Thesis Statement: Women are better leaders than men because they are better at building the skills of their employees and accomplishing company goals.

1 **Body Paragraph 1:** Women are better at helping employees develop their skills.

    ☐ a According to a survey by Zenger and Folkman, female bosses are more interested in their employees and this makes the employees feel a part of the organization. As a result, these employees are more committed to doing their job well.

    ☐ b Chancellor Angela Merkel of Germany is a very powerful leader who kept the economy of Germany strong during the economic crisis in 2009.

2 **Body Paragraph 2:** Women are better at achieving results.

    ☐ a According to research, nations that are culturally diverse have a stronger economy if their leader is a woman (McGregor).

    ☐ b A study by Jack Zenger and Joseph Folkman for the *Harvard Business Review* found that women leaders scored higher than men on their ability to reach goals.

3.14 Apply It to Your Writing

YOUR TURN

Look at the ideas for your essay from Section 1 on page 199. Think of evidence that could strengthen your point of view and write it below. Share your ideas with a partner.

CONCLUDING PARAGRAPH

The **concluding paragraph** tells the readers what you want them to remember about your essay. It is your last chance to restate your argument, say why the topic is important, and convince the readers to agree with your point of view. Writers often create a memorable ending by leaving the readers something to think about: a strong closing statement, quotation, or call to action.

 3.15 Notice

Look at the concluding paragraph of the Student Model essay on pages 204–205. Answer the questions.

1 Where does the writer restate her argument? How is it different from the introductory paragraph?

2 How does the writer remind you why the topic is important? Is it convincing? Why or why not?

3 How does the writer end the essay – with a strong closing statement, a quotation, or a call to action? Is it memorable? Why or why not?

4 Did the writer persuade you to agree with her point of view? Why or why not?

In this section, you will learn the writing and grammar skills that will help make your writing more sophisticated and accurate.

Ⓐ Writing Skill: Avoiding Run-ons and Comma Splices

Writers often write run-on sentences and comma splices when they try to join different ideas together. These errors are easily avoided with coordinating conjunctions and good punctuation.

Below are some examples.

RUN-ONS AND COMMA SPLICES

1 A **run-on sentence** incorrectly combines two independent clauses without a comma and a conjunction such as *and, but,* or *so.*

The run-on sentence can be corrected in three ways:

a by adding a comma and a conjunction

b by adding a semicolon

c by adding a period and capitalizing the first letter of the second independent clause

> INDEPENDENT CLAUSE
> *Natural resources help an economy grow*
> INDEPENDENT CLAUSE
> *diversity is another factor.*

> *Natural resources help an economy grow* **, and** *diversity is another factor.*

> *Natural resources help an economy grow* **;** *diversity is another factor.*

> *Natural resources help an economy grow* **. D** *diversity is another factor.*

2 A **comma splice** incorrectly combines two independent clauses with only a comma.

The comma splice can be corrected in three ways:

a by replacing the comma with a period and capitalizing the first letter of the second independent clause

b by replacing the comma with a semicolon

c by adding a conjunction

> INDEPENDENT CLAUSE   INDEPENDENT CLAUSE
> *A job is a paycheck, it is not a place to have fun.*

> *A job is a paycheck* **. I** *it is not a place to have fun.*

> *A job is a paycheck* **;** *it is not a place to have fun.*

> *A job is a paycheck,* **but** *it is not a place to have fun.*

4.1 Correct Run-ons and Comma Splices

**Work with a partner. Write _RO_ (run-on) or _CS_ (comma splice) next to the items.
Then rewrite them as correct sentences.**

_RO_ 1 Jimmy Carter said the U.S. is a nation of differences those differences are the source of
our strength.

Jimmy Carter said the U.S. is a nation of differences. Those differences are the
source of our strength.

_CS_ 2 The Internet connects people like never before, this has created a global culture and
economy.

_RO_ 3 A job is not just about paying the rent ˏyet it can also increase a person's self-respect.

_RO_ 4 There is a perception that women are not good at computer programming, ᴹany
technology companies have very few women. _believe_

_CS_ 5 Some people think welcoming people from different countries is bad for the economy,ˏ ,but
others feel greater diversity is an advantage.

_CS_ 6 A diverse workforce offers more skills and points of view,ᵀ this helps companies work
better with different cultures in their markets.

B Grammar for Writing: Reduced Relative Clauses

In academic writing, it is important for writers to present their ideas as clearly and efficiently as possible. One way to do this is to reduce relative clauses.

When the relative clause contains the verb *be*, the clause can often be reduced. This is true for identifying relative clauses, as well as for nonidentifying relative clauses (clauses that are set off with commas). Follow the rules below for reducing relative clauses. Note that in the relative clause, the relative pronoun is the subject.

REDUCING TT RELATIVE CLAUSES	
1 Omit the relative pronoun (*who, that, which*) and the verb *be* when they are followed by a verb that ends in *-ing* or *-ed*.	According to a recent study, societies ~~that were~~ **isolated** in preindustrial times continue to be less diverse today. However, the study found that societies ~~that were~~ still **growing** benefited from isolation.
2 Omit the relative pronoun and the verb *be* when they are followed by a prepositional phrase.	The researchers ~~who were~~ for the study concluded that more diverse countries have a stronger economy.
3 Omit the relative pronoun and the verb *be* when they are followed by a noun phrase. If the relative clause is a nonidentifying clause, then the noun phrase becomes an appositive.	Jared Diamond, ~~who is~~ the author of *Guns, Germs, and Steel*, believes that geography is the cause of the West's progress.
4 Do not reduce clauses that include only one adjective. Instead, place the adjective before the noun.	well-known The study ~~that is well known~~ found that geography was the cause of the West's progress.

 **4.2** Combine Ideas

Rewrite the sentences with reduced relative clauses.

1 Some large cities that are on the east and west coasts of the United States have diverse populations.

   Some large cities on the east and west coasts of the United States have diverse populations.

2 New York City, which is known as the Big Apple, is one of the most diverse cities in the United States.

3 When you walk down the streets of New York City, you can hear people who are speaking many different languages.

4 In Toronto, which is a multicultural city, people speak over 140 languages.

5 Immigrants to Canada have skills that are needed for a strong economy.

6 Toronto has a strong network of community groups that are helping immigrants adjust to the city.

7 In both cities, immigrants who are motivated can find the resources to create good lives.

Avoiding Common Mistakes

Research tells us that these are the most common mistakes that students make in academic writing when reducing relative clauses.

1 **Use the correct form of the verb in the reduced clause.**

          studying

   Researchers ~~studied~~ the effects of diversity on the economy do not always agree.

2 **Put the verb after the noun – not before the noun.**

          provided

   The ~~provided~~ facts ^ by the researchers support her argument.

3 **Omit the verb *be* before the noun when you omit the relative pronoun.**

   The author, ~~is~~ an economist, has written many books on the subject of diversity.

4 **For reduced clauses with single adjectives, put the adjective before the noun.**

   multicultural

   The city ~~multicultural~~ ^ has residents from over 100 countries.

 4.3 Editing Task

Find and correct six more mistakes in the paragraph below.

                competing

For many companies ~~competed~~ in today's global market, a diverse workforce is one strategy to increase success, but there are challenges. Some businesses recruited people from different backgrounds believe that it increases creativity, but it can increase conflict, too. While employees with diverse backgrounds offer perspectives unique on problems, they may also be unable to see each other's points of view. Ted Park, is a management consultant, says that employees must be trained to work together. Some employees upset can cause additional problems and conflicts. Training on cultural diversity giving regularly is more effective than training that is given once. Companies thought about diversifying their workforce should prepare carefully for it.

ⒸAvoiding Plagiarism

Time management is particularly important in your college life. If you do not make time for writing papers, you may rush through writing and end up plagiarizing accidentally.

I can't believe it! I have a paper that is due this week, and I haven't even started it! I just started reading some articles to get ideas about my topic, but now I'm afraid I won't finish in time. I'll have to write fast. I feel like just copying and pasting ideas to get it done. I wish I had started earlier. Can you help me get organized for my next assignment?

Arun

Dear Arun,

These days students have many responsibilities and distractions. As a result, they sometimes forget about important due dates for homework. Also, some students have the bad habits of starting their homework late or letting friends distract them from their work. One consequence of these behaviors is that students plagiarize to meet their due dates. Fortunately, there is an easy solution: learning how to plan your time. Learn these skills and you can say goodbye to some of the stress of writing papers.

Good luck!

Professor Wright

STRATEGIES FOR MANAGING YOUR TIME

Procrastinating, or waiting until the last minute to complete a task, is a common problem for college students. When you wait until the last minute to write a paper, you do not have time to think about what you want to write.

Below are reasons that students procrastinate and strategies to stay focused.

REASONS STUDENTS PROCRASTINATE	STRATEGIES TO STAY FOCUSED
Reason 1: Lack of skill or knowledge "I never know what to write or how to start writing. That's why I hate writing papers and I wait until the last minute!"	**Strategy 1: Ask for help.** • Talk to your instructor. • Discuss the assignment with a classmate or friend. • Meet with a friend and encourage each other to write.
Reason 2: Distractions "I keep getting interrupted by my friends texting me and getting on social media."	**Strategy 2: Find a quiet place to study.** • Put your phone away. • Don't check email. • Don't surf the web.
Reason 3: Temptations "I always have something else to do that seems more important, like housework or doing chores. Also, when my friends ask me to go out, it's really hard to say no."	**Strategy 3: Have a dedicated study time every day, and don't let anything interfere with it.** • Say no when a friend asks you to come do something during that time. • Plan to meet *after* you've finished your work. Meeting your friend is your reward. • Don't do things like housework or reading the newspaper to avoid homework.

 4.4 Notice

Work with a partner. Read the case study and discuss the questions below.

   Student A got an assignment on Monday. She didn't understand the question very well. The assignment was due the next Monday. She spent Monday, Tuesday, and Wednesday worrying about it. On Thursday she went to the cafeteria to study. She saw a friend there, and they decided to go to a movie. On Friday, she started to work on her project, but her cousin called. They talked for about an hour. Then she decided to check Facebook. On the weekend, she wanted to ask her teacher a question, but she couldn't because her teacher wasn't available. She decided to do laundry and organize her closet on Saturday, but she kept thinking about that paper! On Sunday night, she wrote her paper. She copied parts of it from the Internet because she didn't have enough time.

1 What are the reasons the student procrastinated?

2 What suggestions would you make to help her avoid procrastinating?

 4.5 Practice

Discuss these questions with a partner.

1 Do you ever procrastinate? Why or why not?

2 What strategies could you use to avoid procrastinating on your next assignment?

In this section, you will follow the writing process to complete the final draft of your essay.

STEP 1: BRAINSTORM

Work with a partner. Follow the steps below to brainstorm ideas for your essay.

STUDENT MODEL

Possible thesis statement: Tech companies should hire women because women need the jobs, they have unique opinions, and they can learn the skills, too.

- Women need these jobs for their families.

- Women can learn these skills, too.

- Women are just as smart as men.

- Women have different ideas than men.

- There's prejudice against women and that's not right.

- Women should have as many opportunities as men.

- If women have good jobs, their families and society are stronger!

- Girls need to learn the skills for these jobs.

- Great women leaders in technology: Facebook, Google, and Yahoo.

---

1 Before you start, notice how the writer of the Student Model essay on pages 204–205 brainstormed. She wrote many ideas. Then she chose a side and circled three reasons she thought were the strongest.

2 Write a possible thesis statement and ideas from Section 1 on page 199 below. Add ideas from the Your Turns throughout the unit.

Possible thesis statement:

Look at your ideas at the bottom of page 225. Circle the three strongest reasons.
Write them below in order of importance.

1 ....

2 ....

3 ....

STEP 2: DO RESEARCH

If your topic requires research, see page 261 for advice on how to find information.

STEP 3: MAKE AN OUTLINE

Complete the outline below with your ideas from Step 1.

ESSAY OUTLINE

I. Introductory paragraph ....

Thesis Statement ....

....

Body Paragraph 1 Point 1   II. ....

Supporting Idea 1   A. ....

Detail   1. ....

Detail   2. ....

Supporting Idea 2   B. ....

Detail   1. ....

Detail   2. ....

Body Paragraph 2 Point 2

III. ....

Supporting Idea 1

    A. ....

Detail

      1. ....

Detail

      2. ....

Supporting Idea 2

    B. ....

Detail

      1. ....

Detail

      2. ....

Body Paragraph 3 Point 3

IV. ....

Supporting Idea 1

    A. ....

Detail

      1. ....

Detail

      2. ....

Supporting Idea 2

    B. ....

Detail

      1. ....

Detail

      2. ....

    V. Concluding paragraph ....

....

STEP 4: WRITE YOUR FIRST DRAFT

Now it is time to write your first draft. Here are some suggestions on how to get started.

1 Use your outline as you write.

2 Focus on making your ideas as clear and convincing as possible.

3 Add a title.

After you finish, read your essay and check for basic errors.

1 Check that all sentences have subjects and verbs.

2 Check that you have used commas and periods correctly.

3 Make sure your thesis statement and topic sentences are clear.

4 Check that your reasons are logical, and make sure the evidence proves them.

STEP 5: WRITE YOUR FINAL DRAFT

1 After you receive feedback on your first draft, review it carefully. Fix any errors.

2 Make a note of errors that were most frequent. Try to avoid them as you write.

3 Review the Academic Vocabulary and Collocations from this unit. Are there any that you can add to your essay?

4 Turn to page 268 and use the Self-Editing Review to check your work one more time.

5 Write your final draft and hand it in.

8 ARGUMENTATIVE ESSAYS 2

GLOBAL STUDIES: ISSUES IN GLOBALIZATION

"Coming together is a beginning; keeping together is progress; working together is success."

Henry Ford (1863–1947)

About the Author:

Henry Ford is the founder of the Ford Motor Company. He is known for developing the assembly line, a way to build cars that was efficient and fast.

Work with a partner. Read the quotation about global issues. Then answer the questions.

1 Choose the best meaning of the quote. Explain your answer.

  a Working in groups is successful only when people cooperate.

  b Working in groups is good.

  c People can get things done when they work in groups.

2 Think of a world problem. How are groups cooperating to solve it?

Ⓐ Connect to Academic Writing

In this unit, you will learn skills to help you argue your point of view on a topic. While some of the writing skills that you will use to do this may be new to you, the skill of persuading people of your opinions is not new. In your everyday life, you use this skill when you and your friends argue about which brand of phone is better or whether the government should control the Internet.

Ⓑ Reflect on the Topic

In this section, you will choose a writing prompt and reflect on it. You will develop these ideas throughout the unit and use them to practice skills that are necessary to write your final essay.

The writing prompt below was used for the Student Model essay on pages 236–237. The student reflected on the topic of a consumer society and used a chart to list reasons for and against it. Thinking about both sides of the argument helped him understand the topic from other people's perspectives.

WRITING PROMPT: At present, the economy is based on a consumer society which, according to the *Cambridge Dictionaries Online* is "a society in which people often buy new goods, especially goods that they do not need, and in which a high value is placed on owning many things." Is this type of society good or bad for us?

GOOD	BAD
- makes us money	- causes pollution
- provides jobs	- people spend too much time shopping
- more rich people – and rich people help others	- people think too much about money
- more choices	- people spend too much money
	- people don't have good relationships

Possible thesis statement: A consumer society is not good for the world because it makes people unhappy and it causes waste and pollution.

 1.1 Notice

Work with a partner. Discuss two more reasons for each column in the chart.

Follow the directions to reflect on your topic.

A Choose a prompt:

- Do you agree or disagree with this proverb: *Give a man a fish and you feed him for a day; teach a man to fish and you feed him for a lifetime.* Use your knowledge of the world and history as well as research to support your argument.
- Should everyone have access to the Internet?
- Many people are leaving their countries because of conflicts. Are other nations responsible for the welfare of these refugees?
- A topic approved by your instructor

B Complete the following tasks:

1 Think about your prompt. What two sides is the prompt asking you to consider?

2 Complete the chart below. Write as many reasons as you can to support each side.

3 Decide on the side you want to support. Write a possible thesis statement and show it to your instructor to make sure you understand how to answer the prompt.

4 Compare charts and possible thesis statements with a partner.

YES / AGREE	NO / DISAGREE

Possible thesis statement: ....

....

In this section, you will learn academic language that you can use in your argumentative essay. You will also notice how a professional writer uses the language and features of argumentation.

Academic Vocabulary

The words below appear throughout the unit. All are from the Academic Word List. Using these words in your writing will make your ideas clearer and your writing more academic.

access (n)	decline (n)	implement (v)	transformation (n)
comprehensive (adj)	estimate (n)	issue (n)	welfare (n)

ACTIVITY **2.1** Focus on Meaning

Work with a partner. Circle the correct definitions.

1 A **decline** in population can hurt a country's economy because the number of working people falls and the country produces fewer products. **Decline** means

   a   a decrease.   b   an increase.

2 The government is going to **implement** a policy that will allow anyone to borrow up to $400,000 so that they can start a small business. This will allow poorer people to be entrepreneurs. To **implement** means

   a   to cancel or stop.   b   to start or make possible.

3 Many people believe that global warming is the most crucial **issue** facing humanity today. **Issue** means

    a a subject or topic that people disagree on.   b an agreement among people.

4 Women in poverty need education. Education can help them see their value as human beings and help them feel empowered. This **transformation** can help them find a way out of poverty. **Transformation** means

    a a radical change.   b a strong support.

5 The United Nations has a **comprehensive** plan to eliminate the global food crisis. The plan includes many strategies to deliver food to poor people around the world. **Comprehensive** means

    a understandable.   b complete.

6 Caring for the **welfare** of older citizens will be difficult if the government cuts spending on health care. **Welfare** means

    a health and happiness.   b income.

7 In government buildings, you must show an ID at the entrance in order to have **access** to them. If you do not have an ID, the security guards will not let you in. **Access** means

    a an appointment.   b an ability or a right to enter.

8 According to one government **estimate**, population numbers will level off in 10 to 12 years. **Estimate** means

    a a plan.   b a guess.

B Academic Phrases

Research tells us that the phrases in bold below are commonly used in academic writing.

ACTIVITY 2.2 Focus on Meaning

Work with a partner. Circle the correct synonyms.

1 Participants in the study were grouped solely **on the basis of** gender. Men formed one group and women formed another. The phrase **on the basis of** can be replaced with

    a based on.   b except for.

2 **With respect to** climate change, all countries must accept responsibility for their actions and production of carbon. The phrase **with respect to** can be replaced with

    a against.   b on the subject of.

3 **In the absence of** a comprehensive plan to fight viruses like the Ebola virus, another epidemic could come at any time. The phrase **in the absence of** can be replaced with

    a because of.   b without.

C Writing in the Real World

The author of "Unrelenting Population Growth Driving Global Warming, Mass Extinction" uses the features of argumentation to convince his audience of his point of view.

Before you read, answer these questions: According to the author, what is the growth in population causing? What are some ideas that the author might discuss?

Now read the article. Think about your answers to the questions above as you read.

UNRELENTING POPULATION GROWTH DRIVING GLOBAL WARMING, MASS EXTINCTION
(adapted)

by Jeremy Hance

1 It took humans around 200,000 years to reach a global population of one billion, yet over the last 40 years we have added an extra billion approximately every dozen years. In fact, the United Nations predicts a total population of 11 billion by century's end. Despite this, few scientists, policymakers, or even environmentalists are willing to publicly connect the **issue** of population growth to the global environmental crisis.

2 "We are already to a point where our population size is unsustainable,[1]" says Jeffrey McKee of Ohio State University. "Millions of people go hungry every day, and an unfathomable[2] number don't even have **access** to clean drinking water. A world of 11 billion people would be regrettable to humans as well as to other species." McKee has also found a direct relationship between the rate of population growth and the number of endangered species in a country.

3 Meanwhile, geographer Camilo Mora with the University of Hawaii argues that overpopulation is making global warming and the loss of species in the world worse. It is also creating large-scale economic and societal problems. If our population is already unsustainable, why has the subject become taboo[3]?

4 For decades scientists have been warning that the world may be entering a period of mass species extinction with dangerous consequences for people and the natural world. While the causes of the global biodiversity **decline** may be numerous, all can be connected to the increasing human population. As Mora states, "It is simple math. We live in a world with limited resources and space. The more we use and take, the less other species have." In fact, a study by McKee and his colleagues has directly linked the rate of national human population growth with a rise in endangered species. The reverse is also true. Of the 12 countries that have already seen their populations decline, nine have also seen their percentage of endangered species drop.

5 Most scientists agree that global warming is the greatest environmental crisis today. Solutions have long focused on renewable energy, forest preservation, and the **transformation** of agricultural practices that preserve the environment. But Mora argues that ignoring population growth makes it incredibly difficult to achieve the carbon cuts needed to reduce global warming. "Achieving a reduction of greenhouse gases will become increasingly difficult even under modest population growth rates given expected improvements in human **welfare** and expected increases in energy consumption."

[1] **unsustainable**: not able to continue at the same rate
[2] **unfathomable**: impossible to understand (in this case, because it is so large)
[3] **taboo**: something that is avoided or forbidden, usually for religious or social reasons

6   So, if a rising population is one of the main forces behind mass extinction and global warming, then why isn't overpopulation on the agenda?[4] "Nobody wants to talk about 'population control,' and rightly so," says McKee. "There are basic human rights of reproduction, family values, cultural values, and even economics that play into these considerations." To complicate matters, many economists argue that slowing population growth would be bad for the economy because fewer young workers in an economy would mean less funding for social programs and the government. Such fears have led many countries, including Russia, Japan, and Iran, to **implement** policies to raise populations, not lower them.

7   But Mora says the belief that population growth is necessary for the economy is wrong. In fact, population growth can hurt an economy because the resulting lack of jobs for younger workers can lead to social unrest. "We can achieve economic growth [through] training and innovation rather than adding more people with limited chances to succeed."

[4] **on the agenda:** scheduled to be discussed

8   Moreover, for a long time, some experts predicted that the world's population would peak at around 9 to 10 billion by mid-century and then begin to fall. However, such **estimates** now appear overly optimistic. While the rate of overall population growth may be slowing, trends do not show a peak population anytime soon.

9   How then do you solve something as sensitive as population growth? Experts say that **access** to family planning and education for women are the best ways to reduce global population. Mora would like to see an education campaign to raise awareness about the impacts of a rising global population. He points to the success of similar campaigns on **issues** like tobacco and HIV.

10 Both Mora and McKee agree that the first step is for scientists to stop avoiding the issue, and to start including it in their work. **With respect to** overpopulation, "[it] must be embraced, not eschewed,"[5] says McKee. "My team's research has shown that considerations of human population density must be part of any **comprehensive** conservation plan. The sooner we open the difficult dialogue, the better."

[5] **eschewed:** intentionally avoided

 2.3 Check Your Understanding

Answer the questions.

1   What effect could a declining population have on economies? Why?

2   According to the article, why is it difficult for many people to talk about overpopulation?

3   What do scientists Jeffrey McKee and Camilo Mora propose doing to solve the overpopulation issue? What is your opinion of the issue of overpopulation?

 2.4 Notice the Features of Argumentative Writing

Answer the questions.

1   Look at paragraph 4. The writer says that there is a direct link between the rate of human population growth and the rise in endangered species. What evidence does he give to support this?

2   Look at paragraph 7. What is the purpose of this paragraph? Does it weaken or strengthen Hance's claim that overpopulation has dangerous consequences?

3   Look at paragraph 8. What prediction about the world's population is mentioned? Does Hance agree or disagree with the prediction? How convincing is Hance in his point of view?

In Section 1, you saw how the writer of the Student Model essay reflected on his topic. In this section, you will analyze the final draft of his argumentative essay. You will learn how to structure your ideas for your own essay.

Ⓐ Student Model

Read the writing prompt again and answer the questions.

WRITING PROMPT: At present, the economy is based on a consumer society which, according to the *Cambridge Dictionaries Online* is "a society in which people often buy new goods, especially goods that they do not need, and in which a high value is placed on owning many things." Is this type of society good or bad for us?

1 What is the prompt asking the writer to argue for or against? Circle the words and phrases in the prompt that you think the writer will use in his thesis statement.

2 Do you think the writer will argue for or against a consumer society? Why?

Read the essay twice. The first time, think about your answers to the questions above. The second time, answer the questions in the Analyze Writing Skills boxes. This will help you notice key features of argumentative essays.

Time to Rethink Our Consumer Society

1   A famous proverb says that money does not buy happiness. Many of the world's consumers today probably do not believe in that wisdom anymore. Shopping for the latest clothes, accessories, and electronic devices[1] is a huge part of many people's lives. This is partly because people are exposed[2] to hundreds of advertisements each day in the real world and in the digital world. Advertisers tell them that buying this thing will make them more attractive, more successful, happier, more intelligent, healthier, and more fun to be around, so they buy it. While a consumer society gives people many choices and some say that improves the quality of life, its effects are very damaging. A consumer society is not good for the world because it leads to unhappiness and it destroys natural resources and the environment.

2   People in a consumer society crave the latest clothes and electronic devices to make them happy, but that happiness does not last. Soon after they purchase the product, they usually feel regret or disappointment because the product does not improve their lives. As a result, they look for a new product to buy. This is a terrible cycle. People do not know

> **1 Analyze Writing Skills**
>
> What is the purpose of the first five sentences in paragraph 1? Circle all that apply.
>
> a to engage the reader
>
> b to explain the topic
>
> c to tell a little about opposing views

> **2 Analyze Writing Skills**
>
> In paragraph 1, underline the thesis statement. Then double-underline the points in the thesis statement that the writer will discuss.

[1]**electronic device:** mobile equipment, such as phone, laptop, electronic reader
[2]**exposed:** having no protection from

that money cannot buy you happiness. In my country, the Dominican Republic, some people have very little money, but they are still happy. They know that happiness comes from family and friends and not from things. According to journalist and best-selling author Malcolm Gladwell, after someone reaches a certain income, money does not make them any happier (49). He says that when an American family earns more than $75,000 per year, the extra money does not make them happier. When someone makes more than that, they can buy more things, but it does not contribute to more happiness. Clearly, more and more money does not make people happier.

3 Analyze Writing Skills

Check (✓) the types of evidence the author gives in paragraph 2.

☐ examples

☐ facts

☐ personal experience

☐ quotations

☐ statistics

3 A consumer society also rapidly uses up[3] valuable natural resources and causes pollution. According to a report by the UNEP (United Nations Environment Programme), the average person in a developed country uses 16 tons of natural resources, such as minerals, metal, and fossil fuels, per year. This report states that this level is not sustainable.[4] Pollution from the production of goods and food is having a negative effect on animal species. According to experts, if consumption levels continue, nearly 40 percent of species could become extinct due to climate change by the year 2050 (Climate Change Impacts). **In the absence** of safety and environmental laws, a consumer society harms both people and the environment.

4 Some experts claim that a consumer society is important for economic growth. They claim that a consumer society creates jobs and provides people with an income. If consumerism stops, then the economy will fail, and this will lead to a worldwide crisis. It is true that a consumer society is good for the economy because it creates goods and jobs. However, is it worth the unhappiness and destruction that it also produces? This cost is too high because it will in the end destroy us. Creating jobs and products is good, but creating them without responsibility to society and the planet is irresponsible. The current model of a consumer society is too destructive to continue.

4 Analyze Writing Skills

Circle the purpose of paragraph 4.

a to support the second point in the thesis statement

b to explain an opposing view and tell why it is partly wrong

c to explain an opposing view and to tell why it is totally wrong

5 In conclusion, a consumer society is not good for the **welfare** of consumers because it creates unhappiness, and it is not good for the Earth because it destroys our resources and causes pollution. The **issue** of consumer society must be addressed. The effects of a consumer society on people and the environment will only continue and get worse. The governments of the world must come together and make decisions that show responsibility and courage.

5 Analyze Writing Skills

Circle the purpose of the last line in paragraph 5.

a to restate the writer's argument

b to give a call to action

Works Cited

"Climate Change Impacts: Wildlife at Risk." *Nature Conservancy*. Nature Conservancy, n.d. Web. 15 Feb. 2014.

Gladwell, Malcolm. *David and Goliath: Underdogs, Misfits, and the Art of Battling Giants*. New York: Little, 2013. Print.

United Nations Environment Programme. *Humanity Can and Must Do More with Less*. UNEP/Intl. Resource Panel, 12 May 2011. Web. 4 Mar. 2014.

[3]**use up**: finish a supply of something
[4]**sustainable:** able to be maintained or continued

3.1 Check Your Understanding

Answer the questions.

1 What is the purpose of the essay?

2 The writer gives two reasons why a consumer society is not good for the world. Think about the evidence he gives for each one. Which reason is stronger? Why?

3 What is your opinion of the consumer society? Do you think that you are part of the consumer society? Explain.

 3.2 Outline the Writer's Ideas

Complete the outline for "Time to Rethink Our Consumer Society." Use the phrases in the box.

consumer society – important for economic growth

cost is too high

leads to unhappiness

Malcolm Gladwell

climate change – 40% of species extinct by 2050

ESSAY OUTLINE

I. Introductory paragraph

Thesis Statement
A consumer society is not good for the world because it leads to unhappiness and it

destroys natural resources and the environment.

Body Paragraph 1
II.

Supporting Idea 1
A. Happy feeling does not last long

Detail
1. Consumers feel regret or disappointment

Detail
2. Terrible cycle

Supporting Idea 2
B. Money cannot buy happiness

Detail
1. Ex: Dominican Republic story

Detail
2.

Body Paragraph 2	III. Uses up valuable natural resources and causes pollution
Supporting Idea 1	A. UN Environment Programme: average person – 16 tons of natural resources
Detail	1. Level is not sustainable
Supporting Idea 2	B. Negative effect on animal species
Detail	1.
Body Paragraph 3 Counterargument	IV.
Support for Counterargument	A. Creates jobs and incomes
Support for Counterargument	B. Economy will fail, worldwide crisis
Refutation	C.
Detail	1. Creating jobs and products without responsibility is bad
	V. Concluding paragraph

B Argumentative Essays with Refutation

As you read in Unit 7, the purpose of an argumentative essay is to convince the reader that your claim is valid. In Unit 7, you focused on explaining your arguments clearly and providing strong evidence to support them.

Arguing also involves explaining why your argument is better in some way than an opponent's argument. This is called a **refutation**. The opponent's argument is called a **counterargument**. In other words, you must create a refutation that shows why a counterargument is weaker than yours. In this unit, you will learn how to refute a counterargument persuasively.

There are many ways to structure an argument that includes refutation. Below is one structure.

1 **Introductory paragraph:** The introductory paragraph starts with a hook to get the reader's attention. Background information explains the issue and its importance and leads the reader to the thesis statement. The thesis statement contains the reasons that the writer will argue in the body paragraphs.

2 **First two or three body paragraphs:** The first two or three body paragraphs build the argument. They explain each reason in the thesis and give clear evidence – such as facts, examples, and research – to convince the reader that the reason is valid.

3 **Last body paragraph:** The body paragraph with refutation appears last. In this paragraph, the writer presents an argument that is against his or her thesis. The writer explains the argument, called a counterargument, recognizes its possible strengths, and then explains particular weaknesses in it.

4 **Concluding paragraph:** The concluding paragraph restates the thesis, emphasizes the importance of the topic, summarizes the main points, and ends with a memorable closing statement, quotation, or call to action.

 3.3 Notice

Look at the Student Model essay on pages 236–237. Answer the questions.

1 How many body paragraphs build the argument?

2 According to the student writer, what is the strength of the counterargument? What is its weakness?

INTRODUCTORY PARAGRAPH

An introductory paragraph for an argumentative essay contains a **hook, background information**, and a **thesis statement**.

A **hook** gets the attention of the readers and lets them see the importance of the topic. Notice how the hook below creates a vivid picture in the readers' mind that engages them so that they want to continue reading the essay.

> *On the street lay a 13-year-old boy. Minutes ago, he was laughing with his friends. Now, he is dead because of gang violence.*

Background information explains the issue and helps set up your thesis. Notice how the background information focuses on information that prepares the reader for the thesis statement.

> *Gangs are a serious problem in many countries. They are usually active in large urban areas, but today more and more can be found in smaller cities and towns. Even young children sometimes join gangs. Many police officers, community leaders, and educators are not sure how to solve the problem.*

The **thesis statement**, also called a **claim,** states a clear point of view. A strong thesis statement often includes the reasons for the point of view.

> *It is essential that communities get more involved in warning preteens about the dangers of gangs because <u>children at this age desperately want to fit in</u> and they <u>are easily influenced by others.</u>*

3.4 Complete an Introductory Paragraph

Work with a partner. Choose one of the thesis statements below and complete the introductory paragraph for it.

Thesis Statement A: *Playing video games wastes time and could cause violent behavior.*

Thesis Statement B: *Playing video games is a great way to relax and socialize.*

Last year, revenue for the video game industry was over $100 billion, and it is expected to grow over 10 billion more this year (Statista).

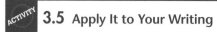 **3.5** Apply It to Your Writing

Look at the possible thesis statement you wrote in Section 1 on page 231.
What background information will help the reader better understand your topic?
Take notes on what you might include.

....

....

....

....

BODY PARAGRAPHS: DEVELOPING YOUR ARGUMENT

As you learned in Unit 7, an argument is a point of view with a summary of the reasons and
evidence to prove that the point of view is valid. Below is the argument for the Student Model
essay on pages 236–237.

> *The effects of a consumer society are damaging to people and the environment. It makes people
> dissatisfied and unhappy because they become addicted to buying and forget that it is people,
> not things, that can make you happy. It destroys natural resources. The amount of natural
> resources that people use now is not sustainable. Current research shows that by 2050 almost
> 40 percent of species will be extinct if nothing is done.*

Each body paragraph develops a writer's argument by explaining and proving one point,
or reason, in a thesis. The writer uses key words from the thesis statement in the topic sentence
to clearly connect them.

Read the thesis statement and topic sentence from an essay on gangs. Notice how the writer
connects the underlined words in the topic sentence to those in the thesis statement.

Thesis Statement: *It is essential that communities get more involved in warning preteens about
the dangers of gangs because <u>children at this age desperately want to fit in</u> and they are easily
influenced by others.*

Topic Sentence for Body Paragraph 1: *Gangs often target preteens because <u>at this age
children need to feel that they belong.</u>*

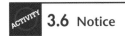 **3.6** Notice

Look at the Student Model essay on pages 236–237. Write the topic sentences for Body Paragraphs 1 and 2 below. Then underline the words in the topic sentences of the body paragraphs that connect to the thesis statement.

THESIS STATEMENT: *A consumer society is not good for the world because it leads to unhappiness and it destroys natural resources and the environment.*

Topic Sentence for Body Paragraph 1: ....

....

Topic Sentence for Body Paragraph 2: ....

....

TYPES OF EVIDENCE

Body paragraphs develop the writer's argument by providing **evidence**. Evidence can include facts, statistics, quotations from experts, examples, and personal anecdotes. They help develop your body paragraphs by making a strong case for your argument. Writers choose their evidence carefully to make sure that it is convincing.

Below are some types of evidence that writers can use to support their points, or reasons.

TYPES OF EVIDENCE

Facts are statements that can be proven to be true.

Gang members are more likely to be killed than nongang members.

Statistics are numbers or other data that often come from surveys, polls, or other research.

According to the Federal Bureau of Investigations (FBI), in 2011 there were 33,000 street, motorcycle, and prison gangs in the United States. This is an increase of 40 percent from 2009.

Quotations are the exact words of another person, usually an expert, authority, or respected individual.

As David L. Kirp, Professor of Public Policy, says, "What happens after school and during the summer also makes a huge difference in shaping children's lives. Research shows that the hours that children spend hanging out on street corners are a better predictor of school failure than race or class."

Examples are specific stories or cases that can help illustrate your point or make it easier to relate to. They can come from the media, from history, or from other sources that you have read or heard about.

When people join gangs, they often have to pass a kind of test. For example, they may have to steal something to prove that they are willing to commit a crime.

Personal experiences are stories or experiences that have happened to you or someone you know.

My cousin was able to leave his gang and actually returned to school to finish his high school education.

Read the supporting evidence from different argumentative essays. Check (✓) the types of evidence.

	Fact (proven by research or true ideas)	Statistics (numbers from research)	Quotation (exact words of sources)	Example (story from the media or history)	Personal experience (story about you or someone you know)
1 Recently in the news, a very popular high school student was killed because he did not want to join a gang.					
2 One successful program to reduce gangs is called Homeboy Industries. It offers job training and counseling.					
3 Research shows that when children go hungry, it can have negative effects on their mental and physical health.					
4 Benjamin Franklin said, "An investment in knowledge pays the best interest."					
5 According to the Hunger Project, a child dies from hunger-related diseases every 10 seconds.					
6 After the latest war in my country, many people were hungry. It was very difficult for me to hear about people in my family who were suffering while I was safe in another country.					

3.8 Match Evidence to Topics

Which piece of evidence from Activity 3.7 best supports each topic sentence? Write it below.

1 **Topic Sentence:** Hunger is the most serious issue facing children in developing countries.

....

....

2 **Topic Sentence:** Gangs are a serious threat to school-age children.

....

....

3 **Topic Sentence:** Poor communities can improve their economy if they invest in the education of their children.

....

....

 3.9 Apply It to Your Writing

Look at your possible thesis statement from page 231. Write evidence that you might use to strengthen your argument. Share it with a partner.

....

....

....

COUNTERARGUMENT AND REFUTATION

An effective way to strengthen an argument in your essay is to include discussion of a counterargument, or an opponent's argument. This is often done in the final body paragraph of an essay. Writers explain the counterargument and offer reasons why the counterargument is weaker than their argument. This is called **refutation**. It is an effective technique because it shows that the writer is knowledgeable about the topic and that he or she has considered other options.

Below are two methods and possible words and phrases to use to structure your counterargument and refutation.

HOW TO STRUCTURE YOUR COUNTERARGUMENT AND REFUTATION

Method 1

First, state the counterargument and acknowledge any strengths in it.

Some people/opponents say/argue that foreign aid does not help a developing country's economy because …

Some experts claim that foreign aid does not help a developing country's economy because …

Critics may argue that foreign aid does not help a developing country's economy because …

Then explain its weakness.

It is true that foreign aid can cause dependency, *but* money that goes to foreign aid programs like microlending and job training makes people more responsible while it also helps the economy.

While many people would agree that foreign aid causes dependency, *this is only partly true.* Foreign aid programs like microlending and job training make people more responsible while they also help the economy.

Method 2

Explain the counterargument and refute the entire argument.

Many people believe that charity can cause dependency. However, this is simply not true. Foreign aid programs like microlending and job training make people more responsible while they also help the economy.

Many people believe that charity can cause dependency. They say that this is because people do not learn to accept responsibility for their lives, *but the opposite is true.* Foreign aid programs like microlending and job training make people more responsible while they also help the economy.

 3.10 Writing Counterarguments and Reasons

Use each sentence and phrase in parentheses to write a counterargument. Then write a possible reason for each counterargument.

1 Technology in the classroom does not improve learning. (Some experts argue that)

   Some experts argue that technology in the classroom does not improve learning. They believe that it actually distracts students from learning.

2 Our economy will suffer as our population ages. (Some opponents say that)

3 People should focus on solving local problems, not international ones. (Critics may
   argue that)

   ....

   ....

4 Fighting global warming will harm the world economy. (Some experts claim that)

   ....

   ....

5 The United Nations is not effective. (Some people say that)

   ....

   ....

ACTIVITY **3.11** Writing Refutations

**Choose two counterarguments in Activity 3.10. Acknowledge the argument using one of
the phrases or sentences in parentheses. Then write a refutation.**

1 (This is not true / This may be partly true)

   Some experts argue that technology in the classroom does not improve learning. They

   believe it actually distracts students from learning. This is not true. Personally, I have

   seen my test scores improve since I started using a tablet to take notes.

2 (This is simply not true / This is only partly true)

   ....

   ....

   ....

   ....

3 (While this may be true up to a point / This is something that many people believe, but it's
   not accurate.)

   ....

   ....

   ....

   ....

   ....

3.12 Apply It to Your Writing

Look at your chart on page 231. Choose the strongest point from the NO/DISAGREE column, and write a counterargument and refutation for it. Be sure to include evidence in your refutation.

Point: ....

Counterargument: ....

....

Refutation: ....

....

CONCLUDING PARAGRAPH

The concluding paragraph restates your argument and emphasizes why the topic is important. It also includes a memorable ending by leaving the reader something to think about, such as a strong closing statement, a quotation, or a call to action.

 3.13 Notice

Work with a partner. Look at the concluding paragraph in the Student Model essay on pages 236–237. Answer these questions.

1 Is the ending memorable? Why or why not?
2 Did the writer convince you to agree with his opinion? Why or why not?

In this section, you will learn writing and grammar skills that will help make your writing more sophisticated and accurate.

Ⓐ Writing Skill 1: Avoiding Faulty Logic

Using faulty or incorrect logic in your writing will weaken your arguments. Two types of faulty logic are overgeneralization and confusing sequence with cause.

AVOIDING OVERGENERALIZATION

Overgeneralization means stating opinions as 100 percent true when they do not apply to everyone.

Below are overgeneralizations and corrected general statements.

OVERGENERALIZATION	CORRECT GENERAL STATEMENT
Everyone believes that investing more in clean energy is a good idea.	**Many people** believe that investing more in clean energy is a good idea.
It is **always** true that solar, wind, and water power are cleaner and safer than traditional fossil fuels.	It is **often** true that solar, wind, and water power are cleaner and safer than traditional fossil fuels.
No one thinks that we will be using much oil and natural gas in the next century.	**Few people** think that we will be using much oil and natural gas in the next century.

To avoid overgeneralizations, do the following:

1 Avoid the pronouns *everyone, everybody, all, no one,* and *nobody.* Instead, use *most people, many people, nearly everyone, some people, few, hardly anyone,* or *almost no one.*

2 Avoid the adverbs of frequency *always* and *never.* Instead, use *almost always, usually, often, sometimes, hardly ever, rarely, seldom,* or *almost never.*

 4.1 Recognizing Overgeneralizations

Underline the words and phrases that cause overgeneralizations in the paragraph below. Correct the underlined words and phrases to make the statements less general. More than one correct answer is possible.

Everyone agrees that clean water is the most serious issue facing the world. According to a recent report by the World Health Organization, 1.7 million people die each year from diseases that come from unsafe water. No one thinks that governments are doing enough to make companies stop polluting the environment, but nobody complains. Companies never clean up the pollution that they create, and they always try to avoid paying fines, too.

AVOIDING CONFUSING SEQUENCE WITH CAUSE

Avoid assigning a causal relationship to two events that are not related. Two events may occur in sequence but without being directly related. For example, imagine you put an umbrella in your bag this morning. Later in the day, it rains. Did putting the umbrella in your bag cause the rain? Of course not. Do not assign cause where there is none. Ask yourself if there is a relationship at all. If not, don't lead the reader to believe there is. This can weaken your argument.

ACTIVITY 4.2 Differentiating Sequence from Cause

Check (✓) the sentences that clearly show a causal relationship.

1 The factories are dumping pollution in the water. The people downstream cannot use the river water for drinking.

2 Water levels in the region have fallen for the last decade. In the last two years, more people are moving into the area to farm.

3 The city put out a warning that its water supply contained dangerous amounts of certain chemicals. The next day sales of bottled water doubled.

4 More countries in the Middle East are now converting salt water to fresh water. The world's oceans are gradually becoming saltier.

5 Rainfall for the last two months has been minimal. Crops are starting to die in the fields.

B Writing Skill 2: Sentence Variety

Sentence variety in writing means including different clause types, sentence types, and sentence lengths. Good writers use a variety of sentence structures to make their writing more natural and interesting to readers. An essay without sentence variety can sound tedious, choppy, and unsophisticated.

Read the paragraph below. Notice the lack of variety in the sentences.

Immigrants come to the United States every year. They come for many reasons. They come to visit their families. Some are escaping persecution at home. Some are coming to find work. Some cannot find work in their country. They are all hoping for a better life. Many of them find it, although not everyone does.

This lack of variety is due to these reasons:

1   Most sentences have the same grammatical structure: subject + verb (+ object).

2   The sentences are about the same length.

3   The subject of the sentences is the same: *immigrants*.

Now read the rewritten version below. Notice how the writer applied sentence variety strategies to improve the flow of ideas.

Strategy 1
Start with a time phrase: The writer started the sentence with *Every year* instead of *Immigrants*.

Strategy 2
Flip the ideas in a sentence: The writer put *The reasons* first instead of *They*.

Strategy 3
Combine sentences: The writer combined sentences with *while*.

Strategy 4
Start with a prepositional phrase: The writer started the sentence with *In some countries* instead of *some*.

Strategy 5
Flip the clauses in a sentence: The writer put the clause with *although* first.

Every year, immigrants come to the United States. The reasons that they come are different. Some come to visit their families, while others come to escape persecution at home. In some countries, it is difficult to find work, so these people come to the United States for jobs. Although not all immigrants succeed, many do find better lives.

4. 3 Adding Variety to Sentences

On a separate sheet of paper, rewrite the paragraph below with more sentence variety. Use the strategies above.

It is crucial that people have safe air to breathe. Poor air quality can make people sick. It can lead to more serious health issues. It can even lead to death. Many countries have problems with air pollution. A recent *New York Times* article by Wong stated that there are 1.2 million deaths caused by air pollution per year in China. The smog is especially bad in Beijing. Officials have been trying to clean it up for many years. Beijing held a marathon race in 2014. It attracted over 25,000 runners. Many runners finished the race. Some did not finish. They were having trouble breathing. Beijing has taken steps to reduce its air pollution, but there is still much to do.

C Grammar for Writing: Modals for Hedging

Modal verbs are used before other verbs to change the tone of a sentence. Modals can also be used to hedge, or limit overgeneralizations.

MODALS FOR HEDGING AND CONTROLLING TONE

1 Writers can use modals such as *can*, *could*, *may*, and *might* to hedge, or soften claims. This more cautious language makes the claims more credible.	Obviously, governments **could** do more to help reduce pollution.
2 Writers can use modals such as *may*, *might*, and *could* to acknowledge a strength in a counterargument in order to expose its weakness.	It **may** be true that globalization does not benefit everyone equally, but the advantages far outweigh its disadvantages. While it **might** be accurate to say the world is warming naturally, studies show that humans are also at fault.
3 Writers can use modals such as *should*, *must*, and *will* to make suggestions, strong recommendations, or predictions.	If we work together on global warming today, we **should** be able to reverse the damage already done. People **must** find a way to balance their need for the latest technology with the waste they contribute to. Unless governments find better ways of working together, terrorism **will** continue to threaten the world

 4.4 Practice Hedging and Controlling Tone

Circle the correct modals to complete the sentences.

1 We **could / must** find a cure for AIDS. Without it more people will die.

2 Unless the city limits the numbers of cars on its roads, air pollution **should / will** only get worse.

3 A small loan to someone who wants to start a business **can / must** actually make a huge difference.

4 I believe that families **may / should** take care of their elderly relatives rather than expect the government to do so.

5 Paying people to stay in school **might / will** seem like a good idea at first, but it's not the best solution.

6 While it **may / should** be true that large fishing companies are depleting fish stocks, small fishing companies are also to blame.

Avoiding Common Mistakes

Research tells us that these are the most common mistakes that students make when using modals for hedging in academic writing.

---

1 Do not use the *-ing* form of the verb after modals. Use the base form instead.

               make
A small donation can ~~making~~ a big difference.

2 Maintain correct word order when *not* is included.

        not
This might be ~~not~~ the best solution.
         ^

3 Use the correct form of the modal in sentences with *if* clauses.

        make
If you ~~will make~~ a donation now, it will help someone in need.

 4.5 Editing Task

Find and correct six more mistakes in the paragraph below.

                                             do
In conclusion, there are certain things that we must ~~doing~~ to end poverty. People need enough food to eat. If they do not eat, they would not have the energy to be productive. They also must have a quality education. This means they should going to school every day and continue their studies when they get older. They should quit not during harvest time or when their families need help with work. If they quit school, they would probably not get a good job later. Finally, people need a way to make money so they can having economic security. If people have these three things together, they not will have to live a life in poverty. They should be able to break the cycle of poverty.

D Avoiding Plagiarism

Synthesis means bringing together ideas from different sources and showing the link between them. When synthesizing, it is important to cite all the sources to avoid plagiarizing.

Help! My instructor assigned us some articles on overpopulation and said that we have to synthesize the authors' ideas in our essays. She said that synthesizing is like comparing ideas. What is synthesis and how do I do it?

Jay

Dear Jay,

Synthesizing ideas is like comparing ideas of authors, but it also means reflecting on the ideas and coming to a conclusion about them: What insight on my topic do I have as a result of these ideas? What have I learned that is new about my topic? Any argument is stronger when you have more than one source to support it, so synthesizing is a good skill for making arguments. While you are reading, don't forget to take good notes to make sure you cite your sources so that you do not plagiarize.

I hope this helps!

Professor Wright

SYNTHESIZING INFORMATION

When writers synthesize information, they look for similarities, differences, and connections between the ideas and reflect on them as a whole.

HOW TO SYNTHESIZE IDEAS FROM TWO OR MORE ARTICLES

1 **Notice similarities and differences between the ideas.**

   Similarities: *Both Paul Ehrlich (Jowit) and Roger Martin (Martin and Klemper) agree that overpopulation is destroying the environment because more people are using up natural resources for food, housing, and business. This destruction will lead to unstable economies, famine, and war.*

   Differences: *Ehrlich believes that overpopulation is an issue because of inequality and greed, and that there is a 90 percent chance that a global catastrophe will occur within the next 30 years (Jowit). On the other hand, Martin is more hopeful and believes that the environmental crisis could be solved by businesses and society working together (Martin and Klemper).*

2 Draw conclusions about the ideas.

*Overpopulation seems to be the basis for other issues, such as changes to the environment, which contribute to climate change. **It makes sense that** solving the overpopulation problem would help solve the problems related to climate change, **so** overpopulation is the more serious problem.*

3 Show how these ideas support your ideas.

*Some experts say that climate change is a more important issue than overpopulation because it is causing significant damage to our environment and plant and animal species. However, at the root of this issue is overpopulation. In fact, **both** Paul Ehrlich (Jowit) and Roger Martin (Martin and Klemper) **argue that** overpopulation is the main cause of the destruction of the environment and that this destruction will cause unstable economies and lead to famine and war.*

Note: The example below does NOT show synthesis because it cites only one source.

Overpopulation does not have to destroy the environment. This destruction is caused by greed. According to Paul Ehrlich, there is actually enough room on this planet for more people to live comfortably, but people are too materialistic, and they do not think about sharing their resources (Jowit).

 4.6 Practice

Check (✓) the texts that are examples of synthesis. Underline the sentences in these texts that show synthesis.

1 Banning plastic bags will save the lives of marine animals. Researchers have found that plastics are a significant source of death for sea animals. The nonprofit group Ocean Crusaders in "Plastic Statistics" states that one million sea birds and 100,000 sea animals die annually from plastic. It makes sense that banning these bags would reduce their numbers, and therefore reduce the number of animal deaths. In fact, Michael Bolinder of Anacostia Riverkeeper found that when plastic bags were banned in 2010 in the District of Columbia, the number of them dropped significantly from over 22 million to around three million.

2 Several specialists who work with women in developing countries have shown that educating women leads to healthier and more financially strong families. Koppell and Sperling both found that education reduced the number of infants who die in poor families. In fact, Koppell says that girls earn up to 20 percent more when they grow up if they attend one extra year in primary school and that statistics show that every year of school increases wages. They also mention that the quality of education is important to have positive results.

3 If governments increased the minimum wage, it would have a positive effect on women. According to *The Impact of Raising the Minimum Wage on Women*, a higher minimum wage would reduce poverty. Eighty percent of the 2.8 million working parents are women, and women usually get lower wages. However, women are also more likely to contribute to the income in a family. The report states that in 2012, there were almost eight million single mothers who were the only breadwinners in their families.

In this section, you will follow the writing process to complete the final draft of your essay.

STEP 1: BRAINSTORM

Work with a partner. Follow the steps below to brainstorm ideas for your essay.

1 Before you start, notice how the writer of the Student Model essay brainstormed.
He included some of the ideas from his chart in Section 1 on page 230. He wrote many ideas
but did not use all of them in his essay. Finally, he circled the points that were the strongest.

GOOD	BAD
- makes us money	(- causes pollution)
- provides jobs	- people spend too much time shopping
- more rich people – and rich people help others	- people think too much about money
- more choices	- people spend too much
	- people don't have good relationships
	(- people are never happy about what they have – they want more and more!)
	- too much waste!
	- people become addicted to shopping
	- people focus too much on what they wear and have
	- pollution is killing plant and animal species

2 Write your ideas from Section 1 on page 231 in the chart below. Include ideas from the Your Turns throughout the unit. Brainstorm more ideas.

YES / AGREE	NO / DISAGREE
-	-
-	-
-	-
-	-
-	-
-	-
-	-

Circle the three strongest points that support your thesis and write them below.

1 ....

2 ....

3 ....

STEP 2: DO RESEARCH

If your topic requires research, see page 261 for advice on how to find information.

STEP 3: MAKE AN OUTLINE

Complete the outline below with your ideas from the previous steps.

ESSAY OUTLINE

I. Introductory paragraph

Thesis Statement

Body Paragraph 1
II.

Supporting Idea 1
A.

Detail
1.

Supporting Idea 2
B.

Detail
1.

Body Paragraph 2
III.

Supporting Idea 1
A.

Detail
1.

Supporting Idea 2
B.

Detail
1.

Body Paragraph 3 Counteragument	IV. ....
Support for Counterargument	A. ....
Detail	1. ....
Refutation	B. ....
Detail	1. ....
	V. Concluding paragraph ....

STEP 4: WRITE YOUR FIRST DRAFT

Now it is time to write your first draft. Here are some suggestions on how to get started.

1 Use your outline and the ideas from Section 3.

2 Focus on making your ideas as clear as possible.

3 Add a title.

After you finish, read your essay and check for basic errors.

1 Check that all sentences have subjects and verbs.

2 Check that you have used commas and periods correctly.

3 Check that you have used commas after dependent clauses that start with words such as *although*, *while*, and *because* when they start a sentence.

4 Make sure that your thesis statement and topic sentences are clear.

STEP 5: WRITE YOUR FINAL DRAFT

1 After you receive feedback on your first draft, review it carefully. Fix any errors.

2 Make a note of errors that were most frequent. Try to avoid them as you write.

3 Review the Academic Vocabulary and Phrases from this unit. Are there any that you can add to your essay?

4 Turn to page 269 and use the Self-Editing Review to check your work one more time.

5 Write your final draft and hand it in.

DO RESEARCH

DEVELOPING KEYWORDS FOR AN INTERNET SEARCH

Using the Internet for research is convenient, but it can be challenging because there is so much information. To search for the information you need, use **keywords** about the topic from your writing prompt.

Alex needed to find information from the Internet for this prompt: *The Internet has changed the shopping habits of consumers over the past two decades. What are the advantages or disadvantages of online shopping?* Read and find out how he did it.

First, I identified the content keywords from the prompt. Then I brainstormed alternative keywords – like synonyms or phrases – for each content word. Next, I typed logical combinations of my keywords into a search engine to find the best information for my essay. Last, I wrote down the title and web address of my results so that I could go back to them later.

Alex's Results

CONTENT KEYWORDS	ALTERNATIVE KEYWORDS	SEARCH RESULTS
advantages	pros, benefits	The Pros & Cons of a Retail Store vs. an Online Store (http://smallbusiness.chron.com/)
disadvantages	cons, problems, issues	Citizens Advice - Buying by Internet, mail order, or phone (http://www.adviceguide.org.uk/)
online shopping	Internet buying, store	What's wrong with online shopping – TIME.com (http://business.time.com/)

 Apply It to Your Writing

On a separate sheet of paper, follow the steps Alex took to find the best information for your essay. Write the content keywords, alternative keywords, and search results in a chart.

SELF-EDITING REVIEW

① INTRODUCTION TO THE ESSAY ENVIRONMENTAL STUDIES: GREEN LIVING

Self-Editing: Review Your Work	Completed
1 Check your introductory paragraph one more time. Include a hook, background information, and a thesis statement.	
2 Check your thesis statement. Make sure it is stated clearly at the end of the introduction.	
3 Check your body paragraphs one more time. Include a topic sentence, supporting sentences, and a concluding sentence in each one.	
4 Check your concluding paragraph. Make sure to restate your main ideas, and offer a suggestion, prediction, or final opinion.	
5 Underline the Academic Vocabulary words and collocations you used. Make sure you used at least two of the words and one collocation.	
6 Underline any infinitives you used, and make sure you avoided common mistakes.	

Self-Editing: Review Your Work	Completed
1 Check one last time that your thesis statement is clear and answers the essay prompt.	
2 If you did research, check that you included sources in your essay and you have included a Works Cited list.	
3 If you paraphrased sources, check that you have used at least three strategies to change the text.	
4 Underline the Academic Vocabulary words and phrases you used. Make sure you used at least two words and one phrase.	
5 Underline verbs (*believe*, *think*) and nouns (*idea*, *belief*) with *that* clauses, and make sure you avoided any mistakes.	
6 Look for mistakes that you typically make, such as using the wrong verb tense or form of the verb, using commas instead of periods, or missing *a/an* and *the*.	

Self-Editing: Review Your Work	Completed
1 Check once again that your thesis statement is clear and answers the prompt.	
2 Make sure that all of your sentences have subjects and verbs.	
3 Underline the Academic Vocabulary words and collocations you used. Make sure you used at least two words and one collocation.	
4 Underline all the words that show similarities and differences. Make sure that you used them correctly.	
5 Underline the relative clauses and make sure that you avoided common mistakes.	
6 Correct the mistakes that you typically make, such as using the wrong past form of verbs or missing *a/an* and *the*.	

Self-Editing: Review Your Work	Completed
1 Check one last time that your thesis statement is clear and answers the essay prompt.	
2 If you did research, check that you included sources in your essay and you have included a Works Cited list.	
3 If you cited online sources, check that you have included all the necessary references.	
4 Underline the Academic Vocabulary words and phrases you used. Make sure you used at least two words and one phrase.	
5 Underline verbs and modals with *if/when* clauses. Make sure you avoided any mistakes.	
6 Be sure all your lists of two or more items are parallel.	
7 Make sure that every paragraph has unity.	
8 Look for mistakes that you typically make, such as using the wrong verb tense or form of the verb, using commas instead of periods, or missing *a/an* and *the*.	

Self-Editing: Review Your Work	Completed
1 Check that your summary essay has an introductory paragraph and a summary paragraph.	
2 Check that the introductory paragraph: • gives the author's name, the title of the article, and the author's main idea in the first sentence • gives background information needed to understand the topic	
3 Check that the summary paragraph: • starts with an introductory sentence • states the points in your own words and in the order in which they appear • includes some explanation for each point • does not include your own ideas	
4 Check that the summary paragraph includes common phrases used in summary essays. Underline those you have included.	

Self-Editing: Review Your Work	Completed
1 Check that your essay has the structure of a summary–response essay. If not, fix it.	
2 Make sure that you have used appropriate ways to create coherence (*this/that/these/those*, pronouns, and articles).	
3 Check that you have used transition words and phrases.	
4 Find and underline any uses of the passive voice. Check for any errors.	
5 Underline the Academic Vocabulary words and phrases you used. Make sure to use at least two words and one phrase.	

Self-Editing: Review Your Work	Completed
1 Check one last time that your argument is clear and answers the essay prompt.	
2 If you did research, check that you included sources in your essay and that you have included a Works Cited list.	
3 Underline the Academic Vocabulary words and phrases you used. Make sure you used at least two words and one phrase.	
4 Underline reduced relative clauses. Make sure you avoided any mistakes.	
5 Correct mistakes that you typically make, such as using the wrong verb tense or form of the verb, using commas instead of periods, or missing *a/an* and *the*.	

8 ARGUMENTATIVE ESSAYS 2 GLOBAL STUDIES: ISSUES IN GLOBALIZATION

Self-Editing: Review Your Work	Completed
1 Check one last time that your thesis statement has a clear point of view and that it answers the essay prompt.	
2 Check for sentence variety.	
3 Underline the Academic Vocabulary words and phrases you used. Make sure you used at least two words and one phrase.	
4 Be sure that you have avoided faulty logic, such as overgeneralization or confusing sequence with cause.	
5 Check that you have used modal verbs to hedge where appropriate.	

SOURCES

The following sources were consulted during the development of Final Draft *Student's Book 3.*

UNIT 1

Sohn, Emily. "Planting Seeds for Better Plastic." *Science News for Students.* Society for Science and the Public, 9 Feb. 2011. Web. 10 Oct. 2014.

Sohn, Emily. "Revving Up Green Machines." *Science News for Students.* Society for Science and the Public, 31 May 2005. Web. 12 June 2012.

UNIT 2

Dweck, Carol. *Mindset: The New Psychology of Success.* New York: Ballantine, 2007. Print.

Ferman, Sara, and Avi Karni. "No Childhood Advantage in the Acquisition of Skill in Using an Artificial Language Rule." *PLoS ONE* 5.10 (2010), 1–10. Web. 29 Apr. 2015.

Ludden, Jennifer. "Going to School May Cost You, But So Will Skipping It." *All Things Considered.* Natl. Public Radio, 11 Feb. 2014. Web. 2 Mar. 2014.

Stevenson, Harold, and James Stigler. *Learning Gap: Why Our Schools Are Failing and What We Can Learn from Japanese and Chinese Education.* New York: Simon, 1992. Print.

UNIT 3

Jolly, David. "Unemployment in Euro Zone Reaches a Record 12%." *New York Times.* New York Times, 2 Apr. 2013. Web. 8 Aug. 2014.

UNIT 4

Agger, Ben. *Oversharing: Presentation of Self in the Internet Age.* New York: Routledge, 2012. Print.

Bindley, Katherine. "Internet Romance Scams Cost Victims $50 Million in 2011." *Huffington Post.* HuffingtonPost.com, 17 May 2012. Web. 6 June 2013.

Cohen, Peter. "Thanks for Not Sharing." *New York Times,* 12 Dec. 2012: A17. Print.

Grant, Adam. "Why Some People Have No Boundaries Online." *Psychology Today.* Sussex Publishers, 11 Sept. 2013. Web. 16 Mar. 2014.

Nixon, Charisse L. "Current Perspectives: The Impact of Cyberbullying on Adolescent Health." *Adolescent Health, Medicine, and Therapeutics* 123.1 (2014), 143–58. Dove Press. Web. 28 Feb. 2015.

Pierce, Tamyra. "Social Anxiety and Technology: Face-to-Face Communication versus Technological Communication among Teens." *Computers in Human Behavior.* 25.6 (2009): 1367–72. *ScienceDirect*, Web. 28 June 2015.

"'Internet Casanova' to Face Charges." *Good Morning America.* ABC News, 22 Feb. 2013. Web. 10 Feb. 2014.

Washington, Edwina Thomas. "An Overview of Cyberbullying in Higher Education." *Adult Learning* 26.1 (2015): 21–27. *Academic Search Complete.* Web. 3 Mar. 2015.

Weed, Julie. "Temptation to Share Online Can Come Back to Haunt Teens." *Seattle Times.* Seattle Times, 9 Mar. 2012. Web. 12 Feb. 2013.

Zuckerberg, Randi. *Dot Complicated: Untangling Our Wired Lives.* New York: Harper, 2013. Print.

UNIT 5

Bird, Jim. "Work-Life Balance Defined." *WorkLifeBalance.com*. WorkLifeBalance.com, 2003. Web. 2 May 2015.

Dr. Irene. "5 Easy Steps for a Balanced Lifestylel." *The Self Esteem Blog*. Self Improvement Blog, 6 Jan. 2015. Web. 2 May 2015.

Edmonds, Molly. "Is There a Link between Music and Happiness?" *HowStuffWorks.com*. HowStuffWorks, 3 June 2009. Web. 28 Jan. 2015.

Expedia.com. *2011 Vacation Deprivation Study*. Expedia, n.d. Web. 3 Feb. 2012.

Groysberg, Boris, and Robin Abrahams. "Manage Your Work, Manage Your Life." *Harvard Business Review*. Harvard Business School Publishing, Mar. 2014. Web. 2 May 2015.

Grynbaum, Michael M., and Marjorie Connelly. "60% in City Oppose Bloomberg's Soda Ban, Poll Finds." *New York Times*. New York Times, 22 Aug. 2012. Web. 2 May 2015.

Harvard School of Public Health. *Obesity Prevention Source*. Harvard College, n.d. Web. 02.11.15.

Joel, Samantha. "Four-Legged Support: The Benefits of Owning a Pet." *Science of Relationships*. ScienceOfRelationships.com, 15 Aug. 2012. Web. 12 Feb. 2015.

National Science Foundation. *Balancing the Scale: NSF's Career-Life Balance Initiative*. National Science Foundation, n.d. Web. 2 May 2015.

Nevarez, Anna. "Vacation Is Not a Luxury – It's a Necessity for a Better Health!" *Examiner.com*. AXS Digital Group, 5 Aug. 2011. Web. 6 June 2013.

"Quinnipiac University Poll." *Yaleruddcenter.org*. Quinnipiac University Polling Institute, 24 Dec 2008. Web. 2 Jan 2012.

Smith, Melinda, Robert Segal, and Jeanne Segal. "Improving Emotional Health: Strategies and Tips for Good Mental Health." HelpGuide.org. *Helpguide.org*, Apr. 2015. Web. 2 May 2015.

Taylor, Steve. "Working Our Lives Away." *Psychology Today*. Sussex Publishers, 6 Jan. 2014. Web. 29 Apr. 2015.

UNIT 6

Boroditsky, Lera. "Lost in Translation." *WSJ.com*. Wall Street Journal, 23 July 2010. Web. 15 May 2013.

McCuskee, Sarah. "Restructuring Urban Healthcare: Beyond the Cultural Model for Immigrants' Healthcare Disparities." *Harvard College Global Health Review*. Harvard College, 1 Feb. 2012. Web. 22 Nov. 2014.

Peek, Liz. "Bilingual Education: Toss It and Teach Kids English." *Fiscal Times*. Fiscal Times, 25 Aug. 2010. Web. 10 Aug. 2014.

Sorace, Antonella, and Bob Ladd. *Raising Bilingual Children*. Washington, DC: Linguistics Society of America, 2004. Web. 13 April 2013.

Taylor, Paul, Mark Hugo Lopez, Jessica Martinez, and Gabriel Velasco. "IV. Language Use among Latinos." *When Labels Don't Fit: Hispanics and Their Views of Identity*. Pew Research Center, 4 Apr. 2012. Web. 10 Nov. 2014.

UNIT 7

Defense Equal Opportunity Management Institute. *Women's History Month 2013 Facts of the Day*. Patrick Air Force Base: DEOMI Press, Mar. 2013. Web. 18 Feb. 2015.

Diamond, Jared. *Guns, Germs, and Steel: The Fates of Human Societies*. New York: Norton, 1997. Print.

Gallo, Carmine. "70% of Your Employees Hate Their Jobs." *Forbes*. Forbes.com,11 Nov. 2011. Web. 2 Feb. 2014.

"Living in Toronto." *Toronto.ca*. City of Toronto, n.d. Web. 17 Feb 2015.

McGregor, Jena. "In Countries with Ethnic Strife, a Link between Female Leaders and GDP Growth." *Washington Post*. Washington Post, 31 Dec. 2013. Web. 12 June 2015.

Moeller, Philip. "Challenges of an Aging American Workforce." *U.S. News and World Report*. U.S. News and World Report, 19 June 2013. Web. 18 Jan. 2015.

UNIT 8

"Do Plastic Bags Bans Help the Environment?" *Tell Me More*. Host Michel Martin. Natl. Public Radio. NPR, 5 June 2012. Web. Transcript. 05 Dec 2014.

"11 Facts about Gangs." *Dosomething.org*. DoSomething.org, n.d. Web. 18 Feb. 2015.

Jowit, Juliette. "Paul Ehrlich, a Prophet of Global Population Doom Who Is Gloomier Than Ever." *The Guardian*. Guardian News and Media, 23 Oct. 2011. Web. 2 Feb 2015.

"Know Your World: Facts about Hunger and Poverty." *Worldwide Organization of Women's Association*. WWOWA, 31 Mar. 2012. Web. 18 Feb. 2015.

Koppell, Carla. "Educate Girls, Develop Nations." *USAID*. USAID Impact, 18 Apr. 2013. Web. 11 May 2015.

Martin, Roger. "Why the Current Population Growth Is Costing Us the Earth." *The Guardian*. Guardian News and Media, 23 Oct. 2011. Web. 20 Feb. 2015.

Martin, Roger L., and Alison Kemper. "Saving the Planet: A Tale of Two Strategies." *Harvard Business Review*. Harvard Business School Publishing, Apr. 2012. Web. 20 Feb. 2015.

National Economic Council, Council of Economic Advisers, Domestic Policy Council, and U.S. Department of Labor. *The Impact of Raising the Minimum Wage on Women*. Whitehouse.gov. White House, 26 Mar. 2014. Web. 29 Apr. 2015.

Sterling, Gene B. "The Case for Universal Basic Education for the World's Poorest Boys and Girls." *Council on Foreign Relations*. Council on Foreign Relations, n.d. Web. 11 May 2015.

Walsh, Bryan. "Why the Real Victim of Overpopulation Will Be the Environment." *Time*. Time, 26 Oct. 2011. Web. 20 Feb. 2015.

"Water, Health and Ecosystems." *World Health Organization*. World Health Organization, n.d. Web. 11 May 2015.

Wong, Edward. "Air Pollution Linked to 1.2 Million Premature Deaths in China." *New York Times*. New York Times, 1 Apr. 2013. Web. 2 Mar. 2014.

INDEX

Words that are part of the Academic Word List are noted with an (A) in this index.

TEXT CREDITS

The authors and publishers acknowledge the following sources of copyright material and are grateful for the permissions granted. While every effort has been made, it has not always been possible to identify the sources of all the material used, or to trace all copyright holders. If any omissions are brought to our notice, we will be happy to include the appropriate acknowledgements on reprinting and in the next update to the digital edition, as applicable.

Text on pp. 18–19 adapted from Platt, John. "Going Off the Grid: Why More People Are Choosing to Live Life Unplugged." *Mother Nature Network*. MNN Holding, 14 Nov. 2012. Web. 24 Mar. 2015.

Text on pp. 48–49 adapted from Kathy Seal's "The Trouble with Talent: Are We Born Smart or Do We Get Smart?" from *Lear's* (July 1993). Copyright © 1993 by Kathy Seal. Reprinted with the permission of the author, www.kathyseal.net.

Text on pp. 78–79 adapted from "Resilience Is About Relationships, Not Just Infrastructure" by Sarah Goodyear, www.citylab.com/weather/2013/01/resilience-about-relationships-not-just-infrastructure/4305/. Reproduced with permission of Sarah Goodyear.

Text on pp. 108–109 adapted from "Generation Overshare" by Marc Savlov, www.austinchronicle.com/screens/2009-03-06/751524/. Reprinted with permission of Marc Savlov.

Text on pp. 142–143 adapted from "Mindful Eating: How to Think More and Eat Less" by Simon Usborne, www.independent.co.uk/life-style/food-and-drink/features/mindful-eating-how-to-think-more-and-eat-less-7682341.html. Reprinted with permission of www.Independent.co.uk.

Text on pp. 161–162 adapted from "More Than Job Satisfaction" by Kirsten Weir, www.apa.org/monitor/2013/12/job-satisfaction.aspx. Copyright © 2013 by the American Psychological Association. Adapted with permission.

Text on pp. 168–169 adapted from "Bilingualism Good for the Brain, Researchers Say" by Amina Khan, http://articles.latimes.com/2011/feb/26/health/la-he-bilingual-brain-20110227. Reprinted with permission of the *Los Angeles Times*.

Text on pp. 195–196 adapted from "Third Culture Kids" by Bilal Ahmed, http://souciant.com/2013/09/third-culture-kids/ Reprinted with permission of Bilal Ahmed.

Text on pp. 202–203 adapted from "Diversity Leads to Economic Growth" by Richard Florida, http://www.theatlanticcities.com/jobs-and-economy/2011/12/diversity-leads-to-economic-growth/687/. Reprinted with permission of Richard Florida.

Text on pp. 234–235 adapted from "Unrelenting Population Growth Driving Global Warming, Mass Extinction" by Jeremy Hance, http://news.mongabay.com/2014/0626-hance-overpopulation-climate-biodiversity.html Reprinted by permission of Jeremy Hance.

The publisher has used its best endeavours to ensure that the URLs for external websites referred to in this book are correct and active at the time of going to press. However, the publisher has no responsibility for the websites and can make no guarantee that a site will remain live or that the content is or will remain appropriate.

CORPUS

Development of this publication has made use of the Cambridge English Corpus (CEC). The CEC is a multi-billion word computer database of contemporary spoken and written English. It includes British English, American English and other varieties of English. It also includes the Cambridge Learner Corpus, developed in collaboration with the University of Cambridge ESOL Examinations. Cambridge University Press has built up the CEC to provide evidence about language use that helps to produce better language teaching materials.

ART CREDITS

NOTES

NOTES